PACEMAKER®

English Composition

TEACHER'S ANSWER EDITION

Parsippany, New Jersey
www.pearsonlearning.com

Contents

Pacemaker® English Composition

Project Staff

Executive Editor: Eleanor Ripp
Project Editor: Monica Glina
Second Editor: Jennifer Watts
Marketing Manager: Jane Walker Neff
Production Editor: Amy Benefiel
Manufacturing Supervisor: Mark Cirillo

ISBN 0-130-23803-1

Printed in the United States of America

10 9 8 7 6 5 4 3 2   02 03 04

Globe
Fearon

1-800-321-3106
www.pearsonlearning.com

A Complete English Composition curriculum that helps all students succeed.

Pacemaker® English Composition is built upon a proven and effective approach to learning that is based on the premise that students learn best at a pace that is right for them. With a controlled reading level, manageable lessons, clearly defined examples, controlled vocabulary support, and frequent practice and review, your students will gain confidence in what they are learning, which will enable them to succeed in school and beyond.

Program Highlights

- The full-color Student Edition makes English-composition skills relevant to students' school and work lives.
- Writing Process unit provides step-by-step instruction to help students learn and practice the writing process.
- Expanded features link learning to life, work, and technology.
- Practice reinforces skills and concepts. Thorough reviews aid in study-skill development and test preparation.
- The improved Workbook connects each exercise to a Student Edition lesson.
- The new Teacher's Answer Edition includes Student Edition pages and point-of-use answers.
- Abundant, easy-to-use reproducibles in the Classroom Resource Binder support and extend lessons.

New!

English Composition

GLOBE FEARON

English Composition

Contents

The Writing Process

STUDENT EDITION includes:

- a new Writing Process unit that walks students through the steps of the writing process using modeling and practice opportunities.
- Unit Openers that list chapters for previewing, planning, and connecting content to students' daily lives.
- Chapter Openers that pre-teach vocabulary and state chapter objectives.
- content that is divided into manageable lessons.
- examples of real-world writing that expose students to different types of writing.
- ample review opportunities that allow students to reinforce their learning.
- relevant features that extend learning, such as Vocabulary Builder, Writing with Style, and Portfolio Project.
- Chapter Reviews that assess vocabulary and content application.
- Unit Reviews that familiarize students with standardized test formats.

TEACHER'S ANSWER EDITION includes:

- instruction on how to use the program in the classroom.
- answers at point-of-use.
- classroom-management notes for each chapter.

CLASSROOM RESOURCE BINDER includes:

- chapter-by-chapter reproducibles that review, reinforce, and enrich key skills and concepts.
- a variety of assessment opportunities.
- organization and planning charts for classroom management.
- ESL notes for every set of Words to Know.
- an introductory activity for every lesson.
- a variety of graphic organizers and visuals.

WORKBOOK includes:

- complete practice for every chapter.
- practice worksheets that assist students with mastery and application of content.
- critical-thinking questions that provide opportunities to extend content.

OTHER STEPS ON THE LADDER TO SUCCESS

- *Pacemaker® English Composition* introduces the writing process. Students focus on using correct grammar and mechanics in the context of writing paragraphs, essays, letters, and more.
- *Pacemaker® Basic English* helps students succeed in English grammar.
- *Pacemaker® Practical English* applies basic English skills to the real world, helping students to develop strong communication skills.

English Composition
Contents

Prewriting
Drafting
Revising
Editing
Publishing
What Is a Sentence?
Sentence Fragments and
   Run-on Sentences
Writing Different Kinds of Sentences
Writing Better Sentences
Choosing the Correct Words
What Is a Paragraph?
Writing Good Paragraphs
Writing Better Paragraphs
Writing to Explain, Inform, or
   Tell a Story
Writing to Persuade
Writing to Describe
Writing to Compare
What Is an Essay?
Writing Your Own Essay
Writing Better Essays
Writing Letters
Writing to Get a Job
Everyday Writing
Writing a Book Report
Writing Answers on Tests
Writing a Report
Creating Characters
Writing a Story
Writing Poetry

Basic English
Contents

Sentences
Punctuation
Common and Proper Nouns
Noun Forms
Pronouns and Antecedents
Pronouns That Ask and Point
Verb Forms
Verb Phrases
Verbs and Sentence Patterns
Adjectives
Adverbs
Prepositions and Prepositional Phases
Other Phrases
Simple and Compound Sentences
Clauses and Complex Sentences
Parts of the Paragraph

Practical English
Contents

Everyday Living
Using Books
Using the Library
Passing Tests
English Skills and Advertising
English Skills for Buying
Job-Hunting
Applying for Jobs
Interviewing
Beginning Work
Learning Job Skills
Communicating at Work
Finding a Place to Live
Getting Around
Managing Money
Working with the Government
Paying Taxes
Getting Health Care
Living Safely
Reading Newspapers and Magazines
Traveling, Eating Out, and Cooking
Writing Personal Messages
Using Criticism

Expectations and requirements for students in today's world have become more rigorous. To meet these challenges, the back-to-basics movement has drawn attention to the importance of all students having a strong understanding of basic English skills. As a result, many states have added a writing component to standardized tests and have begun to hold students accountable for their academic achievement.

To face these challenging academic requirements and more rigorous testing procedures, students must have a firm grounding in the writing process. Once they learn the steps of the writing process, students will be able to organize their ideas and form them into paragraphs.

The Writing Process unit at the beginning of this textbook provides step-by-step instruction to help students work through the writing process. Each page includes an explanation of a specific skill, a model of that skill, and a parallel student activity. Once students master the five main steps of the writing process—prewriting, drafting, revising, editing, and publishing—they will be prepared to build a portfolio of their work.

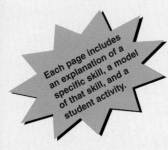

Each page includes an explanation of a specific skill, a model of that skill, and a student activity.

Pacemaker® English Composition will help students to write:

- complete sentences, using correct punctuation.
- well-developed paragraphs.
- explanatory, informative, persuasive, and descriptive paragraphs.
- complete essays.
- letters, résumés, notes, invitations, and advertisements.
- book reports, research papers, and answers on tests.
- imaginative and creative stories and poetry.

> The Writing Process section provides the foundation for the rest of the textbook.

Ideas for writing can come from many sources, like science and your own imagination.

H. G. Wells (1866–1946) studied to be a scientist. Later, he used his scientific knowledge in his writing. Wells became famous when he wrote The Time Machine. *This science-fiction novel tells about a man who travels into the future. Wells also wrote* The War of the Worlds. *It is a story about aliens from Mars that land on Earth. The Martians invade Earth and try to take it over.*

Learning Objectives

- Understand a writing assignment.
- Brainstorm ideas for writing.
- Choose and focus a topic for writing.
- Gather supporting details for an assignment.
- Use an outline to organize details.

WP2   The Writing Process

B-6 ▷ Using a Drafting Checklist

When you draft, you choose your purpose and identify your audience. You write a topic sentence. You write the body of your paragraph, and you write a concluding sentence.

There is one more thing you should do before you go onto the next step of the writing process. You should use a **checklist** to review your draft. A checklist is a list of things to look for and check off when you have done them. Look at the checklist below to make sure that your paragraph contains all of the information you will need.

Drafting Checklist

- ❑ Do I state the purpose of my paragraph?
- ❑ Do I know who my audience is?
- ❑ Do I give my readers all the information they need to understand my topic?
- ❑ Does my topic sentence state the main idea of my topic?
- ❑ Does the body of my paragraph explain my topic?
- ❑ Does my concluding sentence help my readers remember my paragraph?

> Guided questions lead students through the writing process.

Writing Process Activity

Use the drafting checklist to improve your draft about your favorite kind of movie. Add any items to your draft that are missing.

> Writing Process Activities provide opportunities to practice the writing process.

Chapter B • Drafting   WP19

Sample pages from Writing Process unit of the Student Edition.

Captivating color photos spark student interest and connect lessons to real life.

Captions help students understand how skills are used by all writers.

Unit 3 ▶ Paragraphs with a Purpose

Political candidates write with a purpose. Their paragraphs might explain or describe something. They might also try to persuade listeners to vote for them. What other purposes might writers have?

119

Good descriptions are based on observing details.

John Steinbeck
(1902–1968) wrote about life during the Great Depression in the United States. His descriptions of people and places are based on careful observations. Steinbeck's best-known books are The Grapes of Wrath *and* Of Mice and Men. *Both novels show people struggling to survive in hard times. John Steinbeck won the 1962 Nobel Prize for Literature.*

High-interest photos of well-known authors help students connect reading and writing.

Learning Objectives

- Write a descriptive paragraph with specific details to create a picture for the reader.
- Write descriptions that appeal to all the senses.
- Write character descriptions that include physical appearance and personality.
- Identify and write similes and metaphors.

Clear Learning Objectives help students anticipate what they will learn in the chapter and provide opportunities for future assessment.

146   Unit 3 • Paragraphs with a Purpose

Sample pages from Chapter 11 of the Student Edition.

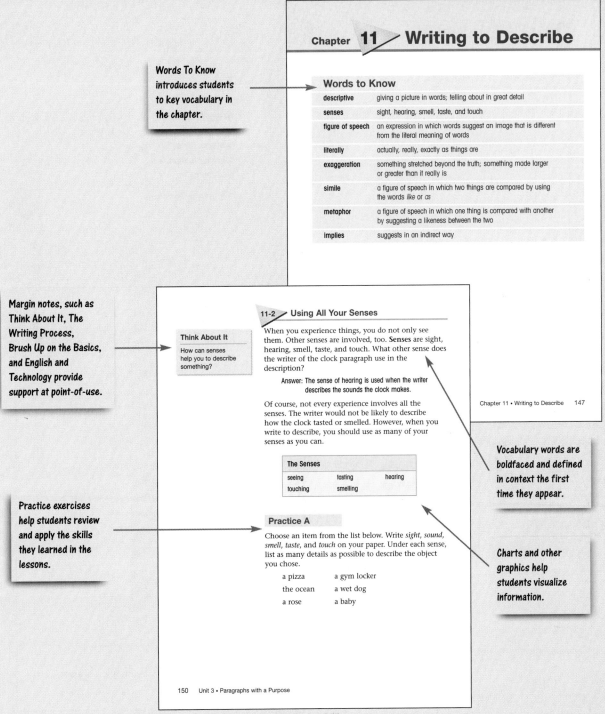

Words To Know introduces students to key vocabulary in the chapter.

Chapter **11** / Writing to Describe

Words to Know

descriptive	giving a picture in words; telling about in great detail
senses	sight, hearing, smell, taste, and touch
figure of speech	an expression in which words suggest an image that is different from the literal meaning of words
literally	actually, really, exactly as things are
exaggeration	something stretched beyond the truth; something made larger or greater than it really is
simile	a figure of speech in which two things are compared by using the words *like* or *as*
metaphor	a figure of speech in which one thing is compared with another by suggesting a likeness between the two
implies	suggests in an indirect way

Margin notes, such as Think About It, The Writing Process, Brush Up on the Basics, and English and Technology provide support at point-of-use.

11-2 / Using All Your Senses

Think About It

How can senses help you to describe something?

When you experience things, you do not only see them. Other senses are involved, too. **Senses** are sight, hearing, smell, taste, and touch. What other sense does the writer of the clock paragraph use in the description?

Answer: The sense of hearing is used when the writer describes the sounds the clock makes.

Of course, not every experience involves all the senses. The writer would not be likely to describe how the clock tasted or smelled. However, when you write to describe, you should use as many of your senses as you can.

The Senses		
seeing	tasting	hearing
touching	smelling	

Vocabulary words are boldfaced and defined in context the first time they appear.

Practice A

Choose an item from the list below. Write *sight, sound, smell, taste,* and *touch* on your paper. Under each sense, list as many details as possible to describe the object you chose.

a pizza	a gym locker
the ocean	a wet dog
a rose	a baby

Practice exercises help students review and apply the skills they learned in the lessons.

Charts and other graphics help students visualize information.

Chapter 11 • Writing to Describe   147

150   Unit 3 • Paragraphs with a Purpose

Sample pages from Chapter 11 of the Student Edition.

▶ Student Edition Full-Page Features

WRITING WITH STYLE
Using Figures of Speech

Figures of speech can give style to your writing. They help the reader see what you are seeing and understand exactly what you mean. Which of the sentences in each pair below creates a clearer picture? Write the correct letter on a separate sheet of paper.

1. **a.** Her hat had lots of colorful feathers and was very fancy.
   b. Her hat was as brilliant as a peacock's tail.

2. **a.** The night was as dark as the inside of a deep cave.
   b. The night was very dark.

3. **a.** The boy was very shy.
   b. The boy was a shy little rabbit hiding in the corner.

4. **a.** The wind howled like a mournful ghost searching for a place to rest.
   b. The wind howled.

5. **a.** Their new quarterback is built like a brick shed.
   b. Their new quarterback is very, very big.

Of course, you do not want to use figures of speech in every sentence you write. You do not even want to use them in every paragraph. Once in a while, they can really help you create a more vivid, precise picture for your reader. You probably figured out by now that the key to descriptive writing is precision, or saying exactly what a thing is.

Writing With Style helps students reinforce the skills they have learned in the chapter.

VOCABULARY BUILDER
Using Suffixes

A suffix is a group of letters added at the end of a word. A suffix changes the meaning of a word. Often, it also changes the word's part of speech. When *-ly* is added to the end of an adjective, it makes the adjective an adverb. For example, when *-ly* is added to the adjective *weird*, it becomes the adverb *weirdly*.

1. On your own paper, use the suffix *-ly* to make the word in parentheses into the adverb that would fit into the sentence. The first one has been done as an example.

   a. The ball hit him (sudden) from behind.   *suddenly*

   b. She (quick) hid the money in her purse.

   c. She laughed (wicked) after she played the trick on him.

   d. There was (most) junk at the garage sale.

   e. He shook his head (sad) and left the room.

2. Add the suffix *-ly* to each of the following adjectives. Then, use each adverb in a sentence.

   a. swift

   b. loud

   c. clear

   d. strange

   e. tight

The Vocabulary Builder helps students develop a strong understanding of how to use words properly.

Sample pages from Chapter 11 of the Student Edition.

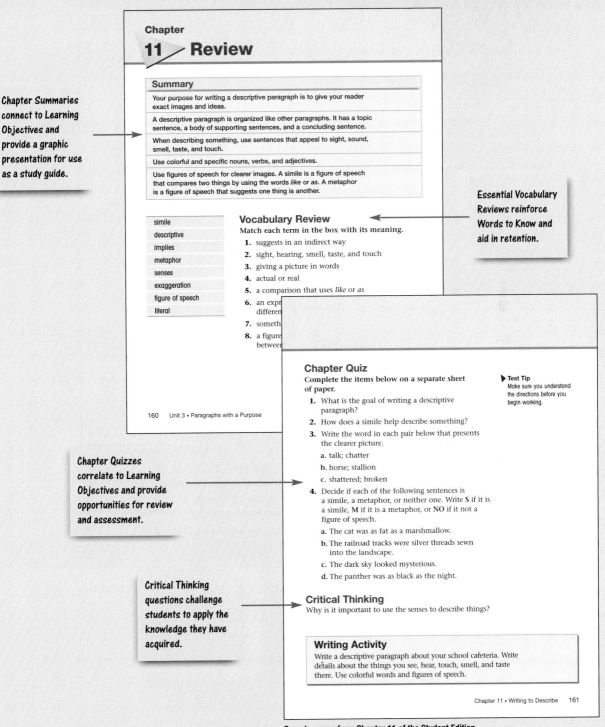

Chapter Summaries connect to Learning Objectives and provide a graphic presentation for use as a study guide.

Chapter

11 ▷ Review

Summary

Your purpose for writing a descriptive paragraph is to give your reader exact images and ideas.

A descriptive paragraph is organized like other paragraphs. It has a topic sentence, a body of supporting sentences, and a concluding sentence.

When describing something, use sentences that appeal to sight, sound, smell, taste, and touch.

Use colorful and specific nouns, verbs, and adjectives.

Use figures of speech for clearer images. A simile is a figure of speech that compares two things by using the words *like* or *as*. A metaphor is a figure of speech that suggests one thing is another.

Essential Vocabulary Reviews reinforce Words to Know and aid in retention.

simile
descriptive
implies
metaphor
senses
exaggeration
figure of speech
literal

Vocabulary Review

Match each term in the box with its meaning.

1. suggests in an indirect way
2. sight, hearing, smell, taste, and touch
3. giving a picture in words
4. actual or real
5. a comparison that uses *like* or *as*
6. an expr...
   differen...
7. someth...
8. a figure...
   between...

160   Unit 3 • Paragraphs with a Purpose

Chapter Quiz

Complete the items below on a separate sheet of paper.

1. What is the goal of writing a descriptive paragraph?
2. How does a simile help describe something?
3. Write the word in each pair below that presents the clearer picture.
   a. talk; chatter
   b. horse; stallion
   c. shattered; broken
4. Decide if each of the following sentences is a simile, a metaphor, or neither one. Write **S** if it is a simile, **M** if it is a metaphor, or **NO** if it not a figure of speech.
   a. The cat was as fat as a marshmallow.
   b. The railroad tracks were silver threads sewn into the landscape.
   c. The dark sky looked mysterious.
   d. The panther was as black as the night.

▶ **Test Tip**
Make sure you understand the directions before you begin working.

Chapter Quizzes correlate to Learning Objectives and provide opportunities for review and assessment.

Critical Thinking

Why is it important to use the senses to describe things?

Critical Thinking questions challenge students to apply the knowledge they have acquired.

Writing Activity

Write a descriptive paragraph about your school cafeteria. Write details about the things you see, hear, touch, smell, and taste there. Use colorful words and figures of speech.

Chapter 11 • Writing to Describe   161

Sample pages from Chapter 11 of the Student Edition.

The hardcover Teacher's Answer Edition provides answers and annotations at point-of-use.

1. a. The <u>snowflakes</u> were like <u>cotton balls</u>.
   b. His <u>tears</u> fell as heavily as <u>rain</u>.
   c. The <u>material</u> is as smooth as <u>silk</u>.
   d. My friend has a <u>neck</u> like a <u>giraffe's</u>.
   e. The <u>house</u> was as silent as a <u>graveyard</u>.

2. Answers will vary. Possible answers:
   a. The rain on the roof sounded like pebbles.
   b. The sun sparkled on the water like diamonds.
   c. Maria is as tall as a tree.
   d. Larry chatters like a bird.
   e. Donna is as thin as a pencil.
   f. The baby's skin was as soft as cotton.

Practice A

1. Copy these sentences on your paper. Underline the two items being compared in each simile.

   a. The snowflakes were like cotton balls.
   b. His tears fell as heavily as rain.
   c. The material is as smooth as silk.
   d. My friend has a neck like a giraffe's.
   e. The house was as silent as a graveyard.

2. Now write some similes of your own by completing the following sentences on a separate sheet of paper.

   a. The rain on the roof sounded like _____.
   b. The sun sparkled on the water like _____.
   c. Maria is as tall as _____.
   d. Larry chatters like _____.
   e. Donna is as thin as _____.
   f. The baby's skin was as soft as _____.

Purpose

Additional activities and strategies to customize this chapter can be found in the Classroom Resource Binder. See the Workbook for **Extra Practice**.

Chapter 12 Writing to Compare

Words to Know

comparison	the act of noting the likenesses and differences of things
similarities	points of likeness; ways that things are alike
differences	points that are not alike; ways that things are different
characteristics	features that make something or someone special and individual

Annotations link practice, assessment, and additional support throughout the program.

12-1 What Is a Paragraph of Comparison?

Making a **comparison** is often a good way to develop a topic. A comparison is the act of noting the likenesses and differences of things. When you have two things that are definite, you can write a paragraph of comparison. You can compare books, people, places, and animals.

The following are examples of comparisons. To *compare* means to point out how two things are alike or how they are different.

black–white

tall–short

happy–sad

fast–slow

friendly–unfriendly

A paragraph of comparison takes two subjects and points out how they are alike and how they are different.

Brush Up on the Basics
A subject names what the sentence is about. (See Grammar 3 in the Reference Guide.)

Sample pages from Chapters 11 and 12 of the Teacher's Answer Edition.

Good descriptions are based on observing details.

John Steinbeck *(1902–1968) wrote about life during the Great Depression in the United States. His descriptions of people and places are based on careful observations. Steinbeck's best-known books are* The Grapes of Wrath *and* Of Mice and Men. *Both novels show people struggling to survive in hard times. John Steinbeck won the 1962 Nobel Prize for Literature.*

Extra Reading See the Pacemaker® Classics series for John Steinbeck's *The Grapes of Wrath.*

To help students tap their prior knowledge of the chapter topic, see the **Chapter Project** in the Classroom Resource Binder.

Learning Objectives

• Write a descriptive paragraph with specific ⬚ to create a picture for the reader.

• Write descriptions that appeal to all the sen⬚

• Write character descriptions that include ph⬚ appearance and personality.

• Identify and write similes and metaphors.

146   Unit 3 • Paragraphs with a Purpose

Teachers can prepare students for standardized tests.

Extra reading opportunities are provided for teachers interested in extending the chapter.

Standardized Test Preparation This unit review follows the format of many standardized tests. A Scantron® sheet, is provided in the Classroom Resource Binder.

Unit 3 **Review**

Read each of the following items. On a separate sheet of paper, write the letter that best answers each one.

1. A piece of writing that tells how to do or make something is called
   - A. an explanatory paragraph.
   - B. a narrative paragraph.
   - C. an informative paragraph.
   - D. an anecdote.

2. A paragraph that begins with a topic sentence that tells about something or someone is usually
   - A. an explanatory paragraph.
   - B. a narrative paragraph.
   - C. an informative paragraph.
   - D. an anecdote.

3. The topic sentence of a persuasive paragraph usually
   - A. answers the *who, what, where, why,* and *when* questions.
   - B. sets up a comparison between two things.
   - C. states an opinion on a subject.
   - D. contains a figure of speech, such as exaggeration.

Critical Thinking Answers will vary. Possible answer: Knowing the purpose of what you are writing is important because it tell you what type of paragraph to write.

Writing Activity For this activity, students are writing a paragraph that compares descriptive writing and comparison writing. Check to make sure that students' ideas are presented clearly and that they have written a well-developed paragraph.

174

4. The body of a descriptive paragraph mainly includes
   - A. facts and figures.
   - B. opinions about the main topic.
   - C. examples from everyday life.
   - D. details that involve the five senses.

5. What figure of speech is used in the following sentence? *The cloud was a soccer ball kicked by the wind.*
   - A. simile
   - B. metaphor
   - C. exaggeration
   - D. connotation

6. Which transition words would be most useful in a paragraph of comparison?
   - A. *unlike* and *similarly*
   - B. *first* and *later*
   - C. *as a result* and *because*
   - D. *before long* and *furthermore*

Critical Thinking
Why is it important to know the purpose of what you are writing? Write your answer on a separate sheet of paper.

WRITING ACTIVITY Choose a paragraph of comparison and a paragraph of description from a textbook. On a separate sheet of paper, write a paragraph that compares them.

Sample pages from Chapters 11 and 12 of the Teacher's Answer Edition.

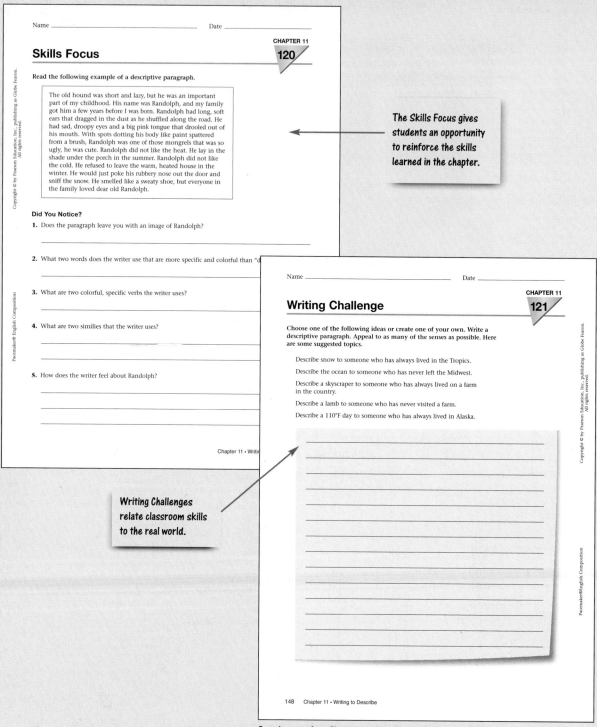

Name _____ Date _____

Skills Focus

Read the following example of a descriptive paragraph.

> The old hound was short and lazy, but he was an important part of my childhood. His name was Randolph, and my family got him a few years before I was born. Randolph had long, soft ears that dragged in the dust as he shuffled along the road. He had sad, droopy eyes and a big pink tongue that drooled out of his mouth. With spots dotting his body like paint spattered from a brush, Randolph was one of those mongrels that was so ugly, he was cute. Randolph did not like the heat. He lay in the shade under the porch in the summer. Randolph did not like the cold. He refused to leave the warm, heated house in the winter. He would just poke his rubbery nose out the door and sniff the snow. He smelled like a sweaty shoe, but everyone in the family loved dear old Randolph.

Did You Notice?

1. Does the paragraph leave you with an image of Randolph?

_____

2. What two words does the writer use that are more specific and colorful than "d

_____

3. What are two colorful, specific verbs the writer uses?

_____

4. What are two similies that the writer uses?

_____

5. How does the writer feel about Randolph?

_____

_____

_____

Chapter 11 • Writi

The Skills Focus gives students an opportunity to reinforce the skills learned in the chapter.

Name _____ Date _____

Writing Challenge

Choose one of the following ideas or create one of your own. Write a descriptive paragraph. Appeal to as many of the senses as possible. Here are some suggested topics.

Describe snow to someone who has always lived in the Tropics.

Describe the ocean to someone who has never left the Midwest.

Describe a skyscraper to someone who has always lived on a farm in the country.

Describe a lamb to someone who has never visited a farm.

Describe a 110°F day to someone who has always lived in Alaska.

Writing Challenges relate classroom skills to the real world.

Sample pages from Chapter 11 of the Classroom Resource Binder.

▶ Workbook

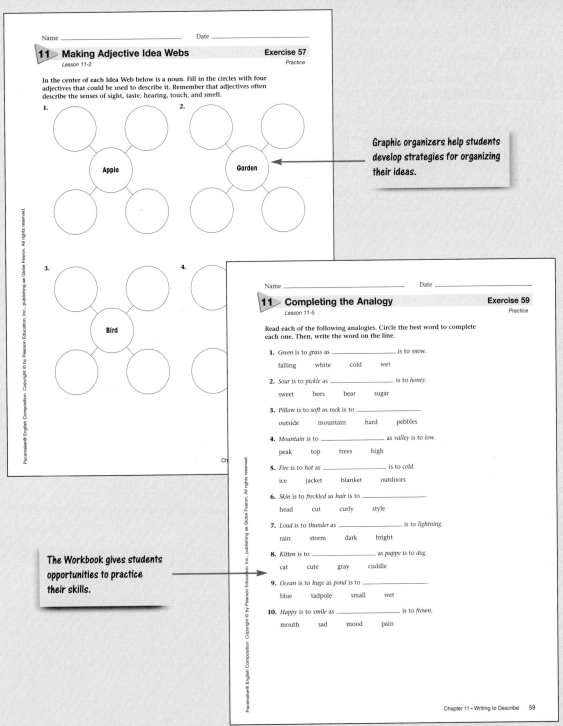

Name _____ Date _____

11▶ Making Adjective Idea Webs   Exercise 57
Lesson 11-2   Practice

In the center of each Idea Web below is a noun. Fill in the circles with four adjectives that could be used to describe it. Remember that adjectives often describe the senses of sight, taste, hearing, touch, and smell.

1.

Apple

2.

Garden

> Graphic organizers help students develop strategies for organizing their ideas.

3.

Bird

4.

Name _____ Date _____

11▶ Completing the Analogy   Exercise 59
Lesson 11-5   Practice

Read each of the following analogies. Circle the best word to complete each one. Then, write the word on the line.

1. *Green* is to *grass* as _____ is to *snow*.
   falling   white   cold   wet

2. *Sour* is to *pickle* as _____ is to *honey*.
   sweet   bees   bear   sugar

3. *Pillow* is to *soft* as *rock* is to _____.
   outside   mountain   hard   pebbles

4. *Mountain* is to _____ as *valley* is to *low*.
   peak   top   trees   high

5. *Fire* is to *hot* as _____ is to *cold*.
   ice   jacket   blanket   outdoors

6. *Skin* is to *freckled* as *hair* is to _____.
   head   cut   curly   style

7. *Loud* is to *thunder* as _____ is to *lightning*.
   rain   storm   dark   bright

8. *Kitten* is to _____ as *puppy* is to *dog*.
   cat   cute   gray   cuddle

9. *Ocean* is to *huge* as *pond* is to _____.
   blue   tadpole   small   wet

10. *Happy* is to *smile* as _____ is to *frown*.
    mouth   sad   mood   pain

> The Workbook gives students opportunities to practice their skills.

Chapter 11 • Writing to Describe   59

Sample pages from Chapter 11 of the Workbook.

USE THESE PROGRAMS FOR EXTRA PRACTICE, RETEACHING, REINFORCEMENT, ENRICHMENT, AND TEST PREPARATION.

GUIDE TO STANDARDIZED TEST PREPARATION

offers tips and strategies for success with most types of test questions and situations.

MASTERING SPELLING

provides students with spelling instruction at the level most appropriate for them. Lessons teach spelling through three approaches: phonics, structural analysis, and word study.

SUCCESS IN WRITING

provides practical focus on the four types of writing: persuasive, expository, narrative, and descriptive. *Grammar Skills for Writers* teaches key grammar skills and concepts.

WRITING FOR PROFICIENCY

helps students develop their writing and mechanical skills. Students learn the four types of writing found on standardized tests: persuasive, expository, narrative, and descriptive

Globe Fearon offers additional materials to help tailor instruction to meet the diverse needs of your students.

For more information on Globe Fearon products, call 1-800-321-3106.

PACEMAKER®

English Composition

Parsippany, New Jersey
www.pearsonlearning.com

REVIEWERS

We thank the following educators, who provided valuable comments and suggestions during the development of this book:

Pacemaker Curriculum Advisor: Stephen Larson, formerly of the University of Texas at Austin

Program Reviewer: Wendi Gdanski, English Teacher, DeWitt-Clinton High School, Bronx, New York

Executive Editor: Eleanor Ripp
Project Editor: Monica Glina
Second Editor: Jennifer Watts
Marketing Manager: Jane Walker Neff
Production Specialist: Amy Benefiel
Manufacturing Supervisor: Mark Cirillo

About the Cover: English skills help people communicate effectively with one another. The images on the cover show the variety of ways that English skills are used in everyday life. Journals are used to express a person's inner feelings. The mouse, the CD-ROM, and the computer disk represent computers, which are used to give and receive information. Computers can also be used to write personal letters or reports for school. People read books for enjoyment and to gather information. Dictionaries give definitions, correct spelling, and pronunciation of words. What are some other ways you can use English skills in your life?

Pacemaker ® English Composition, Third Edition

ISBN 0-130-23802-3

Printed in the United States of America
2 3 4 5 6 7 8 9 10   05 04 03 02

GLOBE FEARON EDUCATIONAL PUBLISHER
Parsippany, New Jersey
www.pearsonlearning.com

Contents

A Note to the Student

The purpose of this book is to help you develop your writing skills to succeed in school and in today's world. You will learn to use the writing process, and you will strengthen your composition skills. You will learn about the parts of a paragraph and an essay. You will learn about different kinds of sentences, and how to capitalize and punctuate them. You will also learn about nouns, pronouns, verbs, adjectives, and adverbs. Writing to express yourself, make somebody laugh, or present your own ideas, can help you communicate your ideas. *English Composition* will lead you down the path to better writing.

This book will walk you through the steps of the writing process. It will show you how to prewrite, draft, revise, edit, and publish your work. The Writing Process section in this book explains *when* you need to do each step and *how* to do it. It provides detailed instructions, explanations, and practices, so that you can create a paragraph that you can feel proud of.

Practicing how to write paragraphs will help you build successful essays. A simple essay is a chain of five good paragraphs. Just as The Writing Process shows how you can transform a general idea into a complete paragraph, it applies to a series of paragraphs as well.

In addition to the Writing Process section, this book introduces different types of writing, and it gives you an opportunity to practice each of them. You will learn to use paragraphs to give information or tell how to do something. You will learn how to write clear descriptions and opinions. By the time you finish this book, you will know how to write notes, letters, book reports, and test answers. You will even be familiar with writing stories and poems.

All through the book, you will find notes in the margins of the pages. These handy notes are there to help you. Sometimes, they lead you to the page on which something is explained in detail. Sometimes, they remind you of something you already know. "The Writing Process" margin note offers information that connects what you are learning to The Writing Process. It provides a cross-reference that directs you to The Writing Process section for more information. "Brush Up on the Basics" connects what you are learning to grammar, capitalization, and punctuation skills. It provides a cross-reference that directs you to the Reference Guide for more information. "Think About It" asks an important question about what you learned. It gives you an opportunity to use what you have learned to answer the question. "English and Technology" connects what you are learning to technology. A Test Tip appears at the end of every chapter. It helps you to prepare for and succeed on tests.

Watch for the study aids throughout the book. At the beginning of every chapter, you will find **learning objectives**. These will help you focus on the important points covered in the chapter. You will also find **Words to Know**, a look ahead at the vocabulary that you will find in the chapter. Finally, you will find a **Chapter Summary** at the end of each chapter before the Chapter Review. The summaries help you to make sure you understand the skills you have just learned.

Everyone who put this book together worked hard to make it useful, interesting, and enjoyable. The rest is up to you. We wish you well in your studies. Our success is in your accomplishment.

The Writing Process

Good plans are the first step of the building process. Workers follow the plans at each stage of the work. Planning is an important first step in writing, too. What kinds of things do you think writers plan?

Caption Accept all reasonable responses. Possible answer: Writers plan what they will write. They also plan and think about who their audience will be.

Ideas for writing can come from many sources, like science and your own imagination.

H. G. Wells (1866–1946) studied to be a scientist. Later, he used his scientific knowledge in his writing. Wells became famous when he wrote The Time Machine. *This science-fiction novel tells about a man who travels into the future. Wells also wrote* The War of the Worlds. *It is a story about aliens from Mars that land on Earth. The Martians invade Earth and try to take it over.*

Extra Reading See the Pacemaker® Classics series for H. G. Wells's *The Time Machine* and *The War of the Worlds.*

To help students tap their prior knowledge of the chapter topic, see the **Chapter Project** in the Classroom Resource Binder.

Learning Objectives

- Understand a writing assignment.
- Brainstorm ideas for writing.
- Choose and focus a topic for writing.
- Gather supporting details for an assignment.
- Use an outline to organize details.

Chapter A / Prewriting

Words to Know

writing process	a five-step process for writing that includes prewriting, drafting, revising, editing, and publishing
prewriting	the planning stage of the writing process
writing assignment	a writing task
topic	the subject of a piece of writing
brainstorming	working with others to list ideas for writing
main idea	the point a writer wants to make about a topic
details	all the small parts of something that make up the whole
outline	a plan that shows how a main idea and its details connect to each other

A-1 ▸ Understanding the Assignment

Writers turn words into sentences and paragraphs and then into essays and stories. To do so, they follow certain steps. These steps are called the **writing process**.

Prewriting is the first step of the writing process. It is a time for thinking and planning before you write. This is an important step in the writing process. It makes writing easier because you do a lot of the work before you even begin to write.

You will often get a **writing assignment**. The writing assignment asks you to complete a writing task. During prewriting, read the assignment carefully. Make sure you understand what to do. That way, you can plan a piece of writing that fills the assignment.

Read the following assignment. What does the assignment ask you to do?

> Decide what <u>your favorite kind of music</u> is. <u>Write a paragraph that explains</u> why you like this type of music. <u>Give three reasons for your choice</u>.

The key words in the assignment are underlined. These key words will help you plan your writing. First, the assignment gives a broad writing **topic**, or the subject of the piece of writing. In this case, the topic is *your favorite kind of music*. Next, it tells you to *write a paragraph that explains*. Finally, the assignment tells you to *give three reasons for your choice*.

Think About It

Why is it important to make a plan before you start writing?

Writing Process Activity

On a separate sheet of paper, copy the following assignment. Underline the key words. Write how the key words help you to plan your writing.

> Write a paragraph about your favorite kind of movie. Explain why you chose this kind of movie. Give three reasons for your choice.

Choosing a Topic

Brainstorming is one way to find writing topics. To brainstorm, you work with a group to list as many ideas as you can think of. Use a word web, like the following one, to put your ideas on paper. At first, do not judge or limit your ideas.

The first assignment on page WP4 asks you to write about your favorite kind of music. The following word web shows how a group of students brainstormed ideas for this topic. Notice how the students put the topic they are asked to write about, Favorite Kind of Music, in the center rectangle. Then, they put their favorite kinds of music in the surrounding circles.

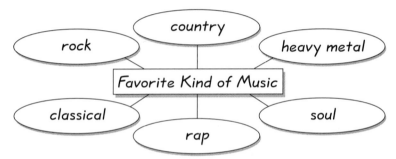

When you finish a word web, think carefully about your ideas. Cross out any ideas you do not want to write about. Place a star next to the one that interests you most.

Writing Process Activity

The second assignment on page WP4 asks you to write about your favorite kind of movie. Brainstorm ideas for this paragraph. On a separate sheet of paper, make a word web. Put the topic you are asked to write about in the center rectangle. Then, put your favorite movies in the surrounding circles. Cross out any ideas that you do not want to write about. Use a star to mark the topic you like most.

A-3 ▸ Focusing the Topic

Once you choose a topic, you need to focus it. When you focus your topic, you make sure that everything you write has to do with your topic. Have you ever looked through a camera that is out of focus? Think about how hard it is to understand what you are looking at. As you focus the camera, things become clearer and easier to see. The same thing happens when you focus your topic. It becomes clearer and easier to understand.

To focus, or narrow, your topic, ask yourself if your topic will work for the assignment. Decide whether you have enough to say about the topic to fill a paragraph. If not, you might need to choose a different idea. Be careful, too, not to choose a topic that is too large for one paragraph. If it is too large, you will have to focus your topic.

When you narrow a topic, you make your topic smaller by focusing on one part of it. You can use a word web to do this. Next to your broad topic, list ideas to narrow it. Then, choose a circle with one of the narrow ideas. Next to that circle, write ideas to further narrow the one in the circle you chose. Put a star next to your favorite idea. This can be the topic of your paragraph.

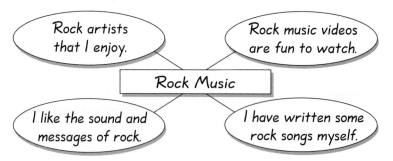

Writing Process Activity

Think about the topic you chose for your paragraph about movies. Use a word web to focus the topic.

Gathering Supporting Details

You have a topic to write about. Now you need to think about what you want to say about the topic. This will be your **main idea**. The next step is to gather **details**. They are often called supporting details. These details support the main idea of the paragraph.

Usually you will need at least three details to support your main idea. You can include more, though. The important thing is to give enough examples so that your ideas are clear.

To gather details, first list your main idea on a sheet of paper. You may already know something about the topic you will write about. If so, you can list the supporting details that you want to use in your paragraph.

> Topic: Rock is my favorite kind of music.
>
> Main Idea: I like the sound of rock music and the messages in the songs.
>
> Supporting Details: The lyrics tell about real-life situations. The ideas in the songs make me think. Rock music has a good beat that I can dance to.

Notice how the student used details to support the main idea.

Writing Process Activity

Look at the movie topic you chose to write about. On a separate sheet of paper, list several details to support your main idea.

The Writing Process

Why is it important to focus the topic before you gather details? (See The Writing Process, page WP6.)

Taking notes helps you to keep a record of the information you find. One way to take notes is to answer the *wh-* questions. The *wh-* questions are *Who? What? When? Where?* and *Why?* As you look through books, magazines, and the Internet ask yourself the *wh-* questions. The answers to these questions are usually important details.

One student read the following paragraph in a book about rock music. Her notes are shown below.

> Bob Mitchell and The Rockets was a famous rock band. Their song "Rock and Roll Around the World" was recorded in 1964. It was the band's first worldwide hit. Young listeners felt that the song said what they were thinking and feeling.

English and Technology

You can always use a word-processing program to save and organize your notes.

See *Pacemaker® Computer Literacy* for more information on word processing.

Who was the first famous rock band?
   Bob Mitchell and The Rockets

What did they do?
   recorded "Rock and Roll Around the World"

When was it recorded?
   in 1964

Where was it a rock hit?
   worldwide

Why was it such a big hit?
   It said what young listeners were
   thinking and feeling.

Writing Process Activity

Think about the kind of movie you want to write about. Use the *wh-* questions to take notes about that kind of movie. Write your notes on a separate sheet of paper.

A-6 ► Organizing Details in an Outline

Once you have enough details, you need to organize them. A good way to organize details is to create an **outline**, or a plan that shows how a main idea and the details connect to each other.

Look at the following outline. Notice that the writing topic is listed first. It has the Roman numeral I next to it. The main idea is listed next. The capital letter A shows the main idea. Finally, each detail is listed under the main idea. The details are numbered from 1 to 3.

I. Rock is my favorite kind of music.

   A. I like the sound of rock and the messages in the lyrics.

      1. The lyrics tell about real-life situations.

      2. The ideas in the songs make me think.

      3. It has a good beat that I can dance to.

This sample outline is for just one paragraph. Sometimes, you will have to write longer pieces. Then, you can add more sections to your outline.

Writing Process Activity

On a separate sheet of paper, organize your ideas about your favorite kind of movie. Use your topic, main idea, and supporting details to create an outline.

Brush Up on the Basics

Use complete sentences when you include details in your writing. (See Grammar 1 in the Reference Guide.)

Chapter

A Review

Summary Have students use the summary to outline the main idea and details of the chapter.

Summary

Writers follow a series of steps called the writing process.
Prewriting is a time for thinking about and planning what you will write.
During prewriting, make sure you understand your writing assignment. Look for key words that will help you plan your writing.
Brainstorming is a way to find a writing topic. Brainstorming means thinking about and listing different ideas.
Choose a writing topic that fits the assignment. You may have to focus, or narrow, your topic to cover it in one paragraph.
Once you have a topic, think about what you want to say about the topic. This statement is the main idea of the paragraph.
Gather details to support the main idea of a paragraph. When taking notes, answer the *wh-* questions to find important details.
Make an outline, or plan, before you write. Use the topic, main idea, and supporting details as the parts of the plan.

topic

details

main idea

prewriting

outline

brainstorming

writing assignment

writing process

More Vocabulary Review is provided in the Classroom Resource Binder.

Vocabulary Review

**Match each term in the box with its meaning.
Write your answers on a separate sheet of paper.**

1. the planning stage of the writing process prewriting

2. thinking about and listing ideas for writing brainstorming

3. the small parts that make up the whole details

4. a plan that lays out the main part of your writing outline

5. what your topic is about main idea

6. a writing task that is given to a student writing assignment

7. the subject of a piece of writing topic

8. a five-step process for writing writing process

Chapter Quiz
1. By reading the assignment carefully, a writer can plan a piece of writing that meets the task.

2. When brainstorming, a writer works with others to think of ideas related to a topic. Brainstorming helps a writer to narrow a topic idea or to think of more ideas to write about.

3. Focusing lets a writer choose a topic that can be covered in one paragraph.

4. The details support, or tell about, the main idea of the paragraph.

Chapter Quiz

Complete the following items. Write your answers on a separate sheet of paper.

1. Why is it important to read the assignment carefully before you begin to write?

2. How would you use brainstorming to find ideas for writing?

3. Why is it important to focus, or narrow, a writing topic?

4. What do details add to a piece of writing?

5. What are two ways to find supporting details for a paragraph?

6. Why is it wise to make an outline before you begin to write?

7. How can an outline help you to organize your topic?

▶ **Test Tip**
Read all of the questions first. Then, begin to answer the questions you are sure of.

5. A writer may already know the topic well enough to be able to come up with some supporting details. A writer can also do research and take notes to answer the *wh-* questions to find supporting details.

6. An outline organizes information and shows how the details relate to the main idea.

7. The topic is written first next to a Roman numeral; the main idea is then written next to a capital letter. Supporting details are then written next to Arabic numerals (such as 1, 2, and 3).

Critical Thinking

What are three reasons prewriting is an important step in the writing process? Write your answer on a separate sheet of paper.

Critical Thinking Answers will vary. Possible answer: Prewriting is a time to think about and plan a writing assignment. By planning beforehand, the task of writing will be easier. Prewriting is a time to gather information to support your topic. Prewriting will make writing more organized.

Writing Activity

Suppose you get an assignment to write a paragraph about your favorite movie. Prepare for the assignment by doing some prewriting. On a separate sheet of paper, begin with brainstorming. Write your main idea and gather supporting details. Then, create an outline for your paragraph.

Writing Activity Check to make sure that students have a narrow enough topic to be covered in one paragraph and that they have at least three logical supporting details.

Drafting is a time to get ideas down on paper.

Arthur Conan Doyle *(1859–1930) was a doctor. He wrote drafts of stories while waiting for patients to come to his office. One day, Doyle created the famous detective Sherlock Holmes. Stories about Holmes became so popular that Doyle gave up medicine to write full-time. Two of his best-known Sherlock Holmes novels are* A Study in Scarlet *and* The Hound of the Baskervilles.

Extra Reading See the Pacemaker® Classics series for Arthur Conan Doyle's *The Adventures of Sherlock Holmes* and *The Hound of the Baskervilles.*

To help students tap their prior knowledge of the chapter topic, see the **Chapter Project** in the Classroom Resource Binder.

Learning Objectives

- Choose a purpose for writing.
- Identify the audience.
- Develop a first draft of a paragraph.
- Write a topic sentence for a paragraph.
- Write the body of a paragraph.
- Write a concluding sentence of a paragraph.
- Use a checklist to review your draft.

Chapter B / Drafting

Words to Know

purpose	the reason for writing something
audience	the people who read a piece of writing
drafting	the writing stage of the writing process
topic sentence	a sentence that states the main idea of a paragraph
body	the main part of a paragraph that gives the supporting details
concluding sentence	a sentence that ends a paragraph
restate	to say or write something again in different words
checklist	a list of things to look for and check off when done

Before you begin to write, ask yourself, *Why am I writing?* The answer is your reason, or **purpose**, for writing. There are four main purposes for writing. These purposes are to explain, to persuade, to inform, and to describe.

Some writing assignments tell you your purpose for writing. Have you ever had to tell someone how something works? If so, your purpose was to explain. Have you ever tried to ask someone to believe in something? Then, your purpose was to persuade.

Some writing assignments tell you your purpose. When you give facts and details, your purpose is to inform. When you show someone what someone or something looks like, your purpose is to describe. Knowing your purpose will help you choose ideas and details to include in your writing.

Writing Process Activity

Think about the paragraph you plan to write about your favorite kind of movie. What is the purpose of your paragraph? On a separate sheet of paper, explain how you chose your purpose for writing.

B-2 ▸ Identifying Your Audience

Another question to ask yourself before you write is, *Who is my audience?* Your **audience** is the person or the people who will read your writing. Often, your audience will be a teacher or your classmates. You may want others to read your writing, too.

Think about how much your readers know about your topic. What are their interests? What kind of information will you need to include? It may be that your audience does not know about your topic. If so, you will need to add information. This will allow your audience to follow what you say. It may be that your audience knows something about your topic. Then, you can skip some of the basic details. Knowing your audience will make you a more effective writer.

Think About It

How can you tell how much your readers know about your topic?

Writing Process Activity

Think about the audience for your paragraph about your favorite kind of movie. Who are your readers? How much do they know about your topic? What information will you need to include so that they will understand your ideas? Write your answer on a separate sheet of paper.

Writing the Topic Sentence

You have already completed the prewriting process for your paragraph. You also know your purpose and audience. Now, you are ready to begin writing. This is the **drafting** stage of the writing process. Do not worry about saying exactly what you want to say at this stage. Your task now is just to put your ideas down on paper.

The draft of your paragraph often begins with a **topic sentence**. The topic sentence states the main idea about the topic. All the other sentences in the paragraph explain or describe this topic sentence.

Look back at your prewriting list from page WP7. What is the most important thing you want to say about your topic? This is the sentence that tells your main idea. The sentence that tells your main idea is your topic sentence.

Look at the following student's notes. Notice how the student's topic sentence states the main idea.

> **Brush Up on the Basics**
>
> A sentence has a subject and a verb and expresses a complete thought. (See Grammar 1 in the Reference Guide.)

Topic: Rock is my favorite kind of music.

Main Idea: I like the sound of it. I like the messages in the songs.

Topic Sentence: Rock is my favorite kind of music because I like the sound of it and the messages in the songs.

Writing Process Activity

Look back at your prewriting list from page WP7 about a kind of movie you like. What is your topic? What is your main idea? On a separate sheet of paper, use these notes to draft your topic sentence.

To start drafting, write your topic sentence at the top of your paper. Now, you are ready to write the **body** of the paragraph. The body is the main part of your paragraph. It contains supporting details. You might use facts, details, or examples to support your topic sentence. All of the supporting details need to tell about the topic sentence.

Your prewriting outline will help you draft the body of your paragraph. The ideas next to numbers 1, 2, and 3 are supporting details. These details will form the body of your paragraph. Write a sentence about each of these ideas. This is the way you build a paragraph.

Compare this paragraph to the outline in Chapter A on page WP9. Notice how the details from the outline make up the body of the paragraph.

> *Rock is my favorite kind of music because I like the sound of it and the messages in the songs. The lyrics tell about real-life situations. The ideas in the songs make me think. It has a good beat that I can dance to.*

Writing Process Activity

Review your outline from Chapter A on page WP9 about your favorite kind of movie. Find the supporting details next to numbers 1, 2, and 3. These details tell why you like the type of movie you have chosen. On a separate sheet of paper, use the details to draft the body of your paragraph. Write the body after your topic sentence.

The Writing Process

Why is it important to identify your audience before you start drafting? (See The Writing Process, WP15.)

B-5 ▸ Writing the Conclusion

Most paragraphs end with a **concluding sentence**. A concluding sentence is a sentence that ends a paragraph. The conclusion is important. It tells the reader that you are finished writing about your idea.

Your concluding sentence can **restate** your main idea. When you restate something, you say it using different words. Try to find an interesting way to end your paragraph so that your audience will remember it.

Look at the following concluding sentence. Notice that it ends the paragraph. The writer uses the concluding sentence to tell readers what they should remember about the paragraph.

> I like rock music most because it expresses what I think and how I feel.

English and Technology

You can use a word-processing program to highlight the topic sentence. Then, you can refer to it when you write your concluding sentence.

Writing Process Activity

Decide how you will conclude your paragraph about your favorite kind of movie. What do you want your audience to remember? On a separate sheet of paper, draft your concluding sentence.

Using a Drafting Checklist

When you draft, you choose your purpose and identify your audience. You write a topic sentence. You write the body of your paragraph, and you write a concluding sentence.

There is one more thing you should do before you go onto the next step of the writing process. You should use a **checklist** to review your draft. A checklist is a list of things to look for and check off when you have done them. Look at the checklist below to make sure that your paragraph contains all of the information you will need.

Drafting Checklist

❑ Do I state the purpose of my paragraph?

❑ Do I know who my audience is?

❑ Do I give my readers all the information they need to understand my topic?

❑ Does my topic sentence state the main idea of my topic?

❑ Does the body of my paragraph explain my topic?

❑ Does my concluding sentence help my readers remember my paragraph?

Writing Process Activity

Use the drafting checklist to improve your draft about your favorite kind of movie. Add any items to your draft that are missing.

Chapter

B / Review

Summary Have students use the summary to outline the main idea and details of the chapter.

Summary

Drafting is a chance to get your ideas down on paper.

A writer chooses the purpose, or reason, for writing. The main purposes for writing are to explain, to persuade, to inform, and to describe.

The writer thinks about the knowledge and interests of an audience.

A paragraph often begins with a topic sentence.

Supporting details form the body of a paragraph.

A paragraph ends with a concluding sentence.

A writer can use a drafting checklist to improve a draft.

body

concluding sentence

checklist

topic sentence

audience

purpose

drafting

restate

1. audience

2. drafting

3. topic sentence

4. purpose

5. body

6. concluding sentence

7. restate

8. checklist

More Vocabulary Review is provided in the Classroom Resource Binder.

Vocabulary Review

Complete each sentence with a term from the box. Write your answers on a separate sheet of paper.

1. Your teacher or classmates will often be the _____ of your writing.

2. The writing stage of the writing process is called _____.

3. The opening sentence of a paragraph is often the _____.

4. One _____ for writing a story is to inform readers.

5. Sentences with supporting details form the _____ of the paragraph.

6. The _____ sums up the paragraph.

7. One way to end a paragraph is to _____ the main idea.

8. A list of things to look for and check off when completed is called a _____.

Chapter Quiz
1. The purpose would be to persuade because you are asking the principal to have the school hold more dances.

2. The draft is a chance for writers to get their ideas down on paper.

3. The topic and main idea from the outline together can form the topic sentence.

Chapter Quiz

Complete the following items. Write your answers on a separate sheet of paper.

1. Suppose that you are writing a letter to the principal. You ask that the school hold more dances. What would be your purpose for writing?

2. What is a draft?

3. How does an outline help you write a topic sentence for a paragraph?

4. What do all the sentences in the body of a paragraph do?

5. What is the purpose of a concluding sentence in a paragraph?

▶ **Test Tip**
If you know the meaning of each vocabulary term, it can help you answer the questions.

4. All the sentences in the body tell about or support the topic sentence or main idea.

5. The purpose of a concluding sentence is to restate the main idea in different words. It sums up and ends the paragraph powerfully.

Critical Thinking

What three points should you remember when you draft a paragraph? Write your answer on a separate sheet of paper.

Critical Thinking Possible answer: When drafting, a writer must first think of the purpose of the writing and who the audience will be. Creating a strong topic sentence is also important at this stage of the writing process. A writer should also use supporting details to create the body of the paragraph.

Writing Activity

For the writing assignment in Chapter A on page WP9, you created an outline about your favorite kind of movie. Now use the outline to draft a paragraph on a separate sheet of paper.

Writing Activity Check to make sure that students use their outline to guide them as they construct their paragraph.

Careful writers revise their drafts to improve their work.

Mark Twain (1835–1910) is one of our country's most popular authors. His writing style is both funny and thoughtful. It shows that he understands people. The Adventures of Tom Sawyer *and* The Adventures of Huckleberry Finn *are two of his most famous novels. Twain often wrote the first drafts of his stories in notebooks while he was traveling. Later, he revised the drafts.*

Extra Reading See the Pacemaker® Classics series for Mark Twain's *The Adventures of Tom Sawyer, The Adventures of Huckleberry Finn,* and *The Prince and the Pauper.*

To help students tap their prior knowledge of the chapter topic, see the **Chapter Project** in the Classroom Resource Binder.

Learning Objectives

- Revise a draft for purpose and audience.
- Revise a draft to organize information.
- Make writing flow smoothly.
- Use a checklist to revise a draft.

Chapter C Revising

Words to Know

revise	to make changes in a piece of writing
define	to give the meaning of a word
organize	to put the parts of something in order
order of importance	organizing sentences from most important to least important
sentence structure	the way in which a sentence is written
combine	to join together

When you **revise** a piece of writing, you make changes to it. To revise your draft, look at it again. You may want to read your writing aloud to see how your words and ideas sound. As you read, look for ways to improve your paragraph.

Think About It

Why is it important to define new words in a paragraph?

Think about your purpose for writing when you revise. Does your paragraph clearly explain your ideas? Also, think about your audience. Your teacher and classmates will read your paragraph. Will the paragraph be clear to them? How much do they know about your topic? Perhaps you have used words or ideas that they do not know. If so, **define**, or give the meaning, of these new words in your paragraph.

Look at the following body of the paragraph. What revisions do you see?

Rock is my favorite kind of music, because
~~I like~~
I like the sound of it, and the messages in
or words,
the songs. The lyrics, tell about real-life
about my own life
situations. The ideas in the songs make me think,
Rock   lively rhythm
~~It~~ has a ~~good beat~~. I can dance to it.

Notice how the student uses details to explain why rock music is his or her favorite kind of music.

Writing Process Activity

Read your paragraph aloud to a classmate. Ask him or her if your explanation is clear. Is there anything that is hard to understand? Revise the paragraph based on what your classmate suggests. Be sure to define any words that your audience may not understand.

When you draft, your task is to put your ideas on paper. Sometimes, those ideas are not in the best order. Revising is a time to **organize** your ideas, or put them in a clear order. Organization will help your audience follow your ideas.

One way to organize your ideas is by **order of importance**, or organizing sentences from most important to least important. To use order of importance, you need to decide what is the most important idea. Then, you need to decide what is the least important idea. Start the body of your paragraph with your topic sentence. This is your most important idea. Then, work your way down to the least important idea.

> **English and Technology**
>
> You can use a word-processing program to cut and paste sentences when you revise for organization.

Look again at the following paragraph. Notice how the writer has changed the order of the sentences.

Rock is my favorite kind of music. I like the sound of it. I like the messages in the songs. The lyrics, or words, tell about real-life situations. The ideas in the songs make me think about my own life. Rock has a lively rhythm. I can dance to it.

Notice how the student has put the most important idea first.

Writing Process Activity

Review your paragraph about your favorite kind of movie. Think about the order of the sentences. Are your reasons listed in their order of importance? If not, organize the sentences in your paragraph on a separate sheet of paper.

C-3 ▶ Making Your Writing Flow

When your writing flows, it is clear and accurate. Look closely at each sentence in your paragraph. Pay close attention to the **sentence structure**, or the way the sentence is put together. First, make sure that each sentence states a complete thought. Then, ask yourself, *Do all my sentences support the main idea?* If you find sentences that do not support your topic sentence, there are two things you can do. You can either get rid of them or you can rewrite them so that they fit.

Good writing has many types of sentences. Some are short, others are long. Do your sentences tend to be short? If so, you can **combine**, or join together, two short sentences. That might make your paragraph read more smoothly. It will help your readers see how your ideas are connected. Some words that help you combine sentences are *and*, *but*, and *or*. Some words that help your sentences sound smoother are *also*, *next*, *first*, *finally*, *in addition*, *for example*, *than*, *most important*, and *however*.

Look at the following paragraph. The writer has combined two sentences. The writer has also added words to make the writing flow more smoothly.

> Rock is my favorite kind of music. **Most important,** The lyrics, or words, tell about real-life situations. **In addition,** The ideas in the songs make me think about my own life. I **also** like the sound of it **and** I like the messages in the songs. **For example,** Rock has a lively rhythm **that** I can dance to it.

Writing Process Activity

Read your paragraph about your favorite kind of movie aloud. Look for ways to combine any short sentences. Add words that make the sentences sound smoother.

C-4 ▶ Using a Revision Checklist

So far, you have revised your paragraph in three ways. You have thought about your purpose and audience. You may also have changed the order of your sentences. You have also revised sentences for structure and variety.

There are other ways to revise as well. Use the following checklist to help you make your writing clear.

The Writing Process

What words can you add to your writing to make it flow? (See The Writing Process, page WP26.)

Revision Checklist

❏ Does my paragraph answer all parts of the assignment?

❏ Does my topic sentence state the main idea clearly?

❏ Are my supporting details clear?

❏ Do all of my sentences flow smoothly?

❏ Can I make my concluding sentence stronger?

Compare the following paragraph with the draft on page WP24. How has revising improved it?

> Rock is my favorite kind of music. Most important, the lyrics, or words, tell about real-life situations. In addition, the ideas in the songs make me think about my own life. I also like the sound of it and the messages in the songs. For example, rock has a lively rhythm that I can dance to. I like rock music because it speaks to what I think and how I feel.

Notice that the student added a concluding sentence.

Writing Process Activity

Use the revision checklist to improve your paragraph about your favorite kind of movie. Will your readers understand your ideas?

Summary Have students use the summary to outline the main idea and details of the chapter.

Summary

Revising is a chance to make changes that improve your draft.
Your writing needs to meet the purpose of the assignment. It also has to meet the needs of the audience.
The sentences in a paragraph are organized. They have an order that makes sense to the reader.
Write sentences of different lengths and types, so that they will flow smoothly.
A revision checklist is a handy tool. Use a checklist whenever you revise your work.

sentence structure
order of importance
combine
define
revise
organize

1. combine
2. organize
3. revise
4. sentence structure
5. define
6. order of importance

More Vocabulary Review is provided in the Classroom Resource Binder.

Vocabulary Review

Match each term in the box with its meaning. Write your answers on a separate sheet of paper.

   1. to join together

   2. to put the parts of something in order

   3. to make changes in a piece of writing

   4. the way in which a sentence is put together

   5. to give the meaning of a word

   6. organizing sentences from most to least important

Chapter Quiz

1. You make changes to a piece of writing.

2. Writers might have to make changes to their writing to meet their original purpose for writing.

3. You might define some words or change some ideas so your audience can better understand your writing.

Chapter Quiz

Complete the following items. Write your answers on a separate sheet of paper.

1. What do you do when you revise a piece of writing?

2. Why is it important to think about your purpose for writing when you revise?

3. What are two ways to revise your writing so your audience understands your ideas?

4. Why is it important to organize your paragraph?

5. What is one way to order the sentences in a paragraph that explains?

6. How can a checklist help you revise your writing?

▶ **Test Tip**
Use a separate sheet of paper to make notes about each question.

4. Organizing your paragraph helps your audience follow your ideas.

5. Order of importance is one way to order a paragraph that explains.

6. A checklist reminds you of the many ways to revise a paragraph.

Critical Thinking

Look over the revisions you have made in your paragraph about your favorite kind of movie. How has revising your paragraph made it clearer? Write your answer on a separate sheet of paper.

Critical Thinking Possible Answer: Revising makes a paragraph stronger, better organized, and easier to follow. It makes sentences flow more smoothly and details clearer.

Writing Activity

Reread the draft you wrote in Chapter B. Then, choose a different audience. Think about how you could revise your paragraph for your new audience. Use the checklist on page WP27 to revise your paragraph.

Writing Activity Be sure that students use the checklist on page WP27 and that their revisions make their paragraphs stronger.

A careful writer edits a piece of writing until it is clear and strong.

Maya Angelou (born 1928) is an African American author and poet. As a young woman, she was a professional singer and dancer. Later, she became a leader in the Civil Rights movement. Angelou's autobiography I Know Why the Caged Bird Sings *tells about her early life. Angelou also worked as a magazine editor. Her writing skills helped her edit her own work and the work of others.*

To help students tap their prior knowledge of the chapter topic, see the **Chapter Project** in the Classroom Resource Binder.

Learning Objectives

- Edit a paragraph for word choice and spelling.
- Edit a paragraph for grammar and mechanics.
- Edit a paragraph for capitalization and punctuation.
- Use a checklist to edit your writing.

Chapter D  Editing

Words to Know

editing	correcting mistakes in a piece of writing
thesaurus	a book that lists words that are similar in meaning
grammar	a set of rules for writing and speaking a language
irregular verbs	verbs that do not use -d or -ed to form their past tense
punctuation marks	marks used to make the meaning of writing clear
proofreading marks	marks used to show editing changes

D-1 ▸ Editing for Word Choice and Spelling

Now that you have revised your paragraph, you are ready to edit it. **Editing** is the fourth step of the writing process. When you edit, you correct mistakes in a piece of writing.

Choosing the right word is part of editing. When you choose the right word, you help your reader see your ideas clearly. The words you choose give your writing a "voice." As you edit, look for words that are used too often or words that do not draw a clear picture. Replace them with more exact words. A thesaurus can help you find more exact words. A **thesaurus** is a book that lists words that are similar in meaning.

As you edit, check your spelling. Make sure you have written the correct form of words that sound the same, like *their* and *there*. Circle any words that you think may be spelled wrong and check them using a dictionary.

Read the following paragraph. What words has the writer changed? Why do you think these changes were made? What spellings will the writer check?

Notice how the student corrected the spelling mistakes.

English and Technology

Many word-processing programs have a thesaurus that you can use to find more exact words.

> The electric guitar is the basic part of rok
> music. Most rock grups use an electric bass,
> drums, and a keyboard, to. Generlly, one singer
> does the vocals.

Writing Process Activity

Read your revised paragraph. Look for words that are used too often. Make sure that you paint a clear picture. Also, check the spelling in your paragraph.

Grammar is a set of rules for writing and speaking a language. Grammar helps your readers to understand your ideas. You know a lot of grammar already just from speaking and listening to others. Still, it is easy to make grammar mistakes.

Here are some points to remember as you edit for grammar.

- Every sentence should state a complete thought. Include a subject and a verb in each sentence.

- Use end marks to help your readers see how your ideas are connected. You can also use a comma followed by a word like *and*, *but*, and *or* to link two sentences.

- Look for **irregular verbs**. Irregular verbs do not use *-d* or *-ed* to form their past tenses. For example, the past tense of *see* is *saw*. Check a dictionary if you are not sure of a verb's forms.

Think About It

Why is it important to help your readers see how your ideas are connected?

Notice how the student edits these sentences for grammar. What correction is made to each of the following sentences?

> *has been*
> From the beginning, rock ∧popular with young
> *written*
> audiences. Young people have ~~wrote~~ most rock
> *es*
> songs○ they have also played them. Rock express∧
> the feelings and experiences of youth.

Writing Process Activity

Edit the grammar of your paragraph about your favorite kind of movie. Look for ways to link your sentences. Also, make any corrections in verb tense that you may have made.

D-3 Editing for Capitalization and Punctuation

Your paragraph is now almost complete. Still, you may have missed a few small errors. Careful writers and editors try to catch them all.

Capitalization is one thing to check. Every sentence should begin with a capital letter. The names of particular people, places, things, and ideas also begin with capitals. Then, check the punctuation of your sentences. **Punctuation marks** are marks that make the meaning of your writing clear. It helps your reader understand how your ideas fit together. Every sentence should end with a period, a question mark, or an exclamation point.

Other punctuation marks are important, too. The apostrophe (') shows ownership in sentences. *This is your dog's bowl* shows that the bowl belongs to your dog. They also show where letters have been left out of contractions. Quotation marks (") show the exact words of a speaker. If Nadia spoke the sentence, it would look like this: *"This is your dog's bowl."* Quotation marks are also used around the names of songs, stories, and poems.

Notice how one student edited the following paragraph for capitalization and punctuation. Why do you think each change was made?

> Bob mitchell and the rockets was a famous rock band. Their song "rock and roll around the world" was recorded in 1964. it was the band's first Worldwide hit. Young listeners felt that the song said what they were thinking and feeling.

Brush Up on the Basics

Use quotation marks at the beginning and at the end of each part of a speaker's words. (See Punctuation 14 in the Reference Guide.)

Writing Process Activity

Edit your paragraph about your favorite kind of movie. Check the capitalization and punctuation.

D-4 ▸ Using an Editing Checklist

Look at the following editing checklist. Use the checklist whenever you edit.

Editing Checklist

❑ Do all the sentences state a complete thought?

❑ Are any words missing?

❑ Are all the words spelled correctly?

❑ Do all the sentences begin with capital letters?

❑ Do all the sentences end with a punctuation mark?

The Writing Process

How is editing different than revising? (See the Writing Process, page WP27.)

You can use special marks, like the ones shown in blue below, to show your editing changes. They are called **proofreading marks**. Using these marks makes editing easier. The marks help you see where a correction needs to be made.

Insert letters or words here.	∧	Make this letter lowercase.	/
Capitalize this letter.	≡	Delete or replace this.	⌿
Indent a new paragraph.	⁊	Check spelling.	◯

Writing Process Activity

On a separate sheet of paper, rewrite the following paragraph. Use the proofreading marks above to correct the errors.

Rock music is the leading popular music today. It was called rock-'n'-roll. In it's early days. Today, people all over the World lissen to rock. Hundreds of Millions of rock CD's are sold every year

Summary Have students use the summary to outline the main idea and details of the chapter.

Summary

Editing is the fourth step of the writing process. Editing is a chance to make final corrections in your writing.

When editing, replace unclear words with more exact ones. A thesaurus can help you choose words to use. Use a dictionary to check the spelling of words.

Make sure each sentence has a subject and verb and states a complete thought. Make sure the forms of all verbs are correct.

Edit for capitalization and punctuation. Every sentence begins with a capital letter and ends with a period, question mark, or exclamation point.

Use an editing checklist when you edit. Use proofreading marks to show the changes you want to make in your writing.

| thesaurus |
| editing |
| proofreading marks |
| irregular verbs |
| punctuation marks |
| grammar |

1. editing
2. irregular verbs
3. thesaurus
4. punctuation marks
5. grammar
6. proofreading marks

More Vocabulary Review is provided in the Classroom Resource Binder.

Vocabulary Review

Complete each sentence with a term from the box. Write your answers on a separate sheet of paper.

1. You correct mistakes in a piece of writing when you are _____.

2. Verbs that do not use -*d* or -*ed* to form their past tense are called _____.

3. A book that lists words that are similar in meaning is called a _____.

4. Commas and periods are types of _____.

5. The rules of _____ tell how language should be written and spoken.

6. Writers use _____ to show the changes they want to make in their work.

Chapter Quiz
1. Correcting mistakes makes a piece of writing better and easier to understand.

2. A thesaurus helps a writer find a more exact word.
3. A dictionary helps a writer check the spelling or meaning of a word.

4. A writer might correct sentences to form a complete thought, to show how ideas are connected, or to correct verb forms.

Chapter Quiz

Complete the following items. Write your answers on a separate sheet of paper.

1. Why is it important to correct mistakes in your writing?

2. When might you use a thesaurus?

3. When might you use a dictionary?

4. What are three types of grammar errors you might edit in your writing?

5. When would you add quotation marks in a paragraph?

6. When would you use an apostrophe?

7. What does each of the following proofreading marks stand for?

    a. ≡

    b. /

    c. ∧

▶ **Test Tip**
If a question asks when you might use something, try to picture how you used it.

5. Quotation marks are added to show the exact words of a speaker or the name of a song, story, or poem.

6. An apostrophe shows ownership; it also shows where letters have been left out of a contraction.

7. **a.** capitalize this letter
    b. make this letter lower case
    c. insert letters or words here

Critical Thinking

What three points should you remember when you edit a paragraph? Write your answer on a separate sheet of paper.

Critical Thinking Answers will vary. Possible answer: A writer should check his or her work carefully for correct word choice and spelling. The writer should also check grammar, capitalization, and punctuation.

Writing Activity

For the writing assignment on page WP27, you revised a paragraph about your favorite movie. Look back at that writing now. Use the checklist on page WP35 and proofreading marks to edit your paragraph.

Writing Activity Check to make sure that students are using the checklist on WP35 and that students are using proofreading marks to show their corrections.

Authors publish their writing to reach a wide audience.

Mary Shelley (1795–1851) was an English author. One stormy night, she was having a party. Some of her friends challenged her to write a scary story. Shelley was only nineteen, but she began to write her story. At first, she shared her story by reading it aloud to friends. Later, she published it for everyone to read. The story was called Frankenstein. *This novel was a huge success around the world. Mary Shelley had created a new type of literature—the horror story.*

Extra Reading See the Pacemaker® Classics series for Mary Shelley's *Frankenstein.*

To help students tap their prior knowledge of the chapter topic, see the **Chapter Project** in the Classroom Resource Binder.

Learning Objectives

- Prepare to publish a piece of writing.
- Publish a piece of writing.
- Understand the purpose of an oral presentation.
- Understand the purpose of a word processing program.

Chapter E  Publishing

Words to Know

publishing	sharing your writing with others
contribute	to give something to others
oral presentation	a talk given to a group
word processing	a computer software, or program, used to type and change text
typeface	a style of type

Publishing means sharing your writing with others. It is the final step of the writing process. All the work you have done so far leads up to publishing.

Sharing your work is important. It is a chance to communicate your ideas to others. You will feel good when others enjoy your work. Good responses will make you want to write more.

Publishing is also a way to **contribute**, or give something to others. You might help your audience learn something. You might help a reader understand his or her thoughts or feelings.

Finally, publishing will prepare you for the future. Later on, whether you are at work or at school, you may have to write reports, letters, and memos. This writing will be shared with many people. It is important to feel comfortable with publishing your work.

There are many ways to publish your writing. You have probably already shared your writing by reading it to a partner or by posting it on a bulletin board. You and your classmates could also gather your paragraphs in a booklet. You might even submit your paragraph to the school newspaper or to a writing magazine.

Writing Process Activity

With a group of classmates, list four ways in which people publish their writing. Describe the audience that you might reach with each type of publishing.

The Writing Process

Why is it important to correct your work before you publish it? (See The Writing Process, pages WP24–WP25.)

E-2 ▸ Publishing Your Work

There are many ways to publish, or share, your work. One way to share your writing is to give an **oral presentation**. An oral presentation is a talk that is given to a group. You can reach your whole class in just a few minutes. As a speaker, your job is to make your talk as interesting as possible.

When you give a talk, try not to read your paragraph word for word. Instead, look at the audience as much as possible. You should be familiar enough with your paragraph to do that. If not, a little practice by yourself will help.

Another way to publish your work is to use word processing. **Word processing** is a computer program used to write something. Word-processing programs are powerful writing tools. They can help you check spelling and grammar. You can also use a word-processing program to print your work in different **typefaces**, or styles of type. You can also vary the size of the type. Suppose, for example, you want to post your paragraph on a bulletin board. Using large-sized type will make your writing easier to read.

Think About It

Why is it important to follow the steps of the writing process for an oral presentation?

Writing Process Activity

Prepare an oral presentation. Present your paragraph to the class. Listen carefully as your classmates present their paragraphs. After the presentations, discuss what you liked about each one.

Chapter

E ▶ Review

Summary Have students use the summary to outline the main idea and details of the chapter.

Summary

Publishing is a chance to share your work with an audience. There are many ways to publish a piece of writing.

Publishing lets you show off your writing skills. It is a chance to contribute information to others. Publishing also prepares you for future writing tasks in school or on the job.

An oral presentation is one way to publish your writing. Speakers try to be relaxed and know their presentation.

Computers make publishing easier. Word-processing programs let a writer print an attractive final copy.

| oral presentation |
| typeface |
| contribute |
| word processing |
| publishing |

1. word processing
2. publishing
3. oral presentation
4. typeface
5. contribute

More Vocabulary Review is provided in the Classroom Resource Binder.

Vocabulary Review

Complete each of the following sentences with a term from the box. Write your answers on a separate sheet of paper.

1. A kind of computer program for writing is _____.

2. The sharing of your writing is called _____.

3. It is important to speak loudly and clearly during an _____.

4. With a computer, you can choose any _____ to print your work.

5. When you publish, you _____ ideas and information to others.

Chapter Quiz

Complete the following items. Write your answers on a separate sheet of paper.

1. What are two reasons to publish your writing?

2. List three ways to publish your paragraph about a favorite kind of movie.

3. Why is it important to be familiar with your paragraph before giving an oral presentation?

4. How do word-processing programs help you to publish a piece of writing?

Critical Thinking

Why is it important to know your audience before you publish your writing? Write your answer on a separate sheet of paper.

Critical Thinking Answers will vary. Students should note that knowing their audience will help them publish their writing in the most effective way.

▶ **Test Tip**
Make sure to reread your answers and correct any mistakes.

Chapter Quiz

1. Publishing can make you feel good about your writing; it lets you contribute to others; it also prepares you for on-the-job writing.

2. It could be read aloud, posted on a bulletin board, or combined with others in a booklet.

3. If I am familiar with my paragraph, I can look at the audience as I speak instead of just reading.

4. Word-processing programs make revising and editing easier; they can also check for spelling and grammar errors.

Writing Activity

For the writing assignment in Chapter D on page WP37, you edited your paragraph about your favorite kind of movie. Now, publish that paragraph for your audience.

Writing Activity You may wish to lay the groundwork for students' options by asking permission to display students' work in your school's library, adding their work to morning announcements, and so on.

Unit **Review**

Read each of the following items. On a separate sheet of paper, write the letter that best answers each one.

1. What does an outline help you do?
   - A. check spelling
   - B. choose better words
   - C. make a writing plan
   - D. publish a paragraph

2. You would draft the body of a paragraph
   - A. before you gather supporting details.
   - B. after you revise for organization.
   - C. before you narrow the topic.
   - D. after you write a topic sentence.

3. During revising, you would
   - A. make sure your paragraph is neatly typed.
   - B. decide on a purpose for writing.
   - C. identify your audience.
   - D. make sure your sentences flow smoothly.

4. Which proofreading mark would you use to show a word should begin with a capital letter?
   - A. ౨
   - B. ⊼
   - C. ≡
   - D. /

5. Publishing your work is important because
   - A. it lets you show off your writing skills.
   - B. it is a way to contribute information to others.
   - C. it prepares you for writing you will have to do on a job.
   - D. all of the above

Critical Thinking Answers will vary. Possible response: Each stage of the writing process helps a writer make a more organized, clearer, and stronger piece of writing. Skipping any of the stages would weaken the writing.

Writing Activity Answers will vary. Encourage students to really think about how they can apply the five stages of the writing process to their own writing.

> **Critical Thinking**
> How does each stage of the writing process help you to create a clear paragraph? Write your answer on a separate sheet of paper.
> **WRITING ACTIVITY** Write a letter to a friend. Explain how your friend could use the writing process to complete an assignment. Write your letter on a separate sheet of paper.

Unit 1 ▶ Writing Sentences

The job of news writers is to communicate current events to readers. They write and copy-edit thousands of words a day. They group these words into sentences. Why are sentences and punctuation important for news writers?

Caption Accept all reasonable responses. Possible answer: Sentences and punctuation allow writers to communicate their ideas clearly and effectively.

1

Writers make their characters come alive through carefully written sentences.

Willa Cather (1873–1947) grew up in Nebraska. Cather's neighbors came from many different countries. When Cather became a writer, she created main characters that were based on her neighbors. Cather made her characters come alive through carefully written sentences. O Pioneers! and My Ántonia are two well-known novels by Willa Cather. They tell about early life on the prairie and the people who settled there.

Extra Reading See the Pacemaker® Classics series for Willa Cather's *O Pioneers!*

To help students tap their prior knowledge of the chapter topic, see the **Chapter Project** in the Classroom Resource Binder.

Learning Objectives

- Explain what makes a group of words a complete sentence.

- Identify the subject and the predicate as the two main parts of a sentence.

- Write and punctuate a complete sentence.

Chapter What Is a Sentence?

Words to Know

sentence	a group of words that expresses a complete thought; a sentence has a subject and a predicate. It begins with a capital letter and ends with a punctuation mark.
subject	the part of the sentence that tells who or what the sentence is about
predicate	the part of the sentence that tells something about the subject
simple subject	the most important noun or pronoun in the sentence; what the sentence is about
noun	a word that names a person, a place, a thing, or an idea
simple predicate	the verb or verb phrase in the sentence
verb	a word that expresses action or being
command	a sentence that gives an order

1-1 ▶ Identifying Sentences

You use sentences every day when you speak and when you write. A **sentence** is a group of words that expresses a complete thought. Sentences are one way that we communicate with each other.

"The bus stops at Main Street," you might say. If so, you have just used a sentence. You may write a note in class and pass it to a friend. You use sentences in the note. You might write, "Will you meet me after school?" That is a sentence. Your teacher might say, "Bring me the note." That is a sentence, too.

What makes these groups of words sentences?

1. Each expresses a complete thought and makes sense on its own.

2. Each contains a **subject** and a **predicate**. The subject tells who or what the sentence is about. The predicate tells what the subject is doing.

Let us look at the first reason. What do we mean when we say that a sentence expresses a complete thought and makes sense on its own?

Read the following group of words.

The gray car raced around the corner.

It is a complete sentence. It has a subject: *gray car*. It has a predicate: *raced around the corner*. It begins with a capital letter and ends with a period. It also makes sense.

English and Technology

How has technology affected the ways that we communicate?

See *Pacemaker® Computer Literacy* for more information about using computers to communicate.

Now, read this group of words.

the gray car

Do these words make sense on their own? Do they express a complete thought? Are you wondering what the writer wants to say about the gray car? *The gray car* is just a phrase. It is not a sentence.

A sentence makes sense by itself. It expresses a complete thought.

Practice A

On a separate sheet of paper, make each of the following groups of words into a complete sentence.

The big, yellow cat _____. (What did it do?)

> **Example:** The big, yellow cat watched the tiny mouse.

1. The army of red ants _____. (What did it do?)

2. Joe Green _____. (What did he do?)

3. _____ turned on the radio. (Who did it?)

4. A terrible thunderstorm _____. (What did it do?)

5. _____ eats everything in sight. (Who or what does it?)

6. The kids in the swimming pool _____. (What did they do?)

7. _____ tore open the letter. (Who did it?)

8. _____ fell to the hard ground. (Who or what did it?)

9. _____ wore an ugly mask. (Who or what did it?)

10. The last dinosaur on Earth _____. (What did it do?)

> **Brush Up on the Basics**
>
> Sentences begin with capital letters and end with punctuation marks. (See Grammar 1 in the Reference Guide.)

Answers will vary. Answers are correct if they express a complete thought, make sense on their own, contain a subject and a predicate, and begin with a capital letter and end with a period.

A sentence must have a subject and a predicate.

Read the following sentence again.

The gray car raced around the corner.

A **simple subject** is the most important noun or pronoun in a sentence. It tells *what* a sentence is about. The simple subject in this sentence is *car*. The simple subject of a sentence is always a **noun** or pronoun. A noun is a word that names a person, a place, a thing, or an idea. *Car* is the *what* in the example above.

simple subject: *car*

The **simple predicate** is the verb or verb phrase in a sentence. The simple predicate in the sentence above is *raced*. The simple predicate of a sentence is always a verb or verb phrase. A **verb** is a word that expresses action or being. The simple predicate tells what the subject did.

Raced tells what the *car* did.

simple predicate: *raced*

Practice B

On a separate sheet of paper, copy each of the following sentences. Notice that each one begins with a capital letter and ends with a period. Underline the simple subject of each sentence once. Underline the simple predicate twice.

Example: <u>Maggie</u> <u>broke</u> the red balloon.

1. Linda screamed.

2. An elephant broke the bars of the cage.

3. Her umbrella had red and yellow stripes.

4. Richard won $2 million.

5. The accident happened at midnight.

Punctuating Sentences

Every sentence begins with a capital letter.

When a sentence just states information, it ends with a period.

> Example: The dog barked at Harry.

Sometimes, a sentence asks a question. Then, it ends with a question mark.

> Example: Who took Harry's dog?

A sentence that expresses very strong feelings, like fear or excitement, ends with an exclamation point.

> Example: Wow, I won tickets to the concert!

The Writing Process

Why is it important to pay attention to punctuation? (See The Writing Process, page WP34.)

Practice A

On a separate sheet of paper, copy each of the following sentences. Capitalize the first word in each sentence. End each sentence with a period, a question mark, or an exclamation point. Remember that most sentences end with periods.

1. the movie begins at seven o'clock
2. will your brother go with us
3. i can't believe there is a spider on your desk
4. the basketball team won again
5. did you finish your work

1. The movie begins at seven o'clock.
2. Will your brother go with us?
3. I can't believe there is a spider on your desk!
4. The basketball team won again.
5. Did you finish your work?

Why is it important to know what a sentence is? Remember that when you write, you are trying to communicate with someone else. You want your ideas to make sense. You want to be understood. It is very hard to understand writing that is not broken into sentences.

> The dark clouds meant rain last night we decided to stay home it was lucky a storm flooded the roads.

The ideas in the writing above are unclear. They run together and are hard to read. Punctuation clears up these ideas. It separates them, so we understand what the writer is saying. Look at the same words written in sentences.

> The dark clouds meant rain. Last night we decided to stay home. It was lucky. A storm flooded the roads.

Communicate clearly. Let your readers know where your ideas begin and end. Write in complete sentences.

Practice B

Answers will vary. Answers are correct if they are complete sentences that begin with a capital letter and end with the appropriate end mark.

On a separate sheet of paper, write five sentences of your own. A topic is suggested for each of your sentences.

1. summer

2. jet planes

3. a special friend

4. a television star

5. your next-door neighbor

A Special Kind of Sentence

A **command** is a sentence that gives an order. The command is a special kind of sentence. Sometimes, commands are used in this book when you are asked to do an activity or to think about something. When you tell someone to do something, or give a command, you can call that person by name.

> Example: Paul, take out the garbage.

In this case, *Paul* is the subject of the sentence.

Another way is just to give the command.

> Example: Take out the garbage.

Take is the simple predicate in this sentence. It seems this sentence has no subject. However, there must be a subject in a complete sentence. In a command, the subject is an understood "you." It is as if the sentence reads the following way.

> You take out the garbage.

A command can end with a period or, if it shows strong feeling, with an exclamation point. The following command shows strong feeling.

> Stop that right now!

Portfolio Project

1. Write and punctuate a sentence that is a command.
2. Write and punctuate a sentence that is a question.
3. Write and punctuate a sentence that expresses strong feeling.

Answers will vary. Answers are correct if they are complete sentences. All must begin with a capital letter. Number 1 must end with a period or exclamation point. Number 2 must end with a question mark. Number 3 must end with an exclamation point.

WRITING WITH STYLE
Making Your Point

There are many ways to make the same point. Part of a writer's job is finding the best way to say something. A writer wants each sentence to be clear, to the point, and pleasant to the ear. Think of how your favorite song states its ideas. How would you *say* the same things? How would you want it to sound? The following sentences are all grammatically correct. They all make the same point. Which sentence do you like best? Why?

1. The frightened young girl tumbled off the cliff.

2. Off the cliff tumbled the young girl who was very frightened and she fell and fell and fell.

3. The girl fell off the cliff.

4. The young girl tumbled in a fright off the edge of the cliff.

You may have chosen Sentence 1 as the best sentence. It is clear and simple, but it still has enough description to give the readers a picture of the event.

VOCABULARY BUILDER
Using Context Clues to Find Meaning

When you read a word you do not know, you may be able to guess its meaning from the context. *Context* means the other words that surround the word you are trying to define. The way a word is used in a sentence very often gives you clues to its meaning.

The car speeding north collided with the car heading south.

You might be able to guess the meaning of the word *collided* from the rest of the sentence, or from its context.

The word *collided* means crashed together.

In each sentence below, one word is in italic type. Decide the meaning of the word in italic type from its context. Write down your definition of the word. Then, check a dictionary to see if you have written a correct definition. Put a star next to your definition if it comes close to the definition in a dictionary.

1. The cans of fruit and vegetables were stored in the kitchen *pantry*.   a cupboard or small room in which food is stored

2. The oil leak might *contaminate* the lake.   pollute, make dirty

3. The new computer worked fine except for one small *defect*.   fault, flaw

4. He seemed *depressed* after his dog died, and he was upset for weeks.   sad, in low spirits

5. The *marlin* struggled on the end of the line, but Susan reeled it in.   a large fish

6. She was having trouble seeing the chalkboard, so she went to an *optometrist*.   a person who examines eyes and prescribes glasses

7. The seven-foot-tall basketball star seemed *gigantic* to the little boy.   huge, very big

8. Martha was *astonished* when a purple elephant appeared in her bedroom!   surprised

Answers should be similar to those given but need not be exact.

fault, flaw

Summary Have students use the summary to outline the main idea and details of the chapter.

Summary

Complete sentences make your writing clearer.

A sentence expresses a complete thought. It makes sense on its own.

A sentence contains a subject and a predicate. Sometimes, the subject is understood, or not stated.

A sentence begins with a capital letter. It ends with a period, a question mark, or an exclamation point.

sentence
subject
predicate
simple subject
noun
simple predicate
verb
command

1. simple predicate
2. noun
3. sentence
4. verb
5. command
6. subject
7. simple subject
8. predicate

More Vocabulary Review is provided in the Classroom Resource Binder.

Vocabulary Review

Match each term in the box with its meaning. Write your answers on a separate sheet of paper.

1. the verb or verb phrase in a sentence

2. a word that names a person, a place, a thing, or an idea

3. a group of words that expresses a complete thought

4. a word that expresses action or being

5. a sentence that gives an order

6. the part of a sentence that tells who or what the sentence is about

7. the most important noun or pronoun in a sentence

8. the part of the sentence that tells something about the subject

Chapter Quiz

1. a. The <u>queen</u> <u>wore</u> a golden crown.

b. The <u>waiter</u> <u>dropped</u> the soup bowl.

c. No

d. No

e. The <u>people</u> <u>talked</u> about the party.

Chapter Quiz

Complete the following items. Write your answers on a separate sheet of paper.

1. Read each of the following items. If it is not a complete sentence, write **No**. If the item is a complete sentence, copy it on your paper. Then, underline the simple subject once and the simple predicate twice.

    a. The queen wore a golden crown.

    b. The waiter dropped the soup bowl.

    c. Hit the ground with a crash.

    d. A small crowd near the park.

    e. The people talked about the party.

2. What makes a group of words a sentence?

3. What punctuation marks can end a sentence?

4. When would you use each type of punctuation mark?

5. How is the subject of a command different from the subjects of other sentences?

▶ **Test Tip**
Read each question carefully so that you know what it is asking.

2. A sentence has both a subject and a predicate and expresses a complete thought. It begins with a capital letter and ends with a punctuation mark.

3. A period, question mark, or exclamation point can end a sentence.

4. A period ends most sentences. A question mark ends a question. An exclamation point can end sentences or commands that show strong feelings.

5. The subject of a command is often not stated. The subject *you* is understood.

Critical Thinking

What are some ways in which you use sentences every day? Write your answer on a separate sheet of paper.

Critical Thinking Answers will vary. Accept all reasonable answers. Answers might include the following: in speech, letters, e-mails, schoolwork.

Writing Activity

Think about something unusual that happened to you recently. How would you describe the event? On a separate sheet of paper, write four sentences about the event.

Writing Activity Answers will vary. Students' responses should be expressed in complete sentences, contain at least four sentences, and be properly punctuated.

Writing complete sentences is a skill all writers must learn.

Zora Neale Hurston *(1891–1960) grew up in Florida. Her parents died when she was nine. Hurston supported herself as a maid and a secretary. At the same time, she taught herself to write, using skills writers must learn. Later, she put herself through Barnard College in New York City. Two of her best-known books are* Jonah's Gourd Vine *and* Their Eyes Were Watching God. *Like Hurston herself, the characters in her novels struggle to overcome hardships.*

Reading Challenge See *Tapestry: A Multicultural Anthology* for an excerpt from Zora Neale Hurston's *Their Eyes Were Watching God.*

To help students tap their prior knowledge of the chapter topic, see the **Chapter Project** in the Classroom Resource Binder.

Learning Objectives

- Identify sentence fragments.
- Correct sentence fragments.
- Identify run-on sentences.
- Correct run-on sentences.
- Write complete sentences that begin with capital letters, end with punctuation marks, and express complete thoughts.

Chapter 2 ▷ Sentence Fragments and Run-ons

See the Workbook for **Extra Practice**.

Words to Know

fragment	a group of words that is not a complete sentence but is punctuated as if it were
run-on sentence	two or more sentences that have not been properly joined
conjunction	a word used to join or link words, phrases, ideas, and sentences; common conjunctions are *and, but,* and *or*

2-1 ▷ Sentence Fragments

A **fragment** is a group of words that is not a complete sentence. A piece broken from a dinner plate is a fragment. A splinter of wood broken from a larger piece is a fragment. In writing, a sentence fragment is a part of a sentence broken from the whole sentence. Sometimes, people mistakenly treat sentence fragments as if they were whole sentences.

> **The coach left the football.** *Under the bench.*

The words in italic type are a sentence fragment. They have been treated like a sentence, but they are not. The group of words has no verb. You learned in Chapter 1 that a sentence always has a predicate, part of which must be a verb. Therefore, *Under the bench* cannot be a sentence.

Be sure that when you begin a group of words with a capital letter and end it with a period, it is really a sentence. Does your sentence express a complete thought? Does it contain a subject and a predicate?

Fragment: The truck in the left lane.

It has no predicate.

Sentence: The truck in the left lane lost its load.

simple subject: *truck*

simple predicate: *lost*

In a sentence fragment, the first word is capitalized. End punctuation is used. However, a fragment does not express a complete thought. As you develop as a writer, you will learn to recognize fragments and to avoid using them. You want your sentences to express whole ideas and feelings, not just fragments of them.

Practice A

Three of the following five items are complete sentences, and two are sentence fragments. On a separate sheet of paper, write the numbers of the fragments. After each number that you write, explain why it is a fragment. Is it missing the subject or the predicate?

1. The beautiful dolls stood in the front window.

2. missing the predicate

2. A tall, dark man in a white coat.

3. The suitcase was stuffed with clothes.

4. missing the subject

4. Screamed and ran from the room.

5. They invited Susan.

Practice B

On a separate sheet of paper, rewrite the items you identified as fragments in Practice A. Make them into complete sentences. Use your imagination to finish the sentences.

Sometimes, sentence fragments can be corrected by joining them to other sentences. At other times, the fragment can be corrected by adding words to it to make a complete sentence.

> Wrong: On the train. The twins saw a movie star.

> Right: On the train, the twins saw a movie star.

> Wrong: The restaurant was too crowded. And noisy as well.

> Right: The restaurant was too crowded and noisy as well.

> or

> Right: The restaurant was too crowded. It was noisy as well.

Practice C

On a separate sheet of paper, correct any sentence fragments you find on page 18. Either turn them into separate, complete sentences, or join them to another sentence.

> Example: The bank robbers in masks. They went into the crowded bank.

> Right: The bank robbers in masks went into the crowded bank.

> or

> Right: The bank robbers wore masks. They went into the crowded bank.

(Practice C continues on next page.) ⫸

Answers may vary but should be similar to the following.

1. On her lucky day, she found a ten dollar bill.

2. The audience clapped loudly for her great magic show.

3. In great pain, the injured skier limped down the mountain.

4. Ken thought he forgot to do his homework, but it was only a dream. *or* Ken thought he forgot to do his homework. It was only a dream.

5. The ball was hit to far left field.

6. The sign showed the way to Cleveland.

7. She hated to do homework after school.

8. Just in time, the bell rang to end the boxing match.

9. Alexander the Great won many battles.

10. Dinner was ready, so we sat down to eat. *or* Dinner was ready. We sat down to eat.

1. On her lucky day. She found a ten dollar bill.

2. The audience clapped loudly. For her great magic show.

3. In great pain. The injured skier limped down the mountain.

4. Ken thought he forgot to do his homework. Was only a dream.

5. The ball was hit. To far left field.

6. The sign showed. The way to Cleveland.

7. Homework after school. She hated to do it.

8. Just in time. The bell rang to end the boxing match.

9. Alexander the Great. He won many battles.

10. Dinner was ready. Sat down to eat.

Sometimes in conversation, we answer questions with fragments. Read the following examples:

Question: Where did you go?

Answer: to the movies

Question: What did you see?

Answer: *Return of the Sea Slime*

In writing, it is always better to answer questions in complete sentences.

Why did you like the book?

Wrong: Because it was exciting.

Right: I liked the book because it was exciting.

This method is especially important when you answer test questions. Writing in complete sentences makes your answers clearer.

Practice D

On a separate sheet of paper, write five sentences about the last time you talked with, went to a movie with, or had fun with a friend or relative. Describe what happened, how people acted, and what you saw. Make sure each of your sentences is a complete thought with a subject and a predicate.

Answers will vary. Answers are correct if they are complete sentences that begin with a capital letter and end with an appropriate end mark.

2-2 ▶ Run-on Sentences

Sometimes, writers forget to separate their sentences. They forget to mark the end of one sentence with a period and the beginning of the next with a capital letter. A sentence that is not properly separated from another sentence is called a **run-on sentence**. Read the following sentences from a job application. The person has been asked why he feels he would make a good worker in a day-care center.

> I am from a large family, I was the oldest child and helped with the younger ones, and, well, I am patient but firm with children.

The item above has been punctuated as if it were one sentence. Really, it is three sentences.

> I am from a large family. I was the oldest child and helped with the younger ones. I am patient but firm with children.

Run-on sentences easily confuse your readers. Avoid run-ons. When you keep your readers in mind, you are helping yourself as well. Your ideas and feelings will come through clearly. Your readers will be able to follow your writing.

Think About It

How can missing periods and missing capital letters cause problems for readers?

A comma cannot separate two sentences. However, an end mark, such as a period, an exclamation point, or a question mark followed by a capital letter can separate sentences.

> Wrong: The little boy laughed, his toy robot worked.

> Right: The little boy laughed. His toy robot worked.

Practice A

Some of the following items are correctly written. Others are run-on sentences. On a separate sheet of paper, number from 1 to 10. Write **C** next to the number if the sentence is written correctly. Write **RO** next to the number if the sentence is a run-on.

1. C
2. RO
3. RO
4. C
5. C
6. RO
7. RO
8. C
9. RO
10. C

1. The alarm clock buzzed. It was time to start another day.

2. The last boy in line got no lunch the food had all been eaten.

3. The movie ended with a kiss it was a silly ending.

4. The bugs escaped from the box. Her collection was ruined.

5. The garbage truck banged and clattered and woke up all the people.

6. The pig grunted loudly, the chickens clucked in the chicken coop.

7. Do you think that was a scary movie my cousin almost fainted when he saw it?

8. Ann fell off her bike and hurt her knee.

9. Mark went to the store he bought milk.

10. The television suddenly went off. The power was out.

How can you correct run-on sentences?

There are two easy ways to correct them.

1. Write two separate sentences.

   Run-on: Popcorn once was free now you pay for each serving.

   Corrected: Popcorn once was free. Now you pay for each serving.

2. Join the sentences with a comma and a **conjunction**. A conjunction is a joining word. The words *and*, *but*, and *or* are conjunctions that are often used to join two sentences.

   Run-on: Popcorn once was free now you pay for each serving.

   Corrected: Popcorn once was free, *but* now you pay for each serving.

> **Brush Up on the Basics**
>
> A conjunction is a joining word that is used to join two sentences. (See Grammar 45 in the Reference Guide.)

Practice B

On a separate sheet of paper, rewrite the following sentences. Underline the comma and the conjunction in each sentence.

Example: I wanted to wear jeans, <u>but</u> it was a costume party.

1. The Smith family brought salad, and the Browns brought dessert.

2. The guitar string broke, and the singer forgot the words to the song.

3. Students must study before a hard test, or they will surely fail.

4. Tim did not study, and he failed.

5. Karen wished on a falling star, but hard work really earned her the job.

1. The Smith family brought salad, <u>and</u> the Browns brought dessert.

2. The guitar string broke, <u>and</u> the singer forgot the words to the song.

3. Students must study before a hard test, <u>or</u> they will surely fail.

4. Tim did not study, <u>and</u> he failed.

5. Karen wished on a falling star, <u>but</u> hard work really earned her the job.

Practice C

On a separate sheet of paper, correct the following run-on sentences. Remember the two easy methods to correct a run-on sentence. Either separate the sentences with periods and use capital letters, or connect the sentences with a comma and a conjunction, such as *and, but,* or *or.*

1. Margie won the prize she really deserved it.

2. The music was loud he liked it that way.

3. The light was red the car roared through the crossing.

4. The basketball went through the hoop the Hawks won the game.

5. Lisa might choose the red tennis shoes she might choose the black ones with the white stripes on the toe.

The Writing Process

How can you use punctuation to fix sentence fragments and run-on sentences? (See The Writing Process, page WP34.)

1. Margie won the prize, and she really deserved it. *or* Margie won the prize. She really deserved it.

2. The music was loud, and he liked it that way. *or* The music was loud. He liked it that way.

3. The light was red, but the car roared through the crossing. *or* The light was red. The car roared through the crossing.

4. The basketball went through the hoop, and the Hawks won the game. *or* The basketball went through the hoop. The Hawks won the game.

5. Lisa might choose the red tennis shoes, or she might choose the black ones with the white stripes on the toe. *or* Lisa might choose the red tennis shoes. She might choose the black ones with the white stripes on the toe.

Rewrite the following paragraph, correcting any sentence fragments or run-on sentences.

Ryan and Marcy wanted to visit the old man. Everyone said the old man was mean they decided to go anyway. The man lived in a rundown house on Oak Street. With his spotted dog. He always seemed so lonely. Ryan and Marcy knew he needed some friends. They brought the man a sandwich. And some apple juice. They rang the old man's doorbell they were a little nervous. Then the old man came to the door. He smiled.

Methods used to correct errors may vary. The paragraph is correct if all sentences are complete, begin with capital letters, end with appropriate end marks, and are not run-on sentences.

Possible answer: Ryan and Marcy wanted to visit the old man. Everyone said the old man was mean, but they decided to go anyway. The man lived in a rundown house on Oak Street with his spotted dog. He always seemed so lonely. Ryan and Marcy knew he needed some friends. They brought the man a sandwich and some apple juice. They rang the old man's doorbell. They were a little nervous. Then the old man came to the door. He smiled.

WRITING WITH STYLE
Telling a Story

Listen closely to people talking. They often use a lot of *ands* and *ums*. They use slang words, too. However, writing is not like everyday speech, unless you are writing dialogue.

Which of the following paragraphs is better? Why?

1. Last Saturday night turned out to be the most frightening night of my life. There was a terrible thunderstorm, and the power went out as I was watching a scary movie about a character named Johnny on television, and then I heard a scraping sound in the basement. Dude, it sounded like Johnny's baseball bat. Well, I was so frightened that I ran to the phone to call for help, and the phone line was dead, which was scary, man, and I knew I had to go downstairs and check on the noise. My heart was pounding as I shined the flashlight around the basement, and there sat my dog scratching his fleas. Like, Johnny was nowhere.

2. Last Saturday night turned out to be the most frightening night of my life. There was a terrible thunderstorm. The power went out as I was watching a scary movie about a character named Johnny on television. Then, I heard a scraping sound in the basement. It sounded like Johnny's baseball bat scraping the floor. I ran to the phone to call for help. The phone line was dead! I knew I had to go downstairs and check on the noise. My heart pounded as I shined the flashlight around the basement. There sat my dog scratching his fleas. Johnny was not around. He is just a character in a movie that scared me. Real life is a dog with fleas.

Selection 2 is the better paragraph. Someone telling the story might be so excited that he or she would run the sentences together with *ands*. However, when writing the story, the narrator can take time to separate his or her thoughts. The writer has created suspense and has scared the readers.

VOCABULARY BUILDER
Choosing the Dictionary Definition

Often, a dictionary will list several definitions for the same word. How do you know which definition is the one you want?

You must look at the word's context. How is the word used in a sentence? Which definition is best when the word is used in that context?

Look at this dictionary entry.

> **boxer** *noun* (1) a person who boxes, especially in competition, (2) any of a breed of large, short-haired dogs of the bulldog type, usually tan or brindled

Which definition would you choose for the word *boxer* in the following sentence?

The boxer barked and showed his teeth when the stranger came near.

In each of the following sentences, one word is in italic type. Look up that word in a dictionary. On a separate sheet of paper, copy the best meaning for the word as it is used in the sentence.

1. In addition to a rifle, the soldier carried a *club* as a weapon.

2. Sam decided to join the school drama *club*.

3. Close the window because a cold *draft* is coming into the room.

4. The first *draft* of his paper contained many mistakes.

5. The soldiers knew they had been beaten and planned their *retreat*.

6. Every weekend, we go to our oceanside *retreat*.

Answers should be similar to those listed but need not be exact.

1. a heavy, wooden stick
2. a group of people who meet for a common purpose
3. a current of air
4. the trial copy of a paper
5. the act of withdrawing
6. a place that is quiet, safe, and peaceful

Chapter

2 / Review

Summary Have students use the summary to outline the main idea and details of the chapter.

Summary

A sentence fragment is not a complete thought. It cannot stand on its own. It should not be punctuated like a sentence.

Do not use sentence fragments in your writing. You can correct fragments by adding words or by combining a fragment with another sentence.

A run-on sentence is formed when sentences are not separated from each other correctly. Run-ons make your writing unclear. They also confuse readers.

A complete sentence should express a complete thought.

A complete sentence should begin with a capital letter and end with a punctuation mark.

fragment

run-on sentence

conjunction

1. false, fragment
2. true
3. false, run-on sentence

More Vocabulary Review is provided in the Classroom Resource Binder.

Vocabulary Review

Write *true* or *false* after each sentence. If the sentence is false, change the underlined word or phrase to make it true. Choose a term from the box. Write your answers on a separate sheet of paper.

1. A <u>run-on sentence</u> is a group of words that is not a complete sentence but is mistakenly punctuated as if it were complete.

2. *And, but,* and *or* are examples of <u>conjunctions</u>.

3. A <u>fragment</u> is made up of two or more sentences that have not been separated correctly.

Chapter Quiz

Complete the following items. Write your answers on a separate sheet of paper.

1. Read each of the following items. If an item is a fragment, write **F** next to its number. If it is a run-on sentence, write **RO**. If it is correct, write C.

   a. The car skidded to a stop it left black tire marks.

   b. Looked left and right then crossed the road.

   c. The puppy barked twice and headed home.

   d. All the tallest members of the class.

   e. I like that author her stories are exciting.

   f. We worked all weekend, but we still did not earn enough money.

   g. The quarterback darted left he passed the ball.

2. What two parts must a sentence have so that it is not a fragment?

3. What two things can you add to correct a run-on sentence?

Critical Thinking

How can fragments and run-ons make writing difficult to understand? Write your answer on a separate sheet of paper.

Chapter Quiz

1. a. RO b. F c. C d. F e. RO f. C g. RO

2. A complete sentence needs both a subject and a predicate.

3. To correct a run-on sentence, you need to add a comma and a coordinating conjunction such as *and, but,* and *or.*

Critical Thinking Answers will vary. Possible answer: It is important to write clearly and accurately so that writers can communicate their ideas in the best possible way. Writing in fragments and run-on sentences makes it difficult for readers to understand a writer's message.

Writing Activity

On a separate sheet of paper, write a paragraph about a person you admire. Describe the person. Give three reasons why you admire this person. Use a conjunction to join ideas in at least one sentence. Correct all fragments and run-on sentences.

Writing Activity Answers will vary. Check to make sure that students' responses do not contain any fragments or run-on sentences. Students should also have at least one sentence in which they join two ideas into one sentence with a conjunction.

A careful writer makes every sentence count.

Edgar Allan Poe *(1809–1849) was a great poet and storyteller. Poe varied his sentences to build suspense and create a feeling of excitement. He made every sentence count. Poe is best known for his poems "Annabelle Lee" and "The Raven." His stories "The Tell-Tale Heart" and "The Black Cat" are also classics.*

Extra Reading See the Pacemaker® Classics series for Edgar Allan Poe's *Tales of Edgar Allan Poe.*

To help students tap their prior knowledge of the chapter topic, see the **Chapter Project** in the Classroom Resource Binder.

Learning Objectives

- Identify and write a simple sentence.
- Identify compound subjects and predicates.
- Identify and write a compound sentence.
- Identify and write a complex sentence.
- Write a variety of sentence types and sentence lengths.

Chapter 3 Writing Different Kinds of Sentences

See the Workbook for **Extra Practice**.

Words to Know

variety	many different forms or kinds of things
simple sentence	a group of words that expresses a complete thought and has one subject-predicate combination
compound subject	two or more subjects with the same predicate
compound predicate	two or more predicates with the same subject
compound sentence	two simple sentences joined by a comma and a conjunction, such as *and, but,* and *or*
subordinate clause	a clause that adds to the meaning of another clause but makes no sense by itself
independent clause	a clause that can stand alone as a complete sentence
complex sentence	a sentence with a subordinate clause and an independent clause
subordinate conjunction	a conjunction that introduces a subordinate clause

If you want people to read what you write, try to make your writing interesting. One way to do this is to use different kinds of sentences. Read the following paragraph.

The Mosquito

The mosquito is an amazing insect. The mosquito has 47 teeth. The mosquito is very small. It can carry twice its weight. The mosquito drinks blood. The mosquito lives in damp places. There are more than 2,000 kinds of mosquitoes. Scientists discover new kinds every year. Some mosquitoes carry disease. Humans look for ways to kill mosquitoes. They are very hard to kill.

What is wrong with the paragraph you just read?

One answer is that all the sentences are too much the same. They sound alike. It is almost as if you were just making a list of facts and not writing sentences. It is as if you were counting items. Read the paragraph aloud. Doesn't it sound dull? Each sentence has one subject and one predicate. They are all just about the same length. Too many of the sentences start with the same words.

Variety means many different forms or kinds of things. The sentences about mosquitoes need more variety. In this chapter, you will learn how to write different kinds of sentences to make your writing more interesting.

A **simple sentence** is a group of words that expresses a complete thought. Most of the sentences you have worked with in Chapters 1 and 2 have been simple sentences. They have just one subject-predicate combination.

This is a simple sentence.

> **The rain splattered the windshield.**

There is one subject: *rain*.

There is one predicate: *splattered*.

One way to vary simple sentences is to use **compound subjects** or **compound predicates**. A compound subject is made up of two or more subjects with the same predicate.

> **The *dog* and *cat* fought in the alley.**

This sentence has a compound subject.

A compound predicate is two or more predicates with the same subject.

> **The rabbit *wiggled* its nose and *hopped* across the cage.**

This sentence has a compound predicate.

> **The *boys* and *girls stood* in the corners and *giggled* on the first day of dancing school.**

This sentence has a compound subject and a compound predicate.

How could compound subjects or compound predicates help the paragraph about mosquitoes?

You might write:

> The mosquito *drinks* blood and *lives* in damp places. (compound predicate)

or

> The mosquito *is* very small but *has* 47 teeth. (compound predicate)

Even though many of the sentences you write will be simple sentences, they do not all have to be the same.

Practice A

On a separate sheet of paper, number from 1 to 10. Write **CS** next to the numbers of the sentences with compound subjects. Write **CP** next to the numbers of the sentences with compound predicates. If neither subject nor predicate is compound, leave a blank after the number.

1. CS
2. CS
3. CP
4. CS
5. CP
6. CP
7. (blank)
8. CP
9. CS
10. CP

1. Men and women played on the college volleyball team.

2. William and I brought peanut butter and banana sandwiches.

3. The driver of the car honked and waved.

4. Pizza and spaghetti were on the menu.

5. The skater twirled gracefully and bowed to the crowd.

6. Big drops of rain fell and ruined our picnic.

7. Most stores closed early for the holiday.

8. Will you stay here or go to the party?

9. The Tigers and the Bears played in Saturday's big game.

10. You should call and make an appointment.

Practice B

On a separate sheet of paper, make each pair of sentences into one sentence by using a compound subject.

Examples: Elvis Presley was a rock star.

Buddy Holly was a rock star, too.

Elvis Presley and Buddy Holly were rock stars.

1. Mr. Wonker wears suspenders.
Mrs. Wonker wears suspenders, too.

2. New York is a big city.
Chicago is also a big city.

3. The Wildcats are a top-rated team.
The Bombers are also a top-rated team.

4. Scott teased Ann.
Brian teased her, too.

5. In the face of danger, Susan was very brave.
Kevin was brave, too.

1. Mr. and Mrs. Wonker wear suspenders.
2. New York and Chicago are big cities.
3. The Wildcats and the Bombers are top-rated teams.
4. Scott and Brian teased Ann.
5. In the face of danger, Susan and Kevin were brave.

Practice C

On a separate sheet of paper, make each pair of sentences into one sentence by using a compound predicate.

Examples: The coach blew her whistle.

She shouted to the team.

The coach blew her whistle and shouted to the team.

1. The magician can saw a person in half.
He can also make a rabbit disappear.

2. Many soldiers in the Spanish-American War got yellow fever.
Many died from yellow fever.

1. The magician can saw a person in half and make a rabbit disappear.
2. Many soldiers in the Spanish-American War got yellow fever and died from it.

(Practice C continues on next page.) ⟹

3. Chris ran the 100-yard dash and won a first-place medal.

4. The lion roared but did not scare anyone.

5. Matt studied hard and passed the test.

3. Chris ran the 100-yard dash.
Chris won a first-place medal.

4. The lion roared.
He did not scare anyone. (Use *but* instead of *and*.)

5. Matt studied hard.
He passed the test. (Use *and* instead of *but*.)

Compound subjects and compound predicates can help you to say things in different ways. They add variety to your sentences and make them more interesting.

3-2 ▶ Compound Sentences

In Chapter 2, you learned that you can join two complete sentences with a comma and a coordinating conjunction, such as *and*, *but*, or *or*. When you do this, you form what is called a **compound sentence**. Read the following example.

> Christine baked the cake, and Larry made the cookies.

In a compound sentence, there is a complete thought with a subject and a predicate on each side of the conjunction.

> Christine baked the cake, *and* Larry made the cookies.

Compound sentences are very useful. Use one sometimes instead of writing two short, simple sentences.

Sometimes, students confuse a simple sentence that has a compound subject or a compound predicate with a compound sentence. To tell the difference, just look on both sides of the conjunction. Is there a subject and a predicate on each side? If so, the sentence is a compound sentence.

> Compound sentence: The wind howled, and the rain pounded.

> Simple sentence: The wind and rain pounded the coast. (no predicate on one side of the conjunction)

The Writing Process

Why is it important to make your writing flow? (See The Writing Process, page WP26.)

On a separate sheet of paper, number from 1 to 10. Decide if each of the following sentences is simple or compound. Write **S** for simple or **C** for compound by each number.

1. Spring and summer are her favorite seasons.

2. Carla likes snow skiing, but John likes water skiing.

3. Adrienne listened to her teacher and wrote her report that afternoon.

4. Howard saved his money, and he bought a plane ticket to London.

5. The Boy Scouts saw Bigfoot, and they told everyone about it.

6. Eric finished his homework, and he had time to check it over.

7. The snake crawled up on the rock and curled up in the sun.

8. The conductor or the clerk will take your ticket.

9. Bars covered the windows, but the burglar got in anyway.

10. The play was held in the smallest theater, and some people had to stand.

1. S
2. C
3. S
4. C
5. C
6. C
7. S
8. S
9. C
10. C

Practice B

On a separate sheet of paper, make each pair of sentences below into one compound sentence. Use the conjunctions *and*, *but*, or *or*.

> Examples: The table was all set. The guests did not arrive.
>
> The table was all set, *but* the guests did not arrive.

1. He was tired and hungry.
   The long trip had been worth the trouble.

2. She did not know where the interesting boy lived.
   She had his phone number.

3. You should be home by midnight.
   You might be locked out.

4. Mark Twain wrote a book called *The Adventures of Huckleberry Finn*.
   He wrote *The Adventures of Tom Sawyer*.

5. In the last inning, the Centerville Tigers scored two runs.
   In the last inning, the Southside Senators made two errors.

1. He was tired and hungry, but the long trip had been worth the trouble.
2. She did not know where the interesting boy lived, but she had his phone number.
3. You should be home by midnight, or you might be locked out.
4. Mark Twain wrote a book called *The Adventures of Huckleberry Finn*, and he wrote *The Adventures of Tom Sawyer*.
5. In the last inning, the Centerville Tigers scored two runs, and the Southside Senators made two errors.

Brush Up on the Basics

There is always a comma before the conjunction in a compound sentence.
(See Punctuation 6 in the Reference Guide.)

Making Choices

The words *and*, *but*, and *or* each suggest a different meaning.

When two ideas are equally important, choose *and*.

> Bill washed the dishes, *and* Sue dried them.

When you want to show contrast between ideas, use *but*.

> He wanted chocolate, *but* he got vanilla.

When you join two ideas in a way that gives a choice between them, use *or*.

> You should answer the phone, *or* it will keep ringing.

Practice C

On a separate sheet of paper, write your own compound sentences.

> Example: Last holiday season, I took a basket of food to a poor family, and my neighbor visited a children's hospital.

1. Tell about something you did during the last holiday season and something your friend did. (Use *and*.)

2. Tell about something that you wanted to do last summer but did not get to do. (Use *but*.)

3. Tell about your first choice for dinner tonight and your second choice. (Use *or*.)

Answers will vary. Answers should be correctly punctuated compound sentences.

3-3 ▶ Complex Sentences

You know that a sentence is a group of words with a subject and a predicate. You know that a sentence expresses a complete thought and can stand alone. Sometimes, you will find a group of words with a subject and a predicate that cannot stand alone. Such a group of words is called a **subordinate clause**. A subordinate clause has a subject and a predicate, but it cannot stand alone.

> Example: after Sharon broke her date

The subject is *Sharon*.

The predicate is *broke*.

However, the subordinate clause does not make sense alone, does it? What happened after Sharon broke her date?

When you join a clause like this with an **independent clause,** or a clause that can stand alone, you make a complex sentence. **A complex sentence** is a sentence with a subordinate clause and an independent clause.

> After Sharon broke her date, she stayed home and studied.

The part that can stand alone is called the independent clause.

> She stayed home and studied.

The part that cannot stand alone is called the subordinate clause.

> After Sharon broke her date,

The words in the box below often begin subordinate clauses. They are called **subordinate conjunctions.** A subordinate conjunction is a conjunction that introduces a subordinate clause.

Subordinate Conjunctions		
after	before	though
when	although	if
unless	whenever	because
since	until	while

This list is not complete. There are many more subordinate conjunctions.

You can vary your writing by using complex sentences.

> Two simple sentences: The storm was coming. Tyler took out the boat.

> One complex sentence: *Although* the storm was coming, Tyler took out the boat.

A subordinate clause can appear at the beginning of a sentence or at the end. The placement of the subordinate clause determines the punctuation in the sentence. When the subordinate clause comes at the beginning of a sentence, it is followed by a comma. When the subordinate clause is at the end of the sentence, no comma is needed.

If it rains, take an umbrella. (subordinate clause at the beginning)

Take an umbrella *if it rains.* (subordinate clause at the end)

Practice

On a separate sheet of paper, write each pair of sentences below as one complex sentence. Use the subordinate conjunctions listed on page 38. Try to use a different subordinate conjunction in each sentence.

Examples: It is snowing.

School might be canceled.

Because it is snowing, school might be canceled.

1. Speed was important.
   Pony Express riders traveled all day and all night.

2. The department store was closed.
   The shoppers stayed downtown.

3. A bodyguard always goes with the rock star.
   The rock star leaves the studio.

4. The clock struck one.
   The mouse ran down.

5. It rained.
   The baseball game was stopped.

Think About It

Why are subordinate conjunctions important when you are explaining the time something happened?

Answers will vary but should be similar to the following.

1. Because speed was important, Pony Express riders traveled all day and all night.

2. Although the department store was closed, the shoppers stayed downtown.

3. A bodyguard always goes with the rock star whenever the rock star leaves the studio.

4. When the clock struck one, the mouse ran down.

5. Whenever it rained, the baseball game was stopped.

WRITING WITH STYLE
Making Writing Interesting

Using different kinds of sentences and different sentence lengths improves your writing. It makes your writing more interesting.

Which of the following selections is better writing? Why?

1. The mongoose is a small animal. It is very fierce. It lives in Africa and southern Asia. It eats all sorts of small creatures. It eats snakes. A mongoose will fight a deadly cobra. The mongoose moves very quickly. The cobra cannot strike it. Mongooses can be tamed. They are often kept around homes. They will drive away snakes.

2. The mongoose is a small, fierce animal that lives in Africa and southern Asia. It eats all sorts of small creatures, including snakes. A mongoose will even fight a deadly cobra. The mongoose moves very quickly, and the cobra cannot strike it. Since mongooses can be tamed, they are often kept around homes to drive away snakes.

If you chose Selection 2 as the better example of good writing, you were correct. Selection 2 uses the variety of sentence types discussed in this chapter. Notice that it contains two simple sentences, one compound sentence, and two complex sentences. In Selection 1, all the sentences are simple, and the writing is choppy and less interesting.

VOCABULARY BUILDER
Using Parts of Speech to Find Word Meaning

A word may have different meanings, depending on how it is used in a sentence. The same word can be more than one part of speech. For example, if you see the word *sail* written all alone on a sheet of paper, you cannot give it any one definition. *Sail* can be used as a noun and a verb, can't it? The word must be used in a sentence before its meaning is clear.

When it is used as a noun, *sail* means a piece of fabric used to catch the wind, as in this sentence:

> He bought a new boat with a yellow *sail*.

When it is used as a verb, *sail* means to move across water or to travel by water, as in this sentence:

> We will *sail* to Hawaii in the spring.

Use a dictionary if you need help in writing the following sentences. Write your sentences on a separate sheet of paper.

1. Write a sentence using *bowl* as a noun.

2. Write a sentence using *bowl* as a verb.

3. Write a sentence using *park* as a noun.

4. Write a sentence using *park* as a verb.

5. Write a sentence using *drive* as a noun.

6. Write a sentence using *drive* as a verb.

Answers will vary. Students' sentences should correctly use the vocabulary word as either a noun or a verb.

Summary Have students use the summary to outline the main idea and details of the chapter.

Summary

There are many ways to communicate the same ideas. Writing different kinds of sentences will make your writing more interesting.

A simple sentence has just one subject and one predicate.

A simple sentence can have a compound subject or a compound predicate.

A compound sentence joins two simple sentences with a comma and a coordinating conjunction.

A complex sentence joins a subordinate clause and an independent clause with a subordinating conjunction.

More Vocabulary Review is provided in the Classroom Resource Binder.

Vocabulary Review

Match each term in the box with its meaning. Write your answers on a separate sheet of paper.

simple sentence

compound sentence

complex sentence

compound subject

compound predicate

independent clause

subordinate clause

1. compound predicate
2. independent clause
3. simple sentence
4. compound sentence
5. compound subject
6. subordinate clause
7. complex sentence

1. two or more predicates with the same subject

2. a clause that can stand alone

3. a group of words that expresses a complete thought

4. two simple sentences joined by a comma and a coordinating conjunction

5. two or more subjects with the same predicate

6. a clause that adds to the meaning of another clause but cannot stand alone

7. a sentence with a subordinate clause and an independent clause

Chapter Quiz

On a separate sheet of paper, number from 1 to 8. Then, read each of the following sentences. If a sentence is simple, write *simple* next to its number. If it is a compound sentence, write *compound*. If a sentence is complex, write *complex*.

1. Although the boat was old, it stayed afloat.

2. The hikers missed the signs, and they soon became lost.

3. Mr. Warren called the police twice yesterday.

4. When a snowstorm hits, the roads are closed.

5. It is a nice autumn day, but winter is on the way.

6. The team from East High and the team from West High play each other on Thanksgiving Day.

7. The mountain rumbled for days before the volcano erupted.

8. The boys and girls are searching for a lost kitten in the backyard.

Chapter Quiz
1. complex
2. compound
3. simple
4. complex
5. compound
6. simple
7. complex
8. simple

Critical Thinking

How can using compound subjects and compound predicates help you to link your sentences? Write your answer on a separate sheet of paper.

Critical Thinking Compound subjects and compound predicates help you link sentences by combining two sentences with a common subject or predicate.

Writing Activity

Reread the paragraph "The Mosquito" on page 30. On a separate sheet of paper, rewrite the paragraph using a variety of sentence types. Use at least one simple sentence, one compound sentence, and one complex sentence

Writing Activity Answers will vary. Accept all reasonable attempts to add sentence variety to the paragraph and to make the passage more interesting.

Powerful, well-written sentences create strong images for readers.

Piri Thomas (born 1928) writes about the people and places he knows well. Thomas's early stories describe his experiences growing up in an inner city. His most famous book is Down These Mean Streets. It shows how inner-city life can affect young people. Thomas creates strong images in his stories by using powerful sentences.

To help students tap their prior knowledge of the chapter topic, see the **Chapter Project** in the Classroom Resource Binder.

Learning Objectives

- Add detail to sentences by using adjectives, adverbs, and prepositional phrases.

- Describe images and ideas clearly by using specific words.

- Choose interesting words.

Chapter 4

Writing Better Sentences

See the Workbook for Extra Practice.

Words to Know

vivid	clear, distinct, colorful
adjective	a word that describes a noun or pronoun
adverb	a word that describes a verb, an adjective, or another adverb
preposition	a word that shows the relationship of a noun or pronoun to some other word in a sentence
prepositional phrase	a preposition and its object taken together
object of the preposition	a noun or pronoun that follows a preposition in the prepositional phrase
synonym	a word with the same or nearly the same meaning as another word
connotation	ideas or feelings associated with a word in addition to its actual meaning

In Chapters 1 through 3, you learned about writing sentences correctly. In this chapter, you will learn how to make those sentences even better. You will learn how to express your ideas clearly and completely.

You write to communicate. You have an image or an idea in your head. You want to give that image to your readers as exactly as possible.

Suppose you saw a man carrying a package that was bigger than he was. You can hardly wait to tell your friends about it. The man looked so tired.

"I saw a man today!" you say to your friends.

"Oh," one of them answers. Your friends do not seem very excited or interested. Why?

You did not communicate your idea. You did not present your image clearly. This chapter will help you communicate more clearly. It will help you write sentences that present **vivid**, or clear, distinct, and colorful, pictures and ideas.

Details are the small parts of something that explain the whole. Using details is one key to good writing. Read some of your own writing and ask yourself, "Is there anything more I could say to make the image or idea clearer to my readers?"

The Writing Process

Why are details important when you write? (See The Writing Process, page WP17.)

Answers will vary. Students' sentences should contain precise language that communicates accurately what students are observing.

Practice

Look out a window or go outside. Focus on one thing that you find interesting or unusual. Look at it closely. On a separate sheet of paper, write one sentence about it. Your goal is to make your readers see that thing just as you see it.

Using Adjectives and Adverbs

Certain kinds of words make the things you describe clearer. For example, an **adjective** is a word that describes a noun. Adjectives make your images clearer to your readers. They tell *what kind*, *which one*, or *how many*.

> She served the *crisp, green* salad.

> She served the *wilted, yellowed* salad.

After reading the first sentence, you might be eager to eat. After reading the second sentence, you might want to skip the salad.

Adjectives can make a difference!

Practice A

Each of the sentences below has a question after it. On a separate sheet of paper, answer each question with an adjective. Then, rewrite the original sentence, adding the adjective.

> Example: The dog barked at the visitor.

> Was the dog vicious or friendly? *friendly*

> Rewrite: *The friendly dog barked at the visitor.*

1. The teacher told Sam to stand up in front of the class.

Was the teacher angry or proud? Rewrite the sentence.

1. The angry teacher told Sam to stand up in front of the class. *or* The proud teacher told Sam to stand up in front of the class.

(Practice A continues on next page.) ⟱

(Practice A continued.)

2. The dark, threatening clouds filled the sky. *or* The puffy, white clouds filled the sky.

3. She offered me the costly diamond necklace. *or* She offered me the cheap plastic necklace.

2. Clouds filled the sky.

Were they dark, threatening clouds or puffy, white clouds? Rewrite the sentence.

3. She offered me the necklace.

Was it a costly, diamond necklace or a cheap, plastic necklace? Rewrite the sentence.

Adverbs describe verbs, adjectives, or other adverbs. Like adjectives, they make the things you describe clearer. Adverbs usually answer the questions *how, when, where, why,* or *to what extent.*

She smiled.

She smiled *coldly.*

She smiled *warmly.*

The adverbs in the sentences above tell *how* she smiled. Adverbs can really change the picture.

Practice B

Each of the sentences below has a question after it. On a separate sheet of paper, answer the question with an adverb. Then, rewrite the original sentence, adding the adverb.

Example: The patient rested.

Did the patient rest comfortably or uncomfortably? *comfortably*

Rewrite: The patient rested comfortably.

1. He was extremely hungry. *or* He was slightly hungry.

1. He was hungry.

Was he extremely hungry or slightly hungry? Rewrite the sentence.

2. Paula wears lipstick.

Does Paula wear lipstick often or never? Rewrite the sentence.

3. The wind blew.

Did the wind blow softly or fiercely? Rewrite the sentence.

Practice C

On a separate sheet of paper, number from 1 to 5. Next to each number, list all of the adjectives or adverbs that appear in each of the following sentences. Identify each word you list as either an adjective or an adverb.

Example: The mad scientist laughed wildly.

mad—adjective

wildly—adverb

1. The graceful cheetah runs swiftly.

2. The tall man sang too loudly.

3. The terrible explosion happened suddenly.

4. The sick child sneezed constantly.

5. The carpenter skillfully sanded the beautiful, dark wood.

Practice D

Look at the suggestions below and on page 50. On a separate sheet of paper, write your own sentences. Use at least one adjective or adverb in each sentence. Underline the adjectives and adverbs that you use.

1. Write a sentence about a highway you have traveled.

2. Write a sentence about a teacher you remember.

2. Paula wears lipstick often. *or* Paula never wears lipstick.

3. The wind blew softly. *or* The wind blew fiercely.

Brush Up on the Basics

Adjectives and adverbs help you to paint a picture for your readers. (See Grammar 41 in the Reference Guide.)

1. graceful–adjective, swiftly–adverb
2. tall–adjective, too–adverb, loudly–adverb
3. terrible–adjective, suddenly–adverb
4. sick–adjective, constantly–adverb
5. skillfully–adverb, beautiful–adjective, dark–adjective

Answers will vary. Check to make sure that students have used adjectives and adverbs correctly and that they have underlined them in each sentence.

(Practice D continues on next page.) ⮕

(Practice D continued.)

3. Write a sentence about spiders.

4. Write a sentence about a hat that you own or would like to own.

5. Write a sentence about a special relative.

4-3 ▶ Using Prepositional Phrases

Prepositions and **prepositional phrases** can make your sentences clearer and more descriptive. A preposition is a word that shows the relationship of a noun or a pronoun to some other word in a sentence. A prepositional phrase sometimes works like an adjective or an adverb.

> The cake *on the table* looked stale.

The prepositional phrase *on the table* describes *cake,* a noun. That prepositional phrase works like an adjective.

> The burglar entered *through the basement window.*

The prepositional phrase *through the basement window* describes the verb *entered.* That prepositional phrase works like an adverb.

A prepositional phrase begins with a preposition and ends with a noun or a pronoun. That noun or pronoun is called the **object of the preposition.**

> Example: They crowded *into the room.*

Into the room is the prepositional phrase.

Into is the preposition.

Room is the object of the preposition.

Some common prepositions are listed in the *Reference Guide, Grammar 48* at the back of this book.

Practice A

Each of the sentences below has a question after it. On a separate sheet of paper, answer the question with a prepositional phrase. Then, rewrite the original sentence, adding a prepositional phrase.

Example: The nervous student spoke.

Did the student speak to the principal or to the class? *to the principal.*

The nervous student spoke *to the principal.*

1. The pitcher hurled the ball.

   Did the pitcher hurl the ball at the batter or at the crowd? Rewrite the sentence.

2. The pot was filled.

   Was the pot filled with gold or with soup? Rewrite the sentence.

3. I like ice cream.

   Do you like ice cream with nuts or with strawberries? Rewrite the sentence.

1. The pitcher hurled the ball at the batter. *or* The pitcher hurled the ball at the crowd.
2. The pot was filled with gold. *or* The pot was filled with soup.
3. I like ice cream with nuts. *or* I like ice cream with strawberries.

Practice B

On a separate sheet of paper, improve the following sentences by adding at least one prepositional phrase.

1. The woman fell.

2. The car skidded.

3. My uncle arrived.

4. The plane landed.

5. The creature appeared.

Answers will vary. Check to make sure students have improved the sentences by adding at least one prepositional phrase.

Portfolio Project

Choose one of the sentences you have written in Practice B on page 51. By using adjectives, adverbs, and prepositional phrases, expand that sentence even more. Be sure that your audience can picture the thing that you are describing. Make that sentence at least ten words long.

4-4 ▸ Using Better Words

You can improve your sentences by making general words more specific.

> I took my *pet there.*

> I took my *lizard to school.*

Which sentence creates a clearer picture? The second sentence is clearer because the word *lizard* is more specific than the word *pet*. The phrase *to school* is more specific than the word *there*.

Practice A

On a separate sheet of paper, rewrite each of the following sentences. Replace each word or phrase in italic type with a more specific word or phrase.

1. I will not eat that *food.*

2. The *car* was parked in the road.

3. The *boat* sailed into the harbor.

4. Mike *put all his things* into his locker.

5. *The girl* is from *another country.*

Some words are more specific than other words. They are more specific because they give a clearer picture and a more vivid meaning.

The duck walked around the park.

The duck waddled around the park.

Why is *waddled* a better word than *walked*?

Walked does not create a clear picture. Using *waddled* helps the reader see *how* the duck walked.

Make the words you use work for you. Use words that "color" your writing.

Practice B

On a separate sheet of paper, list all the verbs that you can think of that could be used in place of *walked*. See how long you can make your list. When you are finished, circle the words that you think are the most colorful and descriptive.

Answers will vary. Possible answers: skipped, tripped, stumbled, strutted, strolled, wandered, and crept.

A **synonym** is a word with the same or nearly the same meaning as another word. Notice that some of the synonyms for *walk* present a favorable picture. For example, the word *strolled* is a pleasant kind of walking.

Words also have **connotations**. A connotation is an idea or feeling associated with a word. They make people think of good things or bad things. For example, *fragrance* is a positive word for smell. *Stench* is a negative word. You can use word connotations to help get your message across to your readers.

Practice C

1. On a separate sheet of paper, write the word or phrase with the most positive connotation in each of the following groups.

    a. strange, odd, interesting

    b. chef, cook, kitchen helper

    c. thin, skinny, slender

    d. argue, discuss, quarrel

    e. job, work, career

2. On a separate sheet of paper, write the word with the most negative connotation in each of the following groups.

    a. proud, conceited, snobbish

    b. reproduction, fake, copy

    c. shy, withdrawn, quiet

    d. say, scream, recite

    e. remind, nag, suggest

1. a. interesting
   b. chef
   c. slender
   d discuss
   e. career

2. a. snobbish
   b. fake
   c. withdrawn
   d. scream
   e. nag

Answers will vary. Possible answer: Mabel *chanted* the words to the song. Her mouth opened wide in her *slender* face, and *elegant* fingers held the song book. She *gazed* at the audience.

Portfolio Project

The following sentences make Mabel sound pretty awful. On a separate sheet of paper, rewrite them to give Mabel a better image. Just change the words in italic type to words with more positive connotations.

Mabel *screeched* the words to the song. Her mouth opened wide in her *thin* face, and her *bony* fingers clutched the song book. She *peered* at the audience.

A Thesaurus: A Book That Can Help You

A thesaurus is a special kind of book. It is a reference book that helps you find synonyms for words. Synonyms are words that mean nearly the same thing. Words are alphabetized in a thesaurus just as they are in a dictionary. If you look up a word, you will find a list of synonyms. A thesaurus can help you find a different word when you think you have used one particular word too many times. It can also help you find more specific words.

For example, if you look up the word *color* in a thesaurus, you might find an entry like the following.

color—*noun* hue, tone, tint, cast, shade, tinge
verb dye, tinge, stain, paint

A person might write, "I chose one *color* for my bedroom, but I wanted a different *color* for the den."

After checking a thesaurus, that person might write, "I chose the *color* for my bedroom, but I wanted a different *shade* for the den."

A thesaurus can help you find words that you might not think of on your own.

Sometimes, a thesaurus will list a word that has a meaning that will not make sense in your sentence. It can also list a word with a different connotation. Be careful not to use a word that changes the meaning of your sentence.

Think About It

How can using a thesaurus help you to make your writing interesting?

WRITING WITH STYLE
Communicating Ideas

Successful writing means successful communication. The writer wants to show the readers some of the ideas, experiences, information, and images inside his or her head.

Compare the two following selections. Which selection presents a clearer image? Which selection lets the readers know more exactly what the writer experienced?

1. I went out on my surfboard last Saturday. It was the first nice day of spring. I did not surf much. I just lay on my board. It was pretty nice. I was happy. Then, I saw what looked like a shark in the water.

2. Some articles had appeared in the paper about shark attacks just off the coast, but I was not thinking about those articles last Saturday. The sky was blue, and it was the first really warm day of spring. I paddled out over the foamy, white waves on my surfboard. I felt lazy that day. I was content to just float and let the waves lift me up and down. The sun was warm on my back. The water was surprisingly warm, too. The sea salt stung my eyes a little, but it did not matter. I was getting a head start on summer fun. Just then, I saw it. The dark black fin cut through the water and raced toward me.

You probably shared the writer's experience more fully when you read Selection 2. What skills that you have read about in this book did the writer use?

VOCABULARY BUILDER
Using Synonyms

1. Match the synonyms in Column A and Column B. Write them in pairs on a separate sheet of paper.

Column A	Column B
a. huge	wicked
b. call	snarl
c. evil	task
d. growl	tremendous
e. brag	summon
f. job	boast

2. Rewrite each sentence below using a synonym for the word in italic type. Write your answers on a separate sheet of paper.

a. The roof collapsed, but no one was *hurt*.

b. The evil character *laughed* as he sped away in the car.

c. He was a *rich* man after he won the lottery.

d. The picture had an *ugly* frame.

e. Do you own that *strange*, spotted dog?

1. **a.** huge, tremendous
   b. call, summon
   c. evil, wicked
   d. growl, snarl
   e. brag, boast
   f. job, task

2. Answers will vary. Possible answers:
   a. injured
   b. chuckled
   c. wealthy
   d. hideous
   e. outlandish

Summary Have students use the summary to outline the main idea and details of the chapter.

Summary

The purpose of writing is to communicate ideas or images.
Choosing words that describe specific details will help you write clearly.
Adjectives describe nouns and pronouns. They can make an idea clearer by telling *what kind*, *which one*, or *how many*.
Adverbs describe verbs, adjectives, and other adverbs. They make ideas clearer by telling *how*, *when*, *where*, *why*, or *to what extent*.
Prepositional phrases work like adjectives or adverbs to make ideas clearer.
Using specific words instead of general ones improves your writing.

synonym

adverb

object of the preposition

adjective

connotation

prepositional phrase

vivid

preposition

1. adjective
2. vivid
3. adverb
4. preposition
5. synonym
6. object of the preposition
7. prepositional phrase
8. connotation

More Vocabulary Review is provided in the Classroom Resource Binder.

Vocabulary Review

Complete each sentence with a term from the box. Write your answers on a separate sheet of paper.

1. A word that adds meaning to a noun or pronoun is an _____.

2. A _____ detail is clear and colorful.

3. A word that adds meaning to a verb, an adjective, or another adverb is an _____.

4. A word that shows the relationship of a noun or pronoun to some other word in the sentence is a _____.

5. A word with nearly the same meaning as another word is a _____.

6. A noun or pronoun that follows a preposition in a phrase is an _____.

7. A _____ is the preposition and the noun or pronoun that follows it.

8. A word that describes the ideas or feelings associated with words is a _____.

Chapter Quiz

Answers will vary. Possible answers:

1. replied, stated, believed, responded, answered.

2. *Station wagon* is a more specific term; it creates a more precise image.

3. a. The spy crept into a dark alleyway.

b. The new lifeguard was quite outgoing.

c. The young panther leapt into the shadows.

Chapter Quiz

Complete each of the following items. Write your answers on a separate sheet of paper.

1. What are two synonyms for *said* that you could use to make your writing clearer?

2. Which word is more specific—*automobile* or *station wagon*? Explain your answer.

3. Copy each of the following sentences. Replace the words in italic type with more vivid words.

   a. The spy *walked* into a dark *place*.

   b. The new *person* was quite *nice*.

   c. The young *animal moved* into the shadows.

4. Rewrite each of the following sentences. Fill in each blank with a vivid adjective or adverb.

   a. The _____ teacher spoke _____ to the class.

   b. The _____ egg made her _____ sick.

   c. Linda was too _____ to drive _____.

▶ **Test Tip**
Answer the easy questions first. Then, go back and complete the harder ones.

4. a. The caring teacher spoke warmly to the class.

   b. The rotten egg made her mildly sick.

   c. Linda was too exhausted to drive safely.

Critical Thinking

How can using vivid language make your writing clearer? Write your answer on a separate sheet of paper.

Critical Thinking Answers will vary. Possible answer: Vivid language helps paint a picture for readers and allows readers to see, hear, smell, feel, or taste what a piece of writing is about.

Writing Activity

On a separate sheet of paper, write a paragraph about your favorite hobby. Use adjectives, adverbs, and prepositional phrases to describe this hobby. Use vivid words to make the hobby come alive for your readers.

Writing Activity Answers will vary. Students' responses should use adjectives, adverbs, and prepositional phrases to make their writing vivid and specific.

Simple language is often more powerful than difficult language.

Gwendolyn Brooks *(1917–2000) was from Chicago, Illinois. In her poetry, Brooks explores the strength and beauty of the human spirit. She uses simple language to show caring, dignity, and hope. Her work makes us aware of the human spirit. In 1950, Brooks won the Pulitzer Prize for "Annie Allen." She was the first African American woman to win this major award.*

To help students tap their prior knowledge of the chapter topic, see the **Chapter Project** in the Classroom Resource Binder.

Learning Objectives

- Identify the subject of a sentence as either singular or plural.
- Write verbs that agree in number with their subjects.
- Write pronouns to replace some nouns.
- Write pronouns that agree with their antecedents in gender and number.

Chapter 5 Choosing the Correct Words

Words to Know

singular	expressing only one
plural	expressing more than one
pronoun	a word used in place of a noun
antecedent	the noun a pronoun replaces
gender	tells if a noun or pronoun is masculine or feminine

5-1 Subject-Verb Agreement

Every sentence has a subject and a verb. The subject and the verb must match each other. If the subject is **singular**, or expresses only one, then the verb must be singular, too. If the subject is **plural**, or expresses more than one, then the verb must be plural, too. A sentence will sound incorrect if the subject and verb do not agree. Study these two sentences.

> Mary wears jeans.

> Mary wear jeans.

Which sentence is correct?

Does the second sentence sound wrong?

In the second sentence, the subject and verb do not agree. In the first sentence, the subject, *Mary*, is singular. The correct form of the verb is the singular *wears*.

Although plural nouns usually end in *s,* the verbs that agree with singular nouns usually end in *s.* Of course, some irregular verbs are exceptions to that rule. Read the charts below.

Singular Nouns	Verbs that Agree with Singular Nouns
dog	barks
duck	quacks
student	asks
doctor	examines

Plural Nouns	Verbs that Agree with Plural Nouns
dogs	bark
ducks	quack
students	ask
doctors	examine

Irregular Exception—Singular	
child	is, was, has

Irregular Exception—Plural	
children	are, were, have

The subject and verb must agree in number.

Practice A

The verb *has* agrees with a singular noun.

The verb *have* agrees with a plural noun.

Look at the subject of each of the following sentences. On a separate sheet of paper, write the correct verb (*has* or *have*).

1. Cats (has, have) eyes that glow in the dark.

2. Music students (has, have) tickets to the concert.

3. My teacher (has, have) the strictest rules.

4. Some animals (has, have) no teeth.

5. Oregon (has, have) more rain than California.

1. have
2. have
3. has
4. have
5. has

Sometimes, subject-verb agreement is tricky. To write the correct verb, you must first recognize the correct subject. For example, the subject of a sentence is not found within a prepositional phrase.

> One [of the boys] was sick.

> All [of the boys] were sick.

In the first sentence, the subject is *one*. The subject is not *boys* because *boys* comes within the prepositional phrase. The subject is singular.

In the second sentence, the subject is *all*. *All* means more than one. The verb must agree with the plural subject.

Certain words often appear before prepositional phrases. These words are singular: *one, either, neither,* and *each*.

These words are plural: *both* and *many*.

Brush Up on the Basics

The letter *s* is often used as a plural ending. However, an *s* added to the end of a verb usually shows the singular verb form. (See Grammar 21 in the Reference Guide.)

Practice B

On a separate sheet of paper, write the subject of each of the sentences below. Then, write the verb that agrees with the subject. You must decide if the subject is singular or plural. Remember that the subject will not be found within a prepositional phrase.

Example: The boys in the back row (was, were) throwing popcorn.

Answer: boys, were

(*Were* agrees with the subject, *boys*.)

1. one, was
2. either, looks
3. both, worry
4. neither, was
5. set, costs
6. one, was
7. houses, were
8. carpet, is
9. both, are
10. list, is

1. One of the old-time radio programs (was, were) a show called *The Shadow*.

2. Either of the two pictures (looks, look) fine over the fireplace.

3. Both of those chefs (worries, worry) about the menu.

4. Neither of his parents (was, were) at home.

5. The set of place mats (costs, cost) ten dollars.

6. Only one of the puppies (was, were) not sold.

7. The houses on the beach (was, were) flooded.

8. The carpet in those rooms (is, are) blue.

9. Both of the neighbors (is, are) willing to help.

10. A list of team members (is, are) posted in the gym.

Should singular or plural verbs be used with compound subjects?

When the singular parts of the compound subject are joined with *or* or *nor*, the subject is considered singular.

Mike, Jill, *or* Ellen *is* going to pick you up for the party.

Neither William *nor* Andy *is* going to the party.

However, if the part of the subject nearer the verb is plural, then the verb must agree with the plural subject.

Neither William nor his *brothers are* **going to the party.**

When the parts of the subject are joined by *and*, the subject is considered plural.

The scissors *and* **the glue** *are* **in the desk.**

The pilot *and* **the flight attendant** *wear* **uniforms.**

Practice C

On a separate sheet of paper, number from 1 to 10. Read each of the following sentences, and write the form of the verb that agrees with the subject.

1. Mitts and Snowball (is, are) both Siamese cats.

2. Rain or darkness (cancels, cancel) baseball games.

3. *The Color Purple* and *Meridian* (is, are) books by Alice Walker.

4. John F. Kennedy and Abraham Lincoln (was, were) both killed while serving as president.

5. Either Sue or Ellen (is, are) fast enough to win the gold medal.

6. Six tablespoons of milk or five tablespoons of water (is, are) needed in the bread dough.

7. Tacos and hamburgers (was, were) served at lunch.

8. Girls and boys (plays, play) on the championship soccer team.

9. Either the guitar player or the piano player (has, have) to leave the band.

10. The red sports car and the black sedan (go, goes) faster than the other cars.

English and Technology

A word-processing program makes it easy for you to correct errors in your writing.

1. are
2. cancels
3. are
4. were
5. is
6. are
7. were
8. play
9. has
10. go

There is one big exception to the rules that you just learned. When the subject of a sentence is *you*, the plural verb form is used—even if *you* is singular.

Right: *You were* the first one in line.

Wrong: You was the first one in line.

Right: *You are* the kindest man.

Wrong: You is the kindest man.

Most often, your ear will tell you if your subjects and verbs agree. Nonagreement does not sound right. However, when you are not sure which verb form is correct, look at the subject. Then, decide if it is singular or plural.

5-2 ▸ Using Pronouns to Replace Nouns

The students walked to class together. The students took the students' seats. The students were prepared for the exam. The students took the exam. The students handed the students' completed exams to Mr. Bennett. The students knew that the students did well.

Something is wrong with the paragraph above. The word *students* is repeated too many times. A **pronoun** can replace the word. That is the job of pronouns. A pronoun replaces a noun.

The students walked to class together. *They* took *their* seats. *They* were prepared for the exam. *They* took the exam. *They* handed *their* completed exams to Mr. Bennett. *They* knew that *they* did well.

The pronouns in the second paragraph about the students have been set in italic type. Notice that the word *students* was replaced.

The noun that the pronoun replaces is called the **antecedent**.

> **The *students* walked to class together.**

> ***They* took *their* seats.**

Students is the antecedent for the pronouns *they* and *their*.

It must always be clear to the readers which word is the antecedent of the pronoun. Never use a pronoun unless you have named the antecedent first.

Practice

In the story below the pronouns are in italic type. On a separate sheet of paper, write each pronoun, and next to it, write its antecedent.

You may have trouble when you get to the last sentence. Think over the problem carefully, and give it your best effort.

> **Example: Marie was happy. She was driving at last.**

> **Pronoun: she; antecedent: Marie**

At last, Marie had turned 16. *She* could hardly wait to get her driver's license. Marie's mother had promised *her* the use of the family car. The car was a 1950 Chevrolet. *It* was red and white, and *it* was considered a classic. *She* loved that car!

Pronoun: she, antecedent: Marie

Pronoun: her, antecedent: Marie

Pronoun: it, antecedent: car

Pronoun: it, antecedent: car

Pronoun: she, antecedent: could be Marie or Marie's mother

(Practice continues on next page.) ⟹

(Practice continued.)

Why did you have trouble with that last sentence? It was because the antecedent was not clear. Was the word *she* in that sentence referring to *Marie* or to *Marie's mother*? Watch out for unclear antecedents in your own writing. The pronoun's antecedent must always be very clear.

Sometimes, writers use the pronoun *they* in writing without making the antecedent clear.

> *They* say that too much television is bad for children.
>
> Who are *they*?

Here are better ways to write the sentence.

> *The National Education Association* says that too much television is bad for children.
>
> *Some parents* say that too much television is bad for children.
>
> *Grade school teachers* say that too much television is bad for children.

Your readers will not get a good picture unless you make that picture very clear.

5-3 ▶ Using the Correct Pronoun

The pronoun that you use must agree with its antecedent. It must agree in **gender**. Gender tells if a noun or pronoun is masculine or feminine.

> Bill is a very funny fellow. *He* always makes jokes during English class. (masculine)
>
> Linda likes to tease Bill. *She* refuses to laugh at Bill's jokes. (feminine)

The pronoun must agree with its antecedent in number (singular or plural).

> The beach *ball* was blue and red. *It* bounced lightly on the sand. (singular)
>
> The *waves* crashed on the shore. *They* carried little shellfish and seaweed. (plural)

Making Choices

How do you choose a pronoun when the antecedent has no particular gender? For instance, look at the word *student*. You can use either the masculine pronoun, as in the following example, or the feminine pronoun.

> If a student cannot attend, *he* should call the office. (masculine)

> If a student cannot attend, *she* should call the office. (feminine)

You can also use both the masculine and feminine pronouns, as in the following example.

> If a student cannot attend, *he* or *she* should call the office.

Sometimes, you can avoid the problem by using a plural noun, as in the following example.

> If *students* cannot attend, *they* should call the office.

The Writing Process

Why is it important to choose the correct word? (See The Writing Process, page WP32.)

Practice

On a separate sheet of paper, fill in the pronouns.

> Example: The car was red. (The car) was $12,000.

> Answer: It

1. Bob bought Fran a bunch of roses. (Bob) wanted to thank her for her help.

2. The clouds moved in from the west. (The clouds) brought rain.

3. Without Connie, the play would have been a flop. Connie made (the play) a success.

1. He
2. They
3. it

WRITING WITH STYLE
Varying Writing

Learn to use a variety of nouns and pronouns to refer to the subject of your writing. For example, if you are writing about tadpoles, think of other words to call them. You could call them *baby frogs*, *they*, *tiny creatures*, and so on. Compare the following two selections. One repeats the same words too many times. The other uses different terms for the same subject. Which selection do you think reads better?

1. Baby frogs and baby toads are constantly changing creatures called *tadpoles*. *Tadpoles* have round heads that are usually the same size as their bodies. *Tadpoles* have long tails to help in swimming. *Tadpoles* are always changing their size and shape. First, the *tadpole's* head begins to take shape. Then, the *tadpole* begins to grow limbs, and the *tadpole's* tail gets shorter. By the time the *tadpole* is a full-grown frog or toad, the *tadpole's* tail has disappeared.

2. Baby frogs and baby toads are constantly changing creatures called *tadpoles*. They have round heads that are usually the same size as their bodies. *Tadpoles* have long tails to help in swimming. These tiny creatures are always changing in size and shape. First, their heads begin to take shape. Then, they begin to grow limbs, and their tails get shorter. By the time the *tadpole* is a full-grown frog or toad, its tail has disappeared.

How many times is a form of the word *tadpole* used in Selection 1? How many times is a form of the word *tadpole* used in Selection 2?

Which selection do you think reads better? Why?

Notice that the word *tadpole* is repeated occasionally in Selection 2. From time to time, the writer needs to remind the readers of the subject.

VOCABULARY BUILDER
Using Antonyms

1. Synonyms are words with similar meanings. Antonyms are words that have opposite meanings. *Big* and *little* are antonyms. *Often* and *seldom* are antonyms.

Match the antonyms in Column A and Column B by writing them in pairs on a separate sheet of paper.

Column A	Column B
a. inside	dry
b. clean	wide
c. wet	evening
d. narrow	outside
e. morning	alike
f. different	dirty

Words often have more than one antonym, just as they often have more than one synonym. *Sad* is an antonym for *happy*. *Sorrowful* and *gloomy* are antonyms for *happy*, too.

2. On a separate sheet of paper, write an antonym for each of the following words.

Example: whisper / shout

a. sharp	**d.** adult
b. heavy	**e.** graceful
c. fresh	**f.** won

1. **a.** inside, outside
   b. clean, dirty
   c. wet, dry
   d. narrow, wide
   e. morning, evening
   f. different, alike
2. Answers may vary. The following are typical answers.
   a. dull
   b. light
   c. stale
   d. child
   e. clumsy
   f. lost

Summary Have students use the summary to outline the main idea and details of the chapter.

Summary

A verb must always agree in number with its subject. To choose the correct form of a verb, find the subject and decide if it is singular or plural.

When you are not sure if the verb is correct, read the sentence aloud. You will probably "hear" an incorrect verb.

Pronouns are used to take the place of nouns.

Using pronouns is a way to avoid repeating the same noun.

Pronouns must always have a clear antecedent.

A pronoun must agree with its antecedent in gender and in number.

plural

gender

pronoun

antecedent

singular

1. antecedent
2. plural
3. pronoun
4. singular
5. gender

More Vocabulary Review is provided in the Classroom Resource Binder.

Vocabulary Review

Match each term in the box with its meaning.
Write your answers on a separate sheet of paper.

1. the noun that a pronoun replaces

2. more than one

3. a word used in place of a noun

4. only one

5. the sex of the person or thing described

Chapter Quiz
1. A noun ending in the letter *s* shows that the noun is plural.

2. A verb ending in the letter *s* shows that the verb is singular.

3. A sentence will sound awkward if the subject and verb do not agree.

Chapter Quiz

Complete the following items. Write your answers on a separate sheet of paper.

1. What does the letter *s* show when used as a noun ending?

2. What does the letter *s* show as a verb ending?

3. Why do effective writers make sure that a subject and a verb agree in a sentence?

4. Read each of the following sentences. Find the error in subject-verb agreement. Rewrite the sentence and correct the error.

   a. Cartoons is created by talented artists.

   b. One of the dancers have a broken leg.

   c. The teacher or the principal are calling Miguel.

   d. You was one of the best singers in the school.

   e. Smoke from the fires make driving impossible.

▶ **Test Tip**
If you are unsure about how to correct a sentence, reread the sentence slowly.

4. a. Cartoons <u>are</u> created by talented artists.

   b. One of the dancers <u>has</u> a broken leg.

   c. The teacher or the principal <u>is</u> calling Miguel.

   d. You <u>were</u> one of the best singers in the school.

   e. Smoke from the fires <u>makes</u> driving impossible.

Critical Thinking

Why is it important for all pronouns to have an antecedent? Write your answer on a separate sheet of paper.

Critical Thinking Answers will vary. Possible answer: It is important for all pronouns to have an antecedent so the reader understands to whom or what the pronoun refers.

Writing Activity

Think about someone who has been important to you. Next, write three sentences describing this person. Tell how he or she has affected your life. Use pronouns to avoid repeating the person's name. Make sure your subjects and verbs agree in all of your sentences.

Writing Activity Answers will vary. Check students' work specifically for correct subject-verb agreement and correct pronoun usage.

Unit 1 **Review**

Read each of the following items. On a separate sheet of paper, write the letter that best answers each one.

1. Which of the following sentences has a verb that does *not* agree with its subject?

   A. Tom and Don read books.
   B. Dina keep a journal.
   C. Mr. Todd or his sons sing all of the time.
   D. You are a good friend.

2. Which of the following groups of words is a fragment?

   A. Ten runners lined up.
   B. The race began.
   C. Running down the track wildly.
   D. Who won the prize?

3. Which of the following groups of sentences is a command?

   A. The popcorn is free.
   B. How much is a ticket?
   C. Danielle, please stand still.
   D. Thirty people will come.

4. Look at the underlined word in this sentence. What part of speech is it? *The queen wore a golden crown.*

   A. adverb
   B. noun
   C. verb
   D. adjective

   Writing Activity Answers will vary. In addition to the content of the letters, check students' work for complete sentences and correct subject-verb agreement and pronoun usage.

5. Which of the following groups of words is an independent clause?

   A. Whenever it snows
   B. Pat scored two runs.
   C. Although it is summer
   D. Since we saw her last

6. Which of the following is a compound sentence?

   A. Jan and Marie swim on the team.
   B. They practice and compete in the fall.
   C. Jan is older, but Marie is faster.
   D. Because they are teammates, the girls have become friends.

Critical Thinking Answers may vary. Possible answer: It is important to write clear, complete sentences so that readers understand your ideas. Writing in incomplete or hard-to-understand sentences makes it difficult for readers to understand what you are trying to say.

Critical Thinking
Why it is important to write clear, complete sentences? On a separate sheet of paper, explain why incomplete or hard-to-understand sentences are a problem in writing.
WRITING ACTIVITY On a separate sheet of paper, write a letter to your teacher. Tell him or her why it is important to write good sentences. Name three things you plan to do to make sure your sentences are clear and complete.

Unit 2 ▷ Writing Paragraphs

Writing a paragraph is like making a piece of furniture. You must have all the parts. The parts must all fit together, too. What are some parts of a paragraph? How do they fit together?

Caption Accept all reasonable responses. Possible answer: Some parts of a paragraph are a topic sentence, the body, and a concluding sentence. They all fit together because they relate to and support each other. Without any one of the parts, the paragraph would fall apart.

Nonfiction writers rely on well-organized paragraphs to communicate their ideas.

Dee Brown *(born 1908) lives in his hometown of Little Rock, Arkansas. He has written many nonfiction books about the U.S. frontier. His most famous book is* Bury My Heart at Wounded Knee. *It describes what happened as people settled in places where Native Americans lived.* Creek Mary's Blood *is another one of Brown's well-known books.*

To help students tap their prior knowledge of the chapter topic, see the **Chapter Project** in the Classroom Resource Binder.

Learning Objectives

- Identify sentences about one idea that belong together in a paragraph.
- Identify the topic sentence within a paragraph.
- Identify the supporting details within the body of a paragraph.
- Identify the concluding sentence within a paragraph.

Chapter 6 / What Is a Paragraph?

Words to Know

paragraph	a group of sentences placed together because they all relate to the same idea
indented	set in from the margin of a page
support	to add strength to
conclusion	the end of a paragraph
summary	a short statement that brings together the important points and details

6-1 / Understanding the Paragraph

Unit 1 discussed how to write good sentences. Usually, you need more than one sentence to explain or to tell about something. Sentences are grouped together in paragraphs. A **paragraph** is a group of sentences placed together because all of the sentences relate to the same idea. Paragraphs make ideas clear and easy to follow. Just as there are skills to learn in writing sentences, there are skills to learn about paragraphing. These skills are worth learning. Paragraphs are important tools in communication.

People recognize a paragraph because it is often **indented**, or set in from the margin of a page. Each new paragraph starts at the next indent. However, there are other ways to identify a paragraph.

They are separated by a line of white space instead, as in this book. How does a writer know when it is time to begin a new paragraph? What makes a paragraph a paragraph?

It is not a mystery. It is not something that only great writers understand. Paragraphing is simple and important. Once you understand what makes a paragraph, your writing will become easier and clearer.

Refer to the following sample paragraph as you read about paragraphs.

The Bermuda Triangle
The Bermuda Triangle is a mysterious place just off the coast of Florida. In 1945, five planes disappeared there. Another plane was sent to find them, but it disappeared, too. No one ever found the missing planes or any plane wrecks. Since then, many more planes and ships have disappeared in the same place. Scientists have studied the area, but they cannot find answers to their questions. The Bermuda Triangle remains a mystery.

There are three basic parts to a paragraph. In fact, you will find that the number three is an important number to remember when you write. Watch for it as you read about English composition.

Paragraph Part 1: Topic Sentence
A paragraph is defined as a group of sentences that are all about one idea. A writer usually identifies the main idea of a paragraph in the first sentence. The statement of that main idea is called the topic sentence.

A good topic sentence lets the readers know right away what is going on. It also helps the writer stick to the point. In our sample paragraph, the topic sentence is "The Bermuda Triangle is a mysterious place just off the coast of Florida."

Paragraph Part 2: Supporting Details

A good paragraph has at least three sentences to **support** the topic sentence. Support adds strength to the topic sentence. All three sentences must back up the statement made in the topic sentence. In the sample paragraph, the job of the supporting sentences is to back up, or to prove, the statement that the Bermuda Triangle is a mysterious place.

Look at the sentences following the topic sentence in the sample paragraph. They make up the body, or main part, of the paragraph. Do they all relate to the main idea? Do they all support the topic sentence?

Brush Up on the Basics
Paragraphs can be different lengths depending on the number of supporting sentences. (See Sentences 1–9 in the Reference Guide.)

Paragraph Part 3: Concluding Sentence

The last sentence in a good paragraph should act as its **conclusion** or **summary**. The conclusion is the end of the paragraph. A summary is a short statement that brings the important points or details together. A conclusion is especially necessary when the paragraph is not part of a larger piece of writing and is going to stand alone. Look at the sample paragraph. The last sentence in it restates the main idea.

The information you have read about paragraphing can be summed up with this diagram.

1   topic sentence
    ↓

2   (a) sentence of support ⎤
    (b) sentence of support ⎬ body
    (c) sentence of support ⎦
    ↓

3   concluding sentence

A strong paragraph should have at least three sentences of support. It may have more, but all sentences must support the topic sentence. If you cannot find three things to write to support your topic sentence, you should probably come up with a different idea.

Practice

On a separate sheet of paper, number from 1 to 4. Answer the following questions.

1. What are the three parts of a paragraph?

2. What does a topic sentence do?

3. The body of a paragraph should include at least how many sentences?

4. What do the sentences in the body of a paragraph do?

1. Topic sentence, body, concluding sentence
2. The topic sentence expresses the main idea of the paragraph.
3. three
4. The sentences in the body of the paragraph support the topic sentence.

You have just learned about a very important skill— paragraphing. Once you understand what makes a good paragraph, you are on your way to becoming a more effective writer.

The topic sentence expresses the main idea of a paragraph. The readers will expect that all other sentences in the paragraph relate to the topic sentence. When you are ready to write a sentence that does not relate to the topic sentence, you should either begin a new paragraph or not include the sentence.

A topic sentence usually appears at the beginning of a paragraph. Putting it first lets the readers know immediately what topic is going to be discussed. The topic sentence in the following paragraph is shown in italic type.

> *Some kinds of mushrooms can be dangerous.* Each year, many people are poisoned when they pick and eat mushrooms that they think are harmless. The "death cap" mushroom that grows in woods around the United States is one of the most deadly. Its poison works like the venom of a rattlesnake. The death cap looks very much like a common mushroom sold in grocery stores, but its poison can kill. Those who pick mushrooms to eat must be careful.

The paragraph above has a clearly written topic sentence at the beginning. It lets the readers know what the paragraph will be about. The topic sentence also helps the writer. It is important to be aware of your own topic sentence when you write. A topic sentence keeps you on track and helps you organize your thoughts.

Think About It

How does a topic sentence help the reader?

Occasionally, a topic sentence will come at the end of a paragraph. The topic sentence in the following paragraph is shown in italic type.

> He was only 5 feet, 3 inches tall. He weighed 130 pounds. He could throw a 30-yard pass. He scored 12 touchdowns in one season. *Despite his size, "Shorty" Hernandez was one of the toughest football players at Mission High.*

Practice

On a separate sheet of paper, find and copy the topic sentence in the paragraphs below and on the next page.

1. The new Riding High Amusement Park has some of the most thrilling rides in America.

2. Spot was a dog hero.

1. The new Riding High Amusement Park has some of the most thrilling rides in America. The giant roller coaster takes riders in a complete upside-down circle. Then it sends them flying toward the ground. The triple Ferris wheel is the tallest in the world. A ride called the Elevator Shaft makes people feel as if they are falling down a dark hole. Visitors go home feeling thrilled and excited.

2. Spot was a dog hero. When Spot and his master, Steven, were lost in a snowstorm, Spot would not leave Steven's side. Spot's fine nose found the trail that led them down the mountainside. When Steven could go no farther, Spot barked and barked until someone heard him. By the time help arrived, Spot had lost his voice from barking so long. The local newspaper named Spot the "hero of the month."

3. The door creaks. Cobwebs hang from the ceiling. A rocking chair moves slowly, but no one is in it. A loud rattle comes from upstairs. Suddenly, a scream pierces the air. The haunted house on Mill Lane is a frightening place.

4. Termites are very destructive insects. They eat wood and paper, and they tunnel their way through the woodwork of houses. These insects snack on books and furniture. Some figures show that they cause as much property loss as fires. Homeowners consider termites dangerous pests.

3. The haunted house on Mill Lane is a frightening place.

4. Termites are very destructive insects.

6-3 Recognizing Supporting Details

Once you have written a topic sentence, you must find details to support it. Three sentences of details give your topic sentence strong support. Supporting details can give facts. They can give samples and make comparisons. They answer questions a person might ask about the topic sentence. The supporting details make up the body of that paragraph.

Later in this book, you will spend time writing your own supporting details. For now, learn to recognize the supporting details in the body of a paragraph. Later on, when you are writing your own paragraph, try to choose a topic you like. Choosing a topic you like will make it easier to find supporting details.

Practice

Remember that every sentence in the body of a paragraph must support the topic sentence. In each of the following paragraphs, one sentence does not support the topic sentence. On a separate sheet of paper, find and copy that sentence.

1. Horses are also used for desert travel.
2. Many said dogs were man's best friend.

1. A camel's ability to go without water is amazing. One way the camel survives without water is by turning some of the fat in its hump into liquid. Camels can drink gigantic amounts of water at one time. Since the camel does not sweat, it does not lose any of the water it drinks. Horses are also used for desert travel. The camel's ability to go without water makes it a perfect desert traveler.

2. Through the ages, people have had many beliefs about cats. Some people thought cats were unlucky. Others insisted that cats brought them good fortune. Many said dogs were man's best friend. In the Middle Ages, some people believed that cats could speak. Sailors believed that a cat on board a ship would bring them a lucky trip. Something mysterious about cats makes people believe they have special powers.

6-4 ▶ Recognizing Concluding Sentences

When a paragraph is going to stand alone, it should have a concluding sentence. The concluding sentence helps the readers recognize that the writer has finished making his or her point. Usually, the concluding sentence summarizes information. It does not add new information. It simply repeats the main idea by using different words.

Look back at the two paragraphs in the Practice on page 84. Each paragraph has a concluding sentence. Notice that it is very much like the topic sentence in each paragraph. The concluding sentence repeats the main idea.

The Writing Process

What is the purpose of a concluding sentence? (See The Writing Process, page WP18.)

Practice

Read each of the following paragraphs. Neither has a concluding sentence. On a separate sheet of paper, write your own concluding sentence for each paragraph.

1. Legends tell us that Robin Hood was a kindly hero. Although he was an outlaw, he stole only from the rich and gave to the poor. He never bothered any group that included poor travelers or women. He never kept the money he stole. He always gave it to needy families.

2. Reading a book can be a wonderful way to pass time. A book can take its readers on adventures. It can introduce new friends or teach facts and information. A book can allow a person to forget the problems of the real world for a little while.

Answers will vary. Possible answers:

1. Seen as a thief by many, Robin Hood was actually a hero who helped many people in need.
2. Take the adventure, if you dare; it will be an enjoyable and rewarding experience.

WRITING WITH STYLE
Using Details

Read the following two paragraphs. One of the paragraphs has a topic sentence followed by supporting details. The other paragraph has sentences that do not support the topic sentence. Which is the stronger paragraph?

1. Paul Bunyan was a hero of American folk tales. Loggers in North American lumber camps once told stories of the giant lumberjack and his blue ox named Babe. According to the tales, Paul Bunyan carved out the Mississippi River and the Grand Canyon. He was also said to have made the Rocky Mountains and the Old Faithful Geyser. These tales about Paul Bunyan are called "tall tales" because they are full of exaggerations. Paul Bunyan was a popular hero from 1850 to 1900, but stories about him are still told and retold today.

2. Pecos Bill was the cowboy hero of tales from the American Southwest. Cowboys once gathered around campfires to sing songs and tell stories about him. According to those stories, Bill was the strongest, smartest, toughest cowboy in the West. Some stories tell how he dug out the Grand Canyon when he was looking for gold. He was a strong man who worked on the American railroads. Casey Jones was an engineer, but the African American hero, John Henry, was said to have built the railroad lines. He drove steel rails into the ground faster than any man alive.

Can you see the differences between Paragraph 1 and Paragraph 2? Paragraph 1 discusses only one topic—folk tales about Paul Bunyan. All of its sentences relate to that topic. The topic sentence of Paragraph 2 suggests that it will only discuss Pecos Bill tales. What happens in that paragraph? There are sentences in it that have nothing to do with Pecos Bill. Can you find these sentences? Why are the right details important?

VOCABULARY BUILDER
Using Antonyms to Make Comparisons

An antonym is a word that has the opposite meaning of another word. Antonyms are useful when discussing the differences between things. They can help you make comparisons. The following sentences are comparisons, and the antonyms are in italic type.

> Richard's job was *dull*, but my job was *exciting*.

> The character named Sam was *kind*, but William was an *evil* character.

> William was the *villain*, and Sam was the *hero*.

On a separate sheet of paper, write your own sentences using antonyms to make some comparisons. Underline the antonyms you use.

> Example: Compare two animals.

> > The dog is usually very *friendly*, but a wolf can be *fierce*.

> Example: Compare two movies.

> > The movie I saw yesterday made me *cry*. The one I saw today made me *laugh*.

1. Compare two friends.

2. Compare two teachers.

3. Compare two houses.

4. Compare two singers.

5. Compare two _____ (topic of your choice).

Answers will vary. Check students' work for comparisons using antonyms.

Summary Have students use the summary to outline the main idea and details of the chapter.

Summary

A paragraph has a topic sentence, a body, and a concluding sentence. The first word of a paragraph is usually indented. Some paragraphs are separated by white space instead.
The topic sentence states the main idea of a paragraph. Often, it is the first sentence.
The body of a paragraph usually has at least three sentences of supporting details.
The concluding sentence usually restates the main idea of a paragraph.
Every sentence in a paragraph should relate to the topic.

More Vocabulary Review is provided in the Classroom Resource Binder.

paragraph
summary
indented
conclusion
support

1. indented
2. support
3. summary
4. conclusion
5. paragraph

Vocabulary Review

Match each term in the box with its meaning.
Write your answers on a separate sheet of paper.

1. set in from the margin of a page
2. to add strength to
3. a short statement that brings together important points and details
4. the end of a paragraph
5. a group of sentences relating to a topic

Chapter Quiz

Complete the following items. Write your answers on a separate sheet of paper.

1. What does a topic sentence do in a paragraph?

2. What do details do in a paragraph?

3. Read the following paragraph. Then, answer the questions.

   The Hopi of Arizona do a special dance. It is called the snake dance. The dancers carry live rattlesnakes in their mouths as they dance, but they are rarely bitten. There are many kinds of nonpoisonous snakes in the United States. The Hopi do the snake dance to ask for rain in the dry land of Arizona.

   a. What is the topic sentence?

   b. What is the main idea?

   c. Which sentence does not belong?

Critical Thinking

How do paragraphs help a reader? Write your answer on a separate sheet of paper.

Critical Thinking Answers may vary. Possible answer: Paragraphs help readers focus on one point at a time.

▶ **Test Tip**
Use your reading skills to look for clues that could be missed easily.

Chapter Quiz

1. The topic sentence tells the reader what the paragraph is going to be about.

2. Details help support a topic sentence. They can give examples, make comparisons, or answer questions.

3. **a.** The Hopi of Arizona do a unique dance.

   b. The Hopi do the snake dance to ask for rain.

   c. There are many kinds of nonpoisonous snakes in the United States.

Writing Activity

On a separate sheet of paper, complete one of the following topic sentences. Then, write at least three supporting sentences and a concluding sentence.

Topic Sentence 1: I would like to work in a _____.

Topic Sentence 2: _____ is the most dangerous career.

Topic Sentence 3: _____ was the best movie last year.

Writing Activity Answers will vary. Check that each student's paragraph contains a topic sentence, a body of at least three supporting sentences, and a strong concluding sentence.

Effective paragraphs include clear description and strong support.

Jack London (1876–1916) *led an adventurous life. He was a sailor and a fisherman. Later, he searched for gold in Alaska. London's tales about the Alaskan Gold Rush are very popular. The paragraphs in his stories clearly describe the people he met and the places he knew. London's best-known novels are* Call of the Wild, White Fang, *and* The Sea Wolf.

Extra Reading See the Pacemaker® Classics series for Jack London's *Call of the Wild* and *The Sea Wolf.*

To help students tap their prior knowledge of the chapter topic, see the **Chapter Project** in the Classroom Resource Binder.

Learning Objectives

- Write clear topic sentences for paragraphs.
- Write paragraphs that contain three parts: topic sentence, supporting details, and concluding sentence.
- Use different types of support for topics, such as facts, figures, examples, details, and description.
- Put supporting details in logical order.

Chapter 7 ▶ Writing Good Paragraphs

See the Workbook for **Extra Practice**.

Words to Know

fact	something that is known to be true
figure	a number
example	one of a group that shows what the rest are like or explains the general rule; a sample
description	a picture in words; the details that create a picture of something
logical	something that makes sense or is reasonable
chronological order	events arranged in the order in which they happened

7-1 ▶ Writing a Topic Sentence

Remember from the last chapter that the topic sentence expresses the main idea of a paragraph. It is usually the first sentence of the paragraph. The topic sentence is in italic type in the following paragraph.

People should not be afraid of spiders. Spiders can be helpful. They eat many harmful insects. Without spiders, these insects would destroy many fruits, grains, and vegetables. Spiders seldom bite people. Most spider bites are not dangerous anyway. Spiders provide beauty, too. Their silken webs are works of art. Humans should not be too quick to kill the helpful spider.

Each of the following paragraphs has a body, supporting details, and a conclusion. However, neither paragraph has a sentence that expresses the main idea. On a separate sheet of paper, write a topic sentence for each paragraph.

Answers will vary. Possible answers:

1. Forty-fifth street is a busy street.

2. This year's basketball team will be the best ever.

1. There are many stores and businesses on 45th Street in New York City. Many people like to shop in these stores. The stores are always busy. Holiday time is a very exciting time because there are even more people on 45th Street than usual. It is a great street to shop.

2. Westlake High School's star basketball player is seven feet tall. He plays center and will probably lead the team to the state championship. Westlake's whole team is fast and skillful. Most of the players are terrific shooters. The coach has led many winning teams. So far this season, Westlake has won every game.

Writing a topic sentence helps you limit your subject so that you can cover it in one paragraph. You cannot, for example, tell everything you know about music in one paragraph. That subject is too big. A topic sentence narrows the larger subject to a topic you can cover in one paragraph.

If the subject was music, the following could be possible topic sentences.

Classical music has a message and delivers it with style.

Some people think records should be rated the same way as films are.

Practice B

The following subjects are too broad and general for one paragraph. Choose one of the subjects and copy it on a separate sheet of paper. Under it, write three topic sentences on that subject. You should be able to use each of these topic sentences to begin a paragraph.

Answers will vary. Check for students' understanding of the process for narrowing topic ideas and for writing strong topic sentences.

movies	relatives	clothes
the beach	feeling lonely	science
dogs	winning contests	teachers

Once you have written a topic sentence, your next task is clear. You must support that topic sentence. You can use different types of sentences for support. You can support your topic sentence with facts and figures, with examples, and with details and description. You may remember from Chapter 4 that details are the small parts of something that explain the whole. A **fact** is something known to be true. A **figure** is a number. An **example** is something that shows what the rest are like. A **description** is a picture in words. The paragraph below has been developed using facts and figures.

The Writing Process

How can the notes you took during prewriting help you provide supporting details? (See The Writing Process, page WP8.)

> Many people laughed when the United States bought Alaska in 1867, but it turned out to be a good buy. Today, Alaska sends gas and oil to other parts of the United States. Fishing is another important Alaskan industry. Alaska is also rich in timber, with more than 100 million acres of forested lands. In addition, there is gold in Alaska, and the state has water to provide electric power. Alaska is not the frozen wasteland that people once thought that it was. It is a land with plenty to offer.

Notice how the writer supported the paragraph about Alaska with facts and figures.

Practice A

On a separate sheet of paper, write a paragraph in which you support your topic sentence by using facts and figures. Use the list of facts and figures on the next page to write a complete paragraph. You will need to write a topic sentence first. Remember to write a concluding sentence for your paragraph.

Babe Ruth was born February 6, 1895, in Baltimore, Maryland.

Babe Ruth played 21 seasons of professional baseball.

In 1927, he set a personal record by hitting 60 home runs in one season.

In his career, he hit 714 home runs.

Ruth batted in 2,209 runs.

He played in 10 World Series.

Answers will vary. Possible answer: Babe Ruth is quite possibly the best baseball player who ever lived. In his 21-season career, he hit 714 home runs, batted in 2,209 runs, and played in 10 World Series. In 1927, he set his personal record of 60 home runs in one season. Only recently have Ruth's accomplishments been challenged, proving this baseball giant's legendary status.

The paragraph below has been developed with an example.

> Mountain climbers should always consider weather before they begin to climb. Last May, five high school students went on a climb when the weather looked bad. They did not listen to warnings of an approaching storm and were caught in a blizzard. They were forced to dig a snow cave and to huddle there throughout the night. At last, rescuers found them and dug them out. All of the climbers were badly frostbitten. Three of them lost toes and fingers. They learned that it can be deadly to climb when the weather looks bad.

Notice how the topic sentence in the paragraph above has been supported by the story of one climb.

Practice B

Choose one of the following topic sentences. On a separate sheet of paper, write a complete paragraph supporting the sentence with one or more examples.

Motorists should never drive over the speed limit.

Gymnastics (or any sport you choose) can be very dangerous.

It is not easy to sew (or any activity you choose).

My aunt (or any relative you choose) is a funny person.

I am sure that cats can think.

Saturday nights are really boring in my town.

Sometimes, you might want to use details and description to develop a paragraph. The following paragraph does just that.

Some people think the junkyard is ugly, but I think it is beautiful. In the spring, tiny wildflowers grow up between the twisted metal of old cars. In the summer, the sun sparkles off of hundreds of pieces of broken glass. Gentle breezes blow scraps of colored cloth and paper across the ground. In the winter, the whole place is covered with a blanket of snow, and silver icicles glitter everywhere. The junkyard has its own special kind of beauty.

Notice how the writer picked very specific details and descriptions to make a point.

English and Technology

You can use a word-processing program to highlight your topic sentences. Then, you can easily refer to it as you write supporting details.

Answers will vary. Students' paragraphs should have a strong topic sentence, a body that presents at least three sentences of support with one or more examples, and a concluding sentence.

Practice C

On a separate sheet of paper, write your own paragraph. Use details and description to develop one of the following topic sentences.

> In the middle of the night, my home can be noisy (or lonely or peaceful).

> I will never forget seeing my favorite performer in concert.

> Sports fans can be fanatics.

> The view from the top of the mountain was worth the climb.

> It is never boring in English class.

> It was a dance to remember.

Answers will vary. Students' paragraphs should contain a strong topic sentence, a body that presents at least three details or descriptions, and a concluding sentence.

Practice D

Look at the following topic sentences. On a separate sheet of paper, write the type of details that you think would best support each one. You might choose facts and figures, examples, or details and description. Sometimes, a topic sentence can be developed in more than one way.

1. The United States produces much of its own energy.

2. Writing paragraphs requires concentration.

3. (Choose your favorite movie) is a great movie.

4. (Choose your favorite sport) is a fantastic sport.

5. Birds may look small and delicate, but they are really very strong.

Answers will vary. The most likely answers are listed here.

1. facts and figures
2. examples or details and description
3. details and description
4. examples or details and description
5. examples, details, facts, and description

Portfolio Project

Write your own paragraph. Select a topic sentence from Practice D on page 97. Use the type of details that you think will best support the topic.

7-3 ▸ Putting Details in Order

A clearly written paragraph presents supporting details in a **logical**, or sensible, order. One way to organize details is by time. This order is called **chronological order**. In fact, certain kinds of paragraphs must be written in chronological order. For example, if you are telling your readers how to do something, it is important to tell them at the beginning of your paragraph what they should do first. Then tell them the rest of the steps in chronological order.

In paragraphs that describe what happened, chronological order is easiest to follow. Most likely, you will tell the details in the order they took place. A description of a full day at a beach, for example, would probably begin in the morning and end in the evening.

Read the following paragraph. Its details are arranged in chronological order.

> A man almost had a terrible accident this morning. He was standing on the corner waiting for the traffic light to change. When the light turned green, he stepped off of the curb. He started across the street without looking to the left or right. A child screamed, and he turned to look. Just then, truck came rumbling around the corner. The truck driver slammed on the brakes just in time to avoid hitting the man.

Think About It

Why might you save the most interesting detail for last?

Notice the sequence of events: (1) the man waits for the traffic light, (2) he steps off of the curb, (3) he starts across the street without looking left or right, (4) a child screams, (5) the truck comes, and (6) the truck driver slams on the brakes. The events are presented in chronological order.

Practice

The following details are out of order. On a separate sheet of paper, write a paragraph using these sentences, but put the details in chronological order. Remember to write a concluding sentence for your paragraph.

Here is your topic sentence.
Ed's home repair ended in disaster.

1. He took the ladder from the garage and leaned it against the house.

2. Suddenly, the ladder began to tip.

3. The next thing Ed knew, he was lying on the ground.

4. Ed decided it was time to patch the gutters.

5. As Ed climbed to the top, he felt dizzy.

Ed's home repair ended in disaster. Ed decided it was time to patch the gutters. He took the ladder from the garage and leaned it against the house. As Ed climbed to the top, he felt dizzy. Suddenly, the ladder began to tip. The next thing Ed knew, he was lying on the ground.

WRITING WITH STYLE
Limiting a Topic

It is important to limit your topic to a size you can support. If your topic is too broad, it is impossible to say anything meaningful in one paragraph. Read the following paragraphs. Paragraph 1 has a topic sentence that presents a topic that is too broad. Paragraph 2 has a topic sentence that limits the topic to a reasonable size.

1. Cars were an important invention. Henry Ford made one of the earliest cars. Cars are mainly for transportation. They can help people get to places quickly. One popular new car is the Firewing GL. Most U.S. families own at least one car. Without cars, Americans' lives would surely be different.

2. This year's Firewing GL has turned out to be a very popular car. It is a great-looking sports sedan that can go up to 180 miles per hour. However, it uses much less fuel than similar models. It can comfortably carry five passengers and a trunk full of luggage. Best of all, the Firewing GL has an amazingly low price.

In Paragraph 1, *cars* was just too broad a topic. By limiting the topic to one type of car in Paragraph 2, the writer was able to present specific details. These details provided focus and made the point.

VOCABULARY BUILDER
Using Base Words

A base word is a word on which other words are built. Sometimes, word parts are added to the beginning or end of base words. For example, *place* is a base word. You could add *mis-* to the beginning of the base word to make *misplace*. You could add *-ment* to the end of the base word to make *placement*.

Understanding base words can help you increase your vocabulary. You can change the meaning of a base word by adding word parts to the beginning or end of the base word.

1. Write the word in each of the following groups that is a base word.

   a. hopeful, hopeless, hope

   b. open, reopen, opened

   c. helpful, help, helpless

   d. take, taken, mistake

   e. comfortable, discomfort, comfort

2. Write the base word of each of the following words.

   Examples: unused = use

           asleep = sleep

           healthy = health

   a. remove   f. remake

   b. secretly   g. interesting

   c. visitor   h. looked

   d. distrust   i. cheerful

   e. truthful   j. discount

1. a. hope
   b. open
   c. help
   d. take
   e. comfort

2. a. move
   b. secret
   c. visit
   d. trust
   e. truth
   f. make
   g. interest
   h. look
   i. cheer
   j. count

Chapter 7 Review

Summary Have students use the summary to outline the main idea and details of the chapter.

Summary
Your topic sentence expresses the main idea of your paragraph.
The topic you write about must be narrow enough to be covered in one paragraph.
The body of a paragraph usually has at least three sentences of supporting details.
Supporting details can be facts and figures, examples, or details and descriptions.
In paragraphs that tell "how to" or "what happened," arrange the supporting details in chronological order.

fact

chronological order

logical

example

description

figure

1. chronological order
2. example
3. logical
4. fact
5. description
6. figure

More Vocabulary Review is provided in the Classroom Resource Binder.

Vocabulary Review

Complete each sentence with a term from the box. Write your answers on a separate sheet of paper.

1. If events are arranged in _____, they are in the order in which they happened.

2. An _____ shows what the rest of a group is like.

3. A statement that makes sense or is reasonable is _____.

4. A _____ is something that can be proven.

5. A _____ is a picture in words.

6. A number that is used in writing is a _____.

Chapter Quiz

Complete the following items. Write your answers on a separate sheet of paper.

1. Why do effective writers limit the topic of a paragraph?

2. What is one way to narrow a topic for a paragraph?

3. What should the supporting sentences in a paragraph do?

4. How would you decide which details to use in a paragraph?

5. What kind of paragraph would have to be organized in chronological order?

Critical Thinking

Why should all of the details in a paragraph support the topic sentence? Write your answer on a separate sheet of paper.

Critical Thinking Answers will vary. Possible answer: The paragraph will be much stronger when it is well supported.

▶ **Test Tip**
Think about the discussions you hold in class. Use some of the suggestions your teachers and classmates gave.

Chapter Quiz

1. Some topics are too large to cover in one paragraph. It is important to narrow the topic to one you can cover in a paragraph.

2. One way to narrow a topic that is too broad is by writing several topic sentences. This process will help you think of ideas that can be covered in one paragraph.

3. The supporting sentences must prove or explain the topic sentence.

4. The details should support the topic sentence.

5. A paragraph that describes a historical event or a personal experience would probably be organized in chronological order.

Writing Activity

On a separate sheet of paper, write your own paragraph. Use one of the following suggestions, or create your own idea. When you have finished, read over your paragraph.

Tell about a time that you felt very happy.

Describe your favorite meal.

Suggest a solution to a problem in your community.

Writing Activity Answers will vary. Students should be able to write a paragraph independently. Their paragraphs should contain a topic sentence, a body of at least three supporting sentences, and a concluding sentence.

Transitions and carefully crafted paragraphs draw readers into a story.

Toni Morrison (born 1931) is a leading American novelist. Her novels focus on the lives of African Americans. Her work is known for its realistic characters and real-life dialogue. Her carefully crafted paragraphs draw her readers into the story. In 1988, Morrison won the Pulitzer Prize for her novel Beloved. *In 1993, Morrison received the Nobel Prize for Literature. Her other novels include* The Bluest Eye, Song of Solomon, Paradise, *and* Jazz.

To help students tap their prior knowledge of the chapter topic, see the **Chapter Project** in the Classroom Resource Binder.

Learning Objectives

- Write topic sentences that make the reader want to read the rest of the paragraph.

- Write topic sentences that are clear and focused.

- Write sentences in the body of the paragraph that support the topic sentence.

- Use transitional words to show the connection between sentences.

Chapter 8

Writing Better Paragraphs

See the Workbook for Extra Practice.

Words to Know

transition	the act of moving from one thing to another
transitional word	a word that helps a reader move from one idea to another; it shows how one idea relates to and connects with another idea

8-1 Writing Interesting Topic Sentences

Of course, all writers want to make their writing as clear and as interesting as possible. Here are some ways to improve your paragraphs.

You know that the topic sentence expresses the main idea in a paragraph. Your readers need a topic sentence. It shows where the paragraph is going. It tells the readers what to expect. The topic sentence can serve another purpose. A good topic sentence should interest your readers in your subject. It should make your readers want to read on and find out what you have to share.

How can you make your topic sentences more lively and interesting? First, get right to the point. Do not waste words. Present your topic clearly and without any unnecessary words.

> Do not write: I am going to write about the way buffaloes are disappearing in the United States.

> Do write: American buffaloes are disappearing in the United States.

> Do not write: I want to tell you some of the reasons I never eat in the school cafeteria.

> Do write: I avoid eating in the school cafeteria.

Practice A

On a separate sheet of paper, number from 1 to 5. Then, read each pair of the following topic sentences. Write the letter of the stronger topic sentence from each pair. Be ready to explain your choices.

1. b
2. b
3. a
4. b
5. a

1. **a.** My paragraph is about hamsters.
   b. Hamsters make friendly, lively pets.

2. **a.** I am supposed to write about a town that I like, so I will write about my birthplace.
   b. I think my birthplace is the most beautiful city in the world.

3. **a.** It is hard to catch a gopher, but it can be done.
   b. There are many ways to catch a gopher, and I am going to tell you about some of them.

4. **a.** Well, last Saturday night I saw a movie, and it was frightening.
   b. *Murders by Night* was a frightening movie.

5. **a.** Skiing is a fun sport.
   b. Skiing is a fun sport, so I am going to write about it.

Remember that the topic sentence should make your readers want to read your paragraph. Make the topic sentence so interesting that your readers have to go on.

One way to add interest to your topic sentence is to express an opinion or state a choice.

Topic sentence *without* an opinion: The beagle is a type of dog.

Topic sentence *with* an opinion: The beagle is not for just anybody.

A topic sentence should give your readers enough information to help them to keep reading.

Which of the following topic sentences would make you most eager to read the paragraph?

1. A scary thing happened to me last night.

2. The sky was dark, the wind was howling, and I was about to have the scariest night of my life.

3. I never thought I could scream in terror, but I did last night.

You probably chose Sentence 2 or Sentence 3. Both of those topic sentences give more detail than Sentence 1. They give the readers enough information to become interested in the topic.

Think About It

How do details help to make a topic sentence interesting?

Practice B

On a separate sheet of paper, number from 1 to 5. Then, read each pair of the following topic sentences. Write the letter of the stronger sentence in each pair. Be ready to explain your choices.

1. a. Somebody once took some candlesticks from our house.
   b. We called it the mystery of the missing candlesticks.

2. a. Leonard A. Cooper is the kindest teacher I have ever had.
   b. Mr. Cooper is my teacher.

3. a. Joey plays baseball.
   b. Joey is a terrific baseball player but a terrible driver.

1. b
2. a
3. b

(Practice B continues on next page.) ⟹

4. b

5. a

4. a. The zoo is a good place to visit.

b. Roaring tigers, deadly snakes, and poisonous spiders are safe to be around—but only at the zoo.

5. a. The television show *Exploring the Universe* takes viewers on exciting adventures.

b. *Exploring the Universe* is a television show.

Practice C

The following five topic sentences are unclear. On a separate sheet of paper, rewrite each one to make it stronger. Make sure that you state the topic directly and that you provide enough information to make it interesting.

Answers will vary. Possible answers:

1. Uncle Ralph is the most unusual member of our family.

2. It happened a long time ago, but I still remember my first day of school.

3. Building a swimming pool in your backyard may seem difficult, but if you follow a few important steps, you'll soon be dipping your toes into your own pool.

4. Stamp collecting can be a fun and educational hobby.

5. Children should not play with matches for many reasons.

1. I want to tell you about my Uncle Ralph (use any relative's name).

2. It happened a long time ago, and I really do not remember it very well, but I will try to tell you something about my first day of school.

3. I do not know too much about it, but this is how to build a swimming pool in your backyard.

4. This paragraph is about stamp collecting.

5. There are many reasons that children should not play with matches, and I am going to tell you some of them.

Unless you are giving directions, avoid using the word *you*. Do not talk directly to your readers. Notice all of the *you*'s in the sentences in Practice C. These sentences are really better off without them.

Making Every Sentence of Support Count

In Chapter 7, you learned to use facts and figures, examples, and details and description to develop your topic sentence. Make sure that every sentence you write in the body of your paragraph counts, too. Avoid sentences that do not support your point. Avoid sentences that repeat or restate an idea already presented in another sentence.

The sentences in italic type in the following paragraph repeat information. They add no new support and should be left out of the paragraph.

> Chimpanzees may be one of the most intelligent animals in the world. *They are very smart.* There are chimps that have been trained to ride bicycles and to eat with forks. They are clever enough to invent all kinds of ways to get to their food. Chimps have been known to pile boxes on top of each other to reach food left in high places. *Even though they are just animals, they are really very intelligent.* Some chimpanzees have been taught to communicate with people through the use of hand signals. Chimpanzees often surprise humans with their ability to learn.

English and Technology

You can search the Internet to find facts and figures to support your ideas.

See *Pacemaker® Computer Literacy* for more information on the Internet.

Practice

Read the following paragraph. Find the sentences that repeat ideas and do not add support to the topic. On a separate sheet of paper, write these sentences.

The Great Mirando made it easy to believe in magic. He came onto the stage dressed in a purple robe that sparkled mysteriously. He made a bowl full of fish disappear. Then, he made a rabbit wearing a baseball cap appear. Mirando's tricks definitely looked real. When he waved his wand, he rose from the ground. Then, he floated above the stage. Maybe it was a trick, but it certainly looked real. When the act ended, Mirando simply clapped his hands and disappeared.

8-3 ▸ Using Transitional Words

Transition means moving or changing from one thing to another. When you are writing a paragraph, you are moving from one sentence to another. You need to make this movement smooth and easy to follow. One of the easiest ways to link your sentences smoothly is through the use of **transitional words.**

Transitional words show the connection between one idea or sentence and another. They serve as guides for your readers as they read your paragraph.

Look at the transitional words on the top of page 111. Notice that the following transitional words are related to time. They help your readers understand how your sentences fit together.

The Writing Process

Why is it important to use transitional words in a paragraph? (See The Writing Process, page WP26.)

Transitional Words Related to Time	
at first	a little later
then	finally
next	afterward
meanwhile	later
at last	soon
before long	after that
at the same time	as

The transitional words in the following paragraph are in italic type. They help readers keep track of time.

> The beginning of our vacation was full of disasters. *First,* our car would not start when we were ready to leave. It took a full hour to fix the problem. *Then,* we discovered that the dog had disappeared. *After* looking around the neighborhood, we found him under the house. *At last,* we pulled out onto the highway. *Before long,* we heard a siren screaming behind us. A police officer pulled us over and told us that we were speeding. *Finally,* with a sixty-dollar speeding ticket and a late start on our vacation, we were on our way.

You will not want to use a transitional word or phrase in every sentence. Too many transitional words or phrases make sentences seem awkward.

Practice A

On a separate sheet of paper, rewrite the paragraph on page 112. Add some transitional words and phrases to help readers follow time order. The list above will help you think of some transitional words.

(Practice A continues on next page.) ⇒

(Practice A continued.)

Everyone knew the tornado was coming. The sky grew very dark. The air became warm and strangely still. The birds stopped singing. My dog ran and hid in the basement. The wind began to howl and whistle. A garbage can rolled down the street, and traffic signals danced crazily on their wires. A voice on the radio warned everyone to take cover.

Answers will vary. Possible answer: Everyone knew the tornado was coming. At first, the sky grew very dark. Then the air became warm and strangely still. The birds stopped singing. A little later, my dog ran and hid in the basement. Soon, the wind began to howl and whistle. Before long, a garbage can rolled down the street, and the traffic signals danced crazily on their wires. After that, a voice on the radio warned everyone to take cover.

Other kinds of transitional words and phrases show how one idea in your paragraph relates to another idea. These transitional words help link your ideas together. They make your sentences flow smoothly. Transitional words make your ideas clearer to your readers, and being clear is one of the goals of good writing.

Notice that the following transitional words show how one idea would relate to another idea. They can link sentences together.

Transitional Words That Link Ideas	
for example	also
on the other hand	in conclusion
for this reason	even so
in addition	in comparison
however	although
as a result	indeed
most importantly	furthermore
another	in fact

In the following example, the transitional words are in italic type. They show the relationships between ideas.

Some people love oysters and others hate them. For some people, oysters are a rare treat. These people consider a really fresh oyster one of the tastiest items in the world. They eat oysters fried, grilled, and in soups and stews. They even make oyster dressing for their turkeys. *In fact,* some people eat their oysters raw. *On the other hand,* others find oysters disgusting. These people think oysters are strange and slimy and salty. *Also,* they dislike the strange, dark-colored insides of the oyster. *Indeed,* although many oyster-haters admit that oysters are a healthy food, most would never eat one.

Practice B

On a separate sheet of paper, list the transitional words or phrases in the following paragraph.

The strangest creatures can be friends. For example, the giant rhinoceros and the tiny tick-bird are the best of pals. Indeed, they help each other survive. The little bird rides around on the rhinoceros's back and eats ticks off of the rhino. Thus, the rhino provides the tick-bird with food. In turn, the tick-bird helps keep the rhinoceros clean and comfortable. Furthermore, when the near-sighted rhinoceros fails to see an enemy coming, the tick-bird chirps a warning. The rhino and the tick-bird are as different as can be. However, they are best friends.

for example
indeed
thus
in turn
furthermore
however

Portfolio Project

Write a paragraph about a day you spent with one of your friends. Use transitional words and phrases to arrange what you did and to move smoothly from one sentence to the next.

Answers will vary. Check students' work specifically for their effective use of transitions.

Transitions can make a difference. Look at the following two paragraphs. They are the same paragraph, but one does not have transitions and the other one does.

1. Without transitions:

Many people think rabbits and hares are the same animals, but that is not true. The animal usually called a jack rabbit is really not a rabbit at all. It is a hare. Hares have always lived in all parts of the world. Rabbits were once found only in Europe. Rabbits are smaller than hares. They have shorter legs and ears. Rabbits dig burrows in the ground. Hares do not build burrows. Hares are much faster than rabbits.

2. With transitions:

Many people think rabbits and hares are the same animals, but that is not true. For example, the animal often called a jack rabbit is not a rabbit at all. It is a hare. Hares have always lived in all parts of the world. Rabbits, on the other hand, were once found only in Europe. They are smaller than hares. Also, rabbits have shorter legs and ears. Although rabbits dig burrows in the ground, hares do not build burrows. Furthermore, hares are much faster than rabbits.

Can you find the transitional words and phrases in the second paragraph? How do these words and phrases improve the flow of the paragraph?

VOCABULARY BUILDER
Using Prefixes

A *prefix* is a group of letters added to the beginning of a word. A prefix changes the meaning of the word. For example, the prefix *re-* means again. In other words, to *recheck* something is to check it again. The following are some common prefixes and their meanings.

Prefix	Meaning	Prefix	Meaning
bi-, duo-	two	multi-	many
tri-	three	pre-	before
non-	not	co-	with, together
re-	again	anti-	against
trans-	across	dis-	opposite

1. Use the list of prefixes above to write the word described by each of the following definitions. The first one has been done as an example. Write your answers on a separate sheet of paper.

    a. to make again   *remake*

    b. three-wheeled cycle

    c. against war

    d. having many purposes

    e. not poisonous

2. Write a word that begins with each of the prefixes listed in the chart.

1. a. remake
   b. tricycle
   c. antiwar
   d. multipurpose
   e. nonpoisonous
2. Answers will vary. Possible answers:
   a. bicycle
   b. tripod
   c. nontoxic
   d. review
   e. transportation
   f. multicolored
   g. pretest
   h. cooperate
   i. anti-drugs
   j. disagree

8 ▷ Review

Summary Have students use the summary to outline the main idea and details of the chapter.

Summary

Avoid unnecessary words in your topic sentences, such as "I am going to write about" or "My paragraph is about."
Write a topic sentence that encourages your readers to read your paragraph. Use enough information to help your readers and to support or express your opinion.
Make sure every sentence in the body of your paragraph supports your topic sentence. Do not include sentences that repeat a detail or restate the topic sentence.
Transitional words and phrases help readers understand the time order of your paragraph. They also show the relationship between sentences.

transition
transitional words

1. true
2. true

More Vocabulary Review is provided in the Classroom Resource Binder.

Vocabulary Review

Write *true* or *false* after each sentence. If the sentence is false, change the underlined word or words to make it true. Choose a term from the box. Write your answers on a separate sheet of paper.

1. *First, then,* and *finally* are <u>transitional words</u> that show time order.

2. Miguel made a <u>transition</u> when he graduated high school.

Chapter Quiz

Complete the following items. Write your answers on a separate sheet of paper.

1. What is the purpose of a topic sentence?

2. What are two reasons to state an opinion or a choice in a topic sentence?

3. How could you rewrite the following topic sentence to make it more interesting? *This paragraph is going to tell about something scary that once happened to me.*

4. List three examples of transitional words that show time order.

5. List three examples of transitional words that show relationships between ideas.

Critical Thinking

How can transitional words and phrases make your writing smoother and easier to read? Write your answer on a separate sheet of paper.

Critical Thinking Transitional words help a reader follow the order of and the relationships between ideas. They help readers understand your writing better by making connections between ideas.

▶ **Test Tip**
Read the directions carefully. Make sure to answer each part of the assignment.

Chapter Quiz

1. The purpose of a topic sentence is to tell readers what your paragraph will be about.

2. Stating an opinion or choice helps get the reader's attention; it makes the topic sentence interesting.

3. Answers will vary. Possible answer: Sometimes real life can be scarier than horror movies.

4. Answers will vary. Transitional words that show time include *at first, then,* and *next.*

5. Answers will vary. Transitional words that show relationships between ideas include *for example, also,* and *on the other hand.*

Writing Activity

On a separate sheet of paper, write a paragraph about a day you will never forget. Use time order to tell what happened. Use transitional words and phrases to guide your readers. Be sure to write a topic sentence that makes your readers want to know about your day. Make sure each supporting sentence adds to the main idea. End with a concluding sentence.

Writing Activity In this activity, students are demonstrating their understanding of presenting ideas in chronological order. Check students' paragraphs for accurate and effective use of time-order transitions.

Unit 2 **Review**

Standardized Test Preparation This unit review follows the format of many standardized tests. A Scantron® sheet is provided in the Classroom Resource Binder.

Read each of the following items. On a separate sheet of paper, write the letter that best answers each one.

1. Which of the following is *not* one of the three main parts of a paragraph?

   A. topic sentence
   B. supporting details
   C. transitional words
   D. concluding sentence

2. A good paragraph usually has at least _____ sentences of support.

   A. two
   B. three
   C. four
   D. five

3. You can support the topic sentence of a paragraph with _____.

   A. time order.
   B. facts and figures.
   C. indented sentences.
   D. a concluding sentence.

4. Which detail does *not* support the following topic sentence?
   The storm did terrible damage.

   A. Forty families were left homeless.
   B. More than 5,000 homes lost their power.
   C. Flooding destroyed downtown businesses.
   D. Sunny skies are predicted for the rest of the week.

5. Which of the following topic sentences is the strongest?

   A. I want to write about Dr. Ortiz.
   B. Dr. Raymond Ortiz is my doctor.
   C. Dr. Raymond Ortiz is the wisest man I have ever met.
   D. This paragraph is about Dr. Ortiz, a doctor in Glenmont.

6. Which transitional word or phrase shows time order?

   A. similarly
   B. furthermore
   C. meanwhile
   D. most importantly

Critical Thinking Answers will vary. In this activity, students write a checklist of tips for writing paragraphs. Check students' lists for such ideas as writing a strong topic sentence; supporting the topic sentence with details and descriptions, facts and figures, and examples; writing a strong concluding sentence; and using effective transitions.

Writing Activity Answers will vary. For this activity, students are demonstrating their mastery for writing strong, effective paragraphs. Check students' work for the qualities they identified in the Critical Thinking exercise.

Critical Thinking

What have you learned about writing better paragraphs in this unit? On a separate sheet of paper, make a checklist with five or more tips for writing paragraphs.

WRITING ACTIVITY On a separate sheet of paper, write a paragraph about a game or sport that you like to play. Follow all the rules you have learned for writing good paragraphs.

Unit ▷3▷ Paragraphs with a Purpose

Political candidates write with a purpose. Their paragraphs might explain or describe something. They might also try to persuade listeners to vote for them. What other purposes might writers have?

Caption Accept all reasonable responses. Possible answer: News writers write to communicate the news. Columnists write to express an opinion but also to entertain readers. Essayists write to explain, inform, or describe something.

Writers can inform readers about different people, places, and events through their stories.

Chinua Achebe
(born 1930) grew up in a village in Nigeria. He loved to listen to the stories of his people. Storytelling is an important part of African culture. Achebe's first novel is titled Things Fall Apart. *It tells the story of his homeland and people. Achebe also wrote* Anthills of the Savannah. *This novel is also set in Nigeria. Since 1990, Achebe has lived and taught in the United States.*

Reading Challenge See the Adapted Classics series for Chinua Achebe's *Things Fall Apart.*

To help students tap their prior knowledge of the chapter topic, see the **Chapter Project** in the Classroom Resource Binder.

Learning Objectives

- Write an explanatory paragraph.
- Write an informative paragraph.
- Write a narrative paragraph.

Chapter 9 > Writing to Explain, Inform, or Tell a Story

Words to Know

explanatory paragraph	a paragraph that explains, clarifies, and gives details
informative paragraph	a paragraph that gives information and shares knowledge
narrative paragraph	a paragraph that tells of events and experiences
anecdote	a short, interesting story about an event or a person
nonfiction	writing that tells about real people and events
fiction	imaginative writing; something made up or invented

9-1 Writing How-To Paragraphs

An **explanatory paragraph** tells how to do something or how to make something. A paragraph in which you give someone directions to your house is an example of an explanatory paragraph.

Look at the following points to remember when you write an explanatory paragraph.

Remember your goal.

> You want to teach your readers something.

Remember to make it clear.

> Write simply. Do not use technical words that the readers will not understand.

Remember to make it easy to follow.

> Use chronological order in a how-to paragraph.
> Use transitional words and phrases to guide your readers.

Read the following sample explanatory paragraph.

One of the easiest tricks to teach a dog is how to sit. To begin the training, stand your dog on your left side. Hold it firmly on a short leash. Then, in a clear, confident voice, command the dog to "sit." As you give the command, pull up slightly on the leash. At the same time, push down on the dog's backside. Once your dog is sitting, repeat the word "sit" several times. Do not let it stand up or lie down. Then, praise your dog cheerfully. Soon, your dog will learn what you expect when you give it the command to "sit." Before long, the dog will be sitting on command without the leash or the tap on the backside.

Practice A

to begin
then
as
at the same time
once
then
soon
before long

On a separate sheet of paper, list the transitional words and phrases you find in the explanatory paragraph above.

Notice that the paragraph was written about a narrow subject. A writer could not write a paragraph on "How to Train a Dog." That topic is too big. He or she could not begin to cover all the points in one paragraph. By limiting the topic to "How to Teach a Dog to Sit," the writer was able to write a full, detailed explanation.

Practice B

Some of the following topics are too broad to be fully covered in a single paragraph. Others would be fine topics for one explanatory paragraph. On a separate sheet of paper, list the topics on page 123 that would be good choices for an explanatory paragraph.

How to cook	How to maintain a car
How to make brownies	How to change a tire
How to play basketball	How to shop
How to shoot a free throw	How to buy the right stereo

Practice C

Think about things you know how to do well. Consider what you do around the house, such as ironing a shirt, making a bed, caring for house plants, washing windows, or cleaning your room. Consider the things you do for fun, like swinging a golf club, doing a back dive, riding a bicycle, learning a new dance step, or planning a party.

Choose a topic to explain. Make sure the topic is not too broad. You would not, for example, be able to explain how to make a dress. There would be too much to cover. You could, however, tell how to sew on a button.

On a separate sheet of paper, list the necessary steps involved in the task. Then, write an explanatory paragraph telling your readers how to do something or how to make something.

Answers will vary. Check to make sure students have a narrow enough topic to be covered in one paragraph. Then, evaluate whether students have written all the necessary steps in the correct order in their paragraphs.

9-2
Writing Paragraphs That Give Information

Often, your purpose in writing will be to tell your readers about something you know. You will be sharing information. Such paragraphs will be developed with details and with facts and figures.

Suppose you know about the life of Chief Joseph. A paragraph written about Chief Joseph is an example of an **informative paragraph.** An informative paragraph gives information and shares knowledge. Read the following example.

> Chief Joseph was a famous leader of the Nez Percé, a Native American nation in the Northwest United States. In 1877, the United States government demanded that the Nez Percé move to a reservation in Idaho. Chief Joseph refused. After losing many battles to the U.S. troops, Chief Joseph and his followers tried to escape to Canada. Forty miles from the Canadian border, Colonel Miles and his troops surprised the Nez Percé. Chief Joseph surrendered to Miles six days later. The courage of Chief Joseph deeply moved many Americans. They began to ask for better treatment for Native Americans.

An informative paragraph often begins with a topic sentence about something or someone. Who was Chief Joseph? He was a famous Nez Percé leader.

Read the following topic sentences. Each one could begin an informative paragraph.

> The Siberian husky is a sturdy, swift sled dog.

> Marian Anderson was an African American opera star.

> Jupiter is the largest of the planets.

Practice

On a separate sheet of paper, write a topic sentence for three of the following topics that could begin an informative paragraph.

hurricane	an electric guitar	a cobra
the Chicago Bears	compact disks	a tidal wave
Maya Angelou	the latest dance	

Portfolio Project

Write an informative paragraph. Use one of the topic sentences that you wrote in the Practice on page 124 as your topic sentence. You may want to use a dictionary and an encyclopedia to find details, facts, and figures to support your topic. You may know enough already to write a good paragraph. Write your paragraph on a separate sheet of paper.

9-3 ▸ A Paragraph That Tells a Story

A paragraph that tells a story about events or experiences is called a **narrative paragraph.** Such a paragraph answers the following question: What happened? Narratives can be different lengths. They can be many pages long, or they can be just one paragraph. A short narrative about an event or person is called an **anecdote.** An anecdote usually describes one event.

A narrative can be **nonfiction,** or true, or **fiction,** or created by the writer. Narratives are usually told in time order. A narrative usually describes some sort of problem. The end of the story comes when that problem is solved.

Think About It

How can an anecdote be helpful when you write a narrative paragraph?

When you write a paragraph that you think of as a story, ask yourself the following questions: *What is the problem in this story? How is that problem solved?* They will help you to create a story for your readers.

When planning your narrative paragraph, you can come up with details by asking yourself a few questions. Whether your story is nonfiction or fiction, ask yourself these questions: *Who? What? Where? When? Why? How?* See the examples on page 126.

Here are some examples.

> Topic sentence: Sue and I almost drowned on our last trip to the beach.
>
> *Who?* Sue and I
>
> *What?* almost drowned when we were caught by the outgoing tide
>
> *When?* late in the afternoon, after the lifeguards had gone off duty
>
> *Where?* Seaside Beach
>
> *Why?* We were caught by the outgoing tide.
>
> *How?* The water was quite warm, and we went out too far.

The Writing Process

How can *wh-* questions help you to create a list of details? (See The Writing Process, page WP8.)

Once you have a list of details, you can write your narrative paragraph. Read the paragraph below that is based on the details about the trip to the beach.

Sue and I almost drowned on our last trip to the beach. We had gone into the ocean at Seaside Beach late one afternoon. Although it was a cloudy day, the water was quite warm. The beach was nearly empty. Everyone, including the lifeguards, had gone home for dinner. We were laughing and splashing. Then, suddenly, our laughs became screams of fear. We realized we had been caught by the outgoing tide and could not get back to shore. Neither Sue nor I was strong enough to fight the tide alone. We were beginning to panic when a group of women came walking up the beach. When they saw us waving our arms, they swam out to help us. They were strong swimmers, and soon we were safe on shore.

What was the problem in the sample paragraph on page 126? How was that problem solved?

Practice A

How would you answer the *who, what, when, where, why,* and *how* questions for one of the following topic sentences? This will be fiction, so you will have to use your imagination to come up with the answers. On a separate sheet of paper, choose and write a topic sentence. Then answer these questions: *Who? What? When? Where? Why? How?*

> The brave dog, Rover, had to struggle to find his way home.
>
> Teresa and I know we saw a bat that night.
>
> Ed and Tonio thought they would never find their way out of the forest.
>
> The baby-sitting job turned into a nightmare.
>
> Finding my lost wallet turned out to be an adventure.
>
> Beth Sanchez became a hero in one day.

Answers will vary. Possible answer for the first sentence is as follows:

Topic sentence: The brave dog, Rover, had to struggle to find his way home.

Who? brave dog, Rover

What? he wandered away from his owners while on a camping trip

When? last night

Where? a dark, lonely forest

Why? he was curious about the wildlife he saw in the forest

How? he struggled to find his way home using his keen sense of smell

Practice B

On a separate sheet of paper, write a narrative paragraph. Use one of the topics from the Practice on page 124, or choose a topic of your own. The paragraph may be fiction or nonfiction.

Answer the *who, what, when, where, why,* and *how* questions before you begin. Also, before you begin to write, answer the following two questions: *What is the problem of my story? How will that problem be solved?*

Answers will vary. Check students' paragraphs for information that would answer the *who? what? when? where? why?* and *how?* questions.

WRITING WITH STYLE
Writing Directions

Before you write an explanatory paragraph, think through the process you are going to describe. List the necessary steps. Ask yourself, *Could I do this task if I were given only these instructions?* Then, write your paragraph by using your list as a guide.

The writer of Paragraph 1 did not think through the process before writing. Could you follow the instructions?

1. You can turn plain popcorn into a special treat by making caramel corn. You just need to mix some caramel with some popcorn. The caramel is made of butter, brown sugar, corn syrup, and salt. It makes the popcorn taste really good. You put the popcorn and the other ingredients together and cook them. You also need to add baking soda and vanilla. Do not forget to stir it often. It is delicious, but it is a lot more fattening than plain popcorn.

You probably decided that the directions in Paragraph 1 were fairly hard to follow. Now, look at Paragraph 2. These directions are complete, detailed, and presented in chronological order. They provide enough information for the readers to actually make caramel corn. That means the paragraph is a success.

2. You can turn plain popcorn into a special treat by making caramel popcorn. First, pop about 6 quarts of popcorn and keep it in a warm oven. Then, begin the caramel syrup by melting 2 sticks of butter. Next, stir 2 cups of brown sugar, 1/2 cup of corn syrup, and 1 teaspoon of salt into the butter. Bring this mixture to a boil. Then, remove the mixture from the heat and add 1/2 teaspoon of baking soda and 1 teaspoon of vanilla. Pour the caramel syrup slowly over the popped corn. Mix it well with a fork. Bake the popcorn-caramel mixture at 250 degrees for one hour. Take the mixture out of the oven and stir it every 15 minutes. When the caramel corn is done, it will smell sweet and delicious. You will want to snack on it right away, but wait until it cools.

VOCABULARY BUILDER
Using Number Prefixes

Knowing about number prefixes can often help you understand words that you do not know. If you know what the prefix means, you can often figure out what the whole word means. Use the following chart to answer the questions. Write your answers on a separate sheet of paper.

Prefix	Meaning	Prefix	Meaning
mono-, uni-	one	sex-, hexa-	six
bi-	two	sept-	seven
tri-	three	oct-	eight
quad-	four	deca-	ten
quint-, penta-	five		

1. What is a unicycle?

2. How many languages can a bilingual person speak?

3. How many babies are born if a mother has triplets?

4. How many feet does an animal have if it is called a quadruped?

5. How many singers are in a quintet?

6. How many sides are in a hexagon?

7. What do you call an eight-sided figure?

8. How many events are in an athletic contest called a decathlon?

1. A unicycle is a one-wheeled cycle.

2. A person who is bilingual can speak two languages.

3. If a mother has triplets, she has three babies.

4. A quadruped has four feet.

5. There are five singers in a quintet.

6. There are six sides in a hexagon.

7. An eight-sided figure is an octagon.

8. There are ten events in a decathlon.

Summary Have students use the summary to outline the main idea and details of the chapter.

Summary

An explanatory paragraph tells how to do something or how to make something.
In an explanatory paragraph, you write details in chronological order.
To guide the reader and keep time order clear, use transitional words and phrases.
Make sure the subject is narrow enough to explain fully in one paragraph.
An informative paragraph gives details, facts, and figures about a topic.
The topic sentence of an informative paragraph is often like a definition.
A narrative paragraph tells the story of an event or a person.
A narrative paragraph usually presents some type of problem and ends with the solution to the problem.

More Vocabulary Review is provided in the Classroom Resource Binder.

Vocabulary Review

explanatory paragraph
anecdote
nonfiction
informative paragraph
fiction
narrative paragraph

1. nonfiction
2. informative paragraph
3. fiction
4. explanatory paragraph
5. anecdote
6. narrative paragraph

Match each term in the box with its meaning. Write your answers on a separate sheet of paper.

1. writing based on real people and events

2. a paragraph that gives information and shares knowledge

3. something made up or invented by an author

4. a paragraph that explains, clarifies, and gives details

5. a short, interesting story about an event or a person

6. a paragraph that tells about events and experiences

Chapter Quiz

Complete the following items. Write your answers on a separate sheet of paper.

1. What are two topics that you might write about in an explanatory paragraph?

2. Why is chronological order important in an explanatory paragraph?

3. What is one purpose for writing an informative paragraph?

4. What does the topic sentence of an informative paragraph often do?

5. Would "my worst day" ever make a good topic for a narrative paragraph? Why or why not?

6. What do writers often do to make their narratives clear?

Critical Thinking

How do the *wh-* questions help you to create a strong paragraph? Write your answer on a separate sheet of paper.

Critical Thinking Answers will vary. Possible response: The *wh-* questions ask questions about a topic that help address the topic sentence and make a paragraph more complete.

▶ **Test Tip**
Make sure you understand the meaning of any new terms that are part of the directions.

1. Answers will vary. An explanatory paragraph might tell how to make or do something or give directions to go somewhere.

2. When steps are given in chronological order, they are clearer and easier to follow.

3. The usual purpose for writing an informative paragraph is to tell readers about something you know.

4. The topic sentence of an informative paragraph often defines something or someone.

5. Describing your worst day ever would make a good topic for a narrative paragraph because it would be explaining the details of the day.

6. To make their narratives clear, writers often describe a problem and tell how it was solved. They also answer the questions *Who? What? When? Where? Why?* and *How?*

Writing Activity

Choose someone who you think is special. On a separate sheet of paper, make some notes that tell what makes that person special. Then, use your notes to write an informative paragraph about that person.

Writing Activity Answers will vary. Check to make sure that students' paragraphs begin with a topic sentence and contain supporting details and a concluding sentence.

Powerful writing about a good cause can persuade readers to help.

Jane Addams (1860–1935) was a social worker. She worked to improve the lives of women, children, and senior citizens. Her most famous book is Twenty Years at Hull House *about a settlement house she began in Chicago, Illinois. Addams's powerful writing earned her both money and respect. Also, she won the Nobel Peace Prize in 1931.*

To help students tap their prior knowledge of the chapter topic, see the **Chapter Project** in the Classroom Resource Binder.

Learning Objectives

- Write a persuasive paragraph.
- Write specific reasons, facts, and figures.
- Identify facts and opinions.
- Use qualifying words and phrases.

Chapter 10 / Writing to Persuade

Words to Know

opinion	a belief, an attitude, or a viewpoint
persuade	to get someone to do something or believe something; to convince
qualify	to limit or make less strong

10-1 / Stating Your Opinion

An **opinion** is a belief, an attitude, or a viewpoint. Sometimes, you write to give your opinion on a subject. Your goal, then, is to present enough reasons and facts to convince the readers that you are right. For example, you might want to **persuade**, or convince, your readers that teenagers are good drivers. You will aim to persuade your readers to accept your opinion.

The first sentence of a persuasive paragraph should present your opinion. It will serve as a topic sentence for the rest of the paragraph.

Your topic must be a clearly stated opinion, something you care about, and something you know enough about to provide at least three statements of support.

The topic television is not suitable for a persuasive paragraph. It does not state an opinion. However, you could narrow the topic, and say what you think about television.

The Writing Process

How can brainstorming help you choose a topic? (See The Writing Process, page WP5.)

Either of the following two sentences would be a strong topic sentence for a persuasive paragraph.

I think Americans watch too much television.

or

In my opinion, television teaches people about the world.

Practice

On a separate sheet of paper, finish each of the following sentences by stating an opinion. Each opinion could serve as a topic sentence for a persuasive paragraph.

1. I think the food in the school cafeteria _____.

2. I feel this city needs _____.

3. In my opinion, _____ was America's best president.

4. I think that _____ is a waste of time.

5. I believe that people under age 25 are _____ drivers.

6. There are several reasons that people should not buy _____.

Answers will vary. Possible answers:
1. I think the food in the school cafeteria is delicious.
2. I feel this city needs more activities for teens.
3. In my opinion, Abraham Lincoln was America's best president.
4. I think that watching television is a waste of time.
5. I believe that people under age 25 are dangerous drivers.
6. There are several reasons why people should not buy fur coats.

10-2 ▶ Supporting Your Opinion

Once you have written your topic sentence, your job is to convince your readers that your opinion is right. Sometimes, you know enough reasons and facts to be persuasive. Sometimes, you must do some research to come up with enough convincing arguments.

In the body of your persuasive paragraph, give specific reasons that support your opinion. Some topics can be supported using what you already know. Read the following example.

> I believe that I should be hired as a waiter in your restaurant. Because I worked as a waiter last summer in Ann's Diner in Seattle, I have had the necessary experience. In fact, before I left Ann's Diner to return to school, I was chosen "Outstanding Employee of the Month." Both the owner, Jill Johnson, and her customers stated that I was a friendly, speedy worker. I never missed a day of work, and I always arrived on the job early. I enjoy being a waiter and believe that I could do an excellent job in your restaurant.

Certain topics might require a little research to find facts and figures. Read the following example.

> The cost of having technology in schools is very high, and the cost will only increase in the future. Computers help students do their homework. However, they cost the United States a lot of money. Right now, technology in schools costs about $3 billion. This is $70 per student. The government is planning to put $15 billion into the schools, or about $300 for each student. It will cost about $11 billion to give every public school a lab with 25 computers. It will cost $47 billion to supply a computer to every five students. Technology in schools proves to have a very costly future.

Often, the supporting details in a persuasive paragraph are listed in order of importance. The most important persuasive detail is left for last. That way, readers are left with the best evidence in their minds. For example, the paragraph about *technology in schools* used the most convincing fact as the last detail in the paragraph. This detail was: *When a computer is supplied to every five students, it will cost $47 billion.*

When writing a persuasive paragraph, remember to do the following things:

- First, write a topic sentence that clearly states your opinion.

- Then, write at least three sentences of support.

- Use transitional words.

- Save the most important detail for last.

- Write a strong conclusion that restates your opinion.

Practice

On a separate sheet of paper, write a persuasive paragraph using the list of details given below. The paragraph should prove that the neighborhood needs a new park.

1. Children are forced to play ball in the street.

2. There are no parks for ten miles.

3. Studies show that children who have places to play are less likely to get into trouble.

4. Everyone, young and old alike, can enjoy the beauty of trees, flowers, and grass.

5. There are several acres of land available to the city for a reasonable price.

Brush Up on the Basics

Make sure that each sentence in your paragraph is a complete sentence. (See Grammar 1 in the Reference Guide.)

Answers will vary. Check to make sure that students are using persuasive words and details to support their opinions.

Answers will vary. By now, students should feel comfortable writing well-developed paragraphs. Encourage students to write their paragraphs independently.

10-3 ▸ Fact or Opinion

There are two kinds of statements. A statement of fact is not the same as a statement of opinion. A statement of fact is something that can be proven right or wrong.

The statement below is an example of fact. It can be proven true by observing that the building is, indeed, in New York City. Everyone would agree it is true.

The Empire State Building is in New York City.

The statement below is an example of opinion. The writer may think it is true, but certainly not everyone would agree.

It is fun to climb the steps of the Empire State Building.

When you write, it is very important to recognize if you are writing facts or opinions.

- A statement of fact can be proven true or false.

- A statement of opinion cannot be proven true or false.

- Certain words act as signals that a statement is an opinion. Words that show approval or disapproval are words of opinion.

- Some opinion words are *better, best, good, bad, pleasant, unpleasant, poor,* and *great.*

  > Ralph is a *better* dog than Spot.
  > (That is someone's opinion.)

- Statements that say what is desirable are statements of opinion. Words like *should, ought to,* and *must* are opinion words.

  > Linda *should* ask Stan to the dance.
  > (That is someone's opinion.)

- Predictions are another kind of opinion. Words and phrases like *will, shall,* and *is going to* signal a prediction. Any statement that predicts what will happen in the future is an opinion.

  > It *is going to* rain this afternoon.
  > (That is someone's opinion.)

Practice

Decide if each sentence on the next page is a statement of fact or a statement of opinion. On a separate sheet of paper, number from 1 to 9. Write **F** for fact or **O** for opinion by each number.

1. Mark Twain was a writer.

2. Mark Twain was a good writer.

3. Speeding is against the law.

4. Carrots are better than celery.

5. Tomorrow, it is going to snow.

6. Dogs are more fun than cats.

7. There are more girls in this class than boys.

8. The Vikings will win the Little League Bowl.

9. Astronauts have landed on the moon.

1. F
2. O
3. F
4. O
5. O
6. O
7. F
8. O
9. F

10-4 ▸ Using Qualifying Words

When you write statements of fact, you can present them just as they are. However, when you write a statement of opinion, you must make it clear that it is not a fact. You must **qualify** it, or make it less strong.

> Do not say: Mrs. Estevez is a terrible boss.

> Do say: In my opinion, Mrs. Estevez is a terrible boss.

The phrase *In my opinion* qualifies the statement. It lets the readers know that you understand that the statement is your opinion and not a fact.

Sometimes, writers make statements that are too general.

> Do not say: Teenagers are safe drivers.
> (You cannot prove that all teenagers are safe drivers.)

> Do say: *Many* teenagers are safe drivers.
> (You could prove that this statement is true.)

Many is a qualifying word.

Think About It

Why is it important to use a qualifying word when you write an opinion?

The following chart lists unqualified and qualified statements.

Unqualified statements	Qualified statements
It will rain tomorrow.	It will probably rain tomorrow.
Dogs bark at cars.	Many dogs bark at cars.
Teachers give too much homework.	Some teachers give too much homework.

The following chart lists some qualifying words.

Qualifying Words		
some	apparently	seems to
several	probably	in my opinion
many	almost	I think
most	usually	often
may	sometimes	it seems
might	supposedly	

Practice

1. a, c, d, f, g, i, j

1. On a separate sheet of paper, write the letters of the statements you think need to be qualified.

   a. Police officers do not smile.

   b. The car is in the garage.

   c. You will need to replace that car in five years.

   d. People who have had hard lives write the best stories.

   e. Portland is the largest city in Oregon.

   f. Women love to dance.

   g. She will make a good lawyer someday.

h. Cruncho Crispos is a cereal.

i. Everyone loves Cruncho Crispos.

j. Dogs chase mail carriers.

2. Rewrite the seven statements that you selected to make qualified statements.

The Great Persuaders

Advertisers are some of the greatest masters of persuasion. Ads make us want things we never knew we wanted before. That is because we are persuaded that a product will somehow improve our lives.

Sometimes, the advertiser will not come out and say, "Buy this. It will make life better." Instead, the ad will suggest that idea. For example, an advertisement might picture a pair of sneakers with wings on them. Such an ad might suggest that a certain kind of sneaker will make a person run very fast.

Another ad could picture a man with three children smiling at him as he cooks with a certain brand of barbecue sauce. This ad would suggest that a father who uses that sauce will have a happy family.

Portfolio Project

Cut three ads out of a newspaper or magazine. Write down some of the reasons given for buying each product. Remember that the reasons might be stated in the ad or suggested by the picture.

2. Answers will vary. Possible answers:

a. Many police officers seem never to smile.

c. You may need to replace that car in about five years.

d. It seems that most people who have had hard lives write the best stories.

f. Many women love to dance.

g. She will most likely make a good lawyer someday.

i. Almost everyone loves Cruncho Crispos.

j. Many dogs hate mail carriers.

WRITING WITH STYLE
Persuading Readers

If you really want your writing to persuade readers, you must sound reasonable. Calm, detailed information is generally more persuasive than heated, emotional opinions. Which paragraph would be more likely to convince a state legislature to pass a seat belt law?

1. I think that this state should require automobile drivers and passengers to wear seat belts. It is so dangerous to drive without belts. People can be killed! People just do not realize how silly it is to ride in a car without a seat belt. There is absolutely no reason to travel in an automobile without a seat belt. Some people say it wrinkles their clothes, but that is crazy. It all comes down to one thing: Seat belts save lives!

2. I think this state should require automobile drivers and passengers to wear seat belts. Safety tests prove that people are less likely to be hurt badly in an automobile accident if they are wearing seat belts. Thirty-two states have already passed laws requiring people to wear seat belts. Those seat belt laws have reduced traffic-related deaths. Some people may say that seat belts are uncomfortable or a bother. I think that is a small price to pay for added safety. It all comes down to one thing: Seat belts save lives!

Notice how Paragraph 1 insults the readers by using words such as *silly* and *crazy*. Paragraph 2 avoids name-calling and provides some facts and figures.

VOCABULARY BUILDER
Using Euphemisms

Euphemisms are words or phrases that make unpleasant things seem better. Euphemisms are often used to persuade people that things are not really so bad. Sometimes people feel they are being polite when they use a euphemism. For example, instead of saying that somebody *did not like something* they might say that something is *okay*. That term sounds less harsh. A company might say that *it let some people go* instead of saying that *it fired some people*.

What do the following euphemisms *really* mean? Write your answers on a separate sheet of paper.

1. stretching the truth

2. news delivery agent

3. passed away

4. restroom

5. house of correction

6. sanitation engineer

7. between assignments

8. otherwise engaged

9. preowned vehicle

10. misguided youth

Answers may vary a bit but should be similar to the following.
1. lying
2. paper delivery person
3. died
4. bathroom or toilet
5. prison or jail
6. janitor or custodian
7. unemployed
8. busy or does not want to see you
9. used car
10. juvenile delinquent

Summary Have students use the summary to outline the main idea and details of the chapter.

Summary

Your goal in a persuasive paragraph is to convince your reader that your opinion is the right one.
The topic sentence of a persuasive paragraph usually states your opinion.
In a persuasive paragraph, you need to provide at least three strong details to support your opinion. Save the most important detail for the last supporting sentence you write.
Write a concluding sentence that restates your opinion in different words.
Be sure the statements that you present as facts are accurate.
Qualify broad statements with such words as *some, might,* and *probably.*

qualify

opinion

persuade

1. opinion

2. persuade

3. qualify

More Vocabulary Review is provided in the Classroom Resource Binder.

Vocabulary Review

Complete each sentence with a term from the box. Write your answers on a separate sheet of paper.

1. A belief that you have about something is your _____.

2. Some writing is used to _____ others to believe or do something.

3. If a statement is too general, a writer might _____ it.

Chapter Quiz

1. A fact is something that is true. An opinion is a belief.

2. A writer should state an opinion in the topic sentence of a persuasive paragraph so that the reader knows the writer's opinion.

3. Supporting details help to support the writer's opinion.

Chapter Quiz

Complete the following items. Write your answers on a separate sheet of paper.

1. What is the difference between a fact and an opinion?

2. Why should a writer state an opinion in the topic sentence of a persuasive paragraph?

3. Why must the body of a persuasive paragraph contain supporting details?

4. What are two sources you can use to find supporting details for a persuasive paragraph?

5. Is the following statement an opinion or a fact? How do you know? *Dan should go to college.*

▶ **Test Tip**
When you are asked to give your opinion, make sure to support it with facts.

4. A writer could research books or the Internet for more details to support the paragraph.

5. The statement is an opinion. Sentences with words like *should* state an opinion or a wish.

Critical Thinking

What is a strong way to end your paragraph?
Write your answer on a separate sheet of paper.

Critical Thinking Answers will vary. Possible answer: The strongest way to end a paragraph is to restate the topic sentence as the concluding sentence.

Writing Activity

The following opinions show two sides of one issue.

- Too much TV confuses people about what is real and what is not real.

- Television has made Americans smarter and more aware of current issues.

Choose one opinion. On a separate sheet of paper, make a list of details that support your side. Then, write a persuasive paragraph. Include a topic sentence, at least three sentences of support, and a concluding sentence.

Writing Activity Answers will vary. Check students' work for inclusion of the techniques learned in this chapter.

Good descriptions are based on observing details.

John Steinbeck
(1902–1968) wrote about life during the Great Depression in the United States. His descriptions of people and places are based on careful observations. Steinbeck's best-known books are The Grapes of Wrath *and* Of Mice and Men. *Both novels show people struggling to survive in hard times. John Steinbeck won the 1962 Nobel Prize for Literature.*

Extra Reading See the Pacemaker® Classics series for John Steinbeck's *The Grapes of Wrath.*

To help students tap their prior knowledge of the chapter topic, see the **Chapter Project** in the Classroom Resource Binder.

Learning Objectives

- Write a descriptive paragraph with specific details to create a picture for the reader.
- Write descriptions that appeal to all the senses.
- Write character descriptions that include physical appearance and personality.
- Identify and write similes and metaphors.

Chapter **11** Writing to Describe

Words to Know

descriptive	giving a picture in words; telling about something in great detail
senses	sight, hearing, smell, taste, and touch
figure of speech	an expression in which words suggest an image that is different from the literal meaning of words
literally	actually, really, exactly as things are
exaggeration	something stretched beyond the truth; something made larger or greater than it really is
simile	a figure of speech in which two things are compared by using the word *like* or *as*
metaphor	a figure of speech in which one thing is compared with another by suggesting a likeness between the two
implies	suggests in an indirect way

11-1 ▸ Organizing a Descriptive Paragraph

In Chapter 4 you read about one of a writer's primary goals. That goal was to take images and ideas from the writer's own head and put them, as exactly as possible, into the reader's head. When you write a **descriptive** paragraph, you will be trying to describe something to a reader as clearly as possible.

A descriptive paragraph is organized just like the other types of paragraphs described in this book.

1   topic sentence

2   (a) sentence of support ⎤
    (b) sentence of support ⎬ body
    (c) sentence of support ⎦

3   concluding sentence

1. The topic sentence tells the reader what you are describing. Read this example.

    The grandfather clock was very old and very valuable, but, best of all, it recalled memories of my grandparents' house.

2. The body of the descriptive paragraph provides details for your reader. It gives enough details for the reader to picture and experience what you are describing. Read this example.

    The clock was much taller than I was as a ten-year-old boy. It was made of fine, smooth, dark brown wood. The wood was perfect except for two scratches. Those two long, light-colored scratches ran down the left side of the clock. They showed where the cat had tried to climb up the side. The clock had a bright, white face painted with gold numbers. I always called them "fancy numbers" because of their curly ends. Two heavy brass balls hung on chains down the front of the clock. I would stare at the balls through the clock's glass door. They were, I decided, just about the size of grapefruits. My favorite part of the magnificent clock was its sound. The clock had loud, strong, even ticks that echoed through the room. Then, each hour, came the long, mellow tones of the striking chimes.

3. The concluding sentence summarizes the topic and may express your feelings about it. Read this example.

    I loved that old clock because it was a part of my childhood.

When writing a descriptive paragraph, remember your purpose. Your purpose now is to give your reader an image that is as exact as possible. You want to describe something as it really appeared to you.

Be sure to limit your topic. You cannot write a complete description if your topic is too broad. For example, it would be hard to fully describe your town in one paragraph. However, you could describe one street corner or one bus stop or one house.

The Writing Process

Why is it important to know your purpose for writing? (See The Writing Process, WP14.)

Using All Your Senses

When you experience things, you do not only see them. Other senses are involved, too. **Senses** are sight, hearing, smell, taste, and touch. What other sense does the writer of the clock paragraph use in the description?

> Answer: The sense of hearing is used when the writer describes the sounds the clock makes.

Of course, not every experience involves all the senses. The writer would not be likely to describe how the clock tasted or smelled. However, when you write to describe, you should use as many of your senses as you can.

The Senses		
seeing	tasting	hearing
touching	smelling	

Practice A

Answers will vary. Accept all reasonable answers for how each item might be described under each sense. Following is a possible answer for pizza.

Sight: colorful

Sound: crunchy

Smell: cheesy

Taste: salty

Touch: chewy

Choose an item from the list below. Write *sight*, *sound*, *smell*, *taste*, and *touch* on your paper. Under each sense, list as many details as possible to describe the object you chose.

a pizza	a gym locker
the ocean	a wet dog
a rose	a baby

Practice B

Suppose you had lost your sense of sight for a short time. Write a paragraph describing something by using only your four other senses. Here are some suggestions, but you may write about any other topic that interests you.

a summer day   a busy street corner

a trip to a movie   a park

a library   a date

Portfolio Project

Close your eyes. Listen for a while, and then list the sounds you hear. Now write a paragraph describing those sounds and how they make you feel.

Answers will vary. Accept all reasonable answers for how each item might be described under all the senses except sight. Following is a possible answer for a summer day.

Sound: chirping birds, rustling leaves

Smell: clean and fresh

Taste: sweet

Touch: warmth from the sun

Answers will vary.

11-3 ▸ It Takes More Than Adjectives

When people think about describing something, they often think first of using adjectives. For example, if someone were describing a dog, that person might write, "It was a *big*, *brown*, *shaggy* dog with *ugly*, *long*, *sharp*, *white* teeth." All the words in italics are adjectives, or words that describe nouns. However, long lists of adjectives can bore your reader. Try it for yourself. Read the sample sentence above aloud. How does it sound to you? Adjectives are useful in a description, but it is not a good idea to use too many.

There are other ways you can describe your subject. For example, verbs can also be descriptive. Let the verbs you use paint a picture for your reader. For example, a dog that *howls* is different from a dog that *whines*. A dog that *growls* is different from a dog that *yaps*.

The nouns you use can also be descriptive. If you call a dog a *hound*, it changes the image. If you call the dog a *beast*, the reader will get a much different picture than if you call it a *pup*. What other nouns can you think of to use in place of dog?

Practice

For each of the following three boldfaced words, list at least three other words that present a clearer picture and have a more specific meaning. Write your answers on a separate sheet of paper.

Answers will vary.
Possible answers:
1. shout, whisper, yell
2. ship, row boat, yacht or cruise ship
3. trek or expedition, vacation, voyage or cruise

1. talk

> talk loudly
>
> talk quietly
>
> talk angrily

2. boat

> big, ocean-going boat
>
> little boat with oars
>
> luxury boat

3. trip

> long, hard trip
>
> short, holiday trip
>
> trip on the ocean

Understanding Connotation

Connotation refers to the feelings and ideas words stir up in us. For instance, the words, *parakeet* and *canary* suggest pets. These words have positive connotations. On the other hand, the term *caged bird* suggests, or connotes, a sad, trapped creature. Although all of these words describe birds, their connotations are very different. Remember to consider the connotations of the words you choose in your descriptive writing.

Portfolio Project

What feelings and ideas do you associate with each word listed below? Write a one-sentence description of each word. Compare your descriptions with those of others in your class. Are any of your descriptions similar?

poodle	German shepherd
rain	thunderstorm
cottage	mansion
avenue	road

What Is in a Name?

Names have different connotations, as well. Why might a person called Bobby as a child decide to go by the name Robert as an adult? If you are describing a fictional character, you can create a picture in your reader's mind just by choosing a certain name.

11-4 Describing Characters

Sometimes, you may write a description of a person. You may be asked to describe a character from a book, or you may be describing a real person you know. When describing a character, you need to think about more than just what that character looks like. You also must think about the character's personality.

Practice

Answers will vary. Check to make sure that students have used precise language and words that connote the feelings they want.

1. Think of a person about whom you feel strongly. The person can be real or fictional. Then use the categories listed below to work up a characterization of that person. On a separate sheet of paper, write as many descriptive words as you can for each item.

    Hair

    Eyes

    Nose

    Ears

    Mouth

    Skin

    Height, weight, and shape

    Usual clothing

    What he or she likes to do

    What he or she does not like to do

    How he or she acts around other people

    What kind of mood he or she is usually in

    Any unusual characteristics he or she has

    Something he or she might say

2. Use the notes you made in Part 1 to write two descriptive paragraphs. In the first paragraph, describe the person's physical appearance. In the second paragraph, describe what the person is like.

11-5 Figures of Speech: Using Similes and Metaphors

A **figure of speech** is an expression that is not meant **literally**, or exactly as things are. The expression, *The package is as light as a feather*, does not mean that the package really weighs as much as a feather. The expression is a figure of speech. There are different kinds of figures of speech. One kind is **exaggeration**. An exaggeration is something that is made larger or greater than it really is. The sentence *I am so hungry I could eat a horse* is an example of an exaggeration.

Another kind of figure of speech is the **simile**. A simile is a comparison between two different things, saying one is like the other. A simile must use the word *like* or *as* to make the comparison. *She is as sweet as pie* is a simile.

Sometimes, writers use similes when they are describing something. A carefully thought out simile can help the reader get a much clearer picture. The reader can imagine exactly how something looks, tastes, or feels.

Here are a few more similes.

His shirt was as white as snow.

He came into the classroom like a tornado.

He acted as playful as a kitten with a ball of string.

Practice A

1. Copy these sentences on your paper. Underline the two items being compared in each simile.

   a. The snowflakes were like cotton balls.

   b. His tears fell as heavily as rain.

   c. The material is as smooth as silk.

   d. My friend has a neck like a giraffe's.

   e. The house was as silent as a graveyard.

2. Now write some similes of your own by completing the following sentences on a separate sheet of paper.

   a. The rain on the roof sounded like _____.

   b. The sun sparkled on the water like _____.

   c. Maria is as tall as _____.

   d. Larry chatters like _____.

   e. Donna is as thin as _____.

   f. The baby's skin was as soft as _____.

Margin answers:

1. a. The <u>snowflakes</u> were like <u>cotton balls</u>.
   b. His <u>tears</u> fell as heavily as <u>rain</u>.
   c. The <u>material</u> is as smooth as <u>silk</u>.
   d. My friend has a <u>neck</u> like a <u>giraffe's</u>.
   e. The <u>house</u> was as silent as a <u>graveyard</u>.

2. Answers will vary. Possible answers:
   a. The rain on the roof sounded like pebbles.
   b. The sun sparkled on the water like diamonds.
   c. Maria is as tall as a tree.
   d. Larry chatters like a bird.
   e. Donna is as thin as a pencil.
   f. The baby's skin was as soft as cotton.

A **metaphor** is another figure of speech. It **implies**, or suggests, a comparison of unlike things without using the word *like* or *as*. A metaphor simply calls one thing another or gives one thing the characteristics of another thing.

> Example: My father is a bear when he wakes up in the morning.

That metaphor calls the father a bear. It does not use the word *like* or *as*.

Practice B

1. Copy the following sentences on your paper. Underline the two items being compared in each metaphor.

   a. The sun was a golden giant.

   b. Happiness is a chocolate ice cream cone.

   c. Joy is the morning of the first snowfall.

   d. The wind was a howling animal.

   e. The ice turned the tree branches into bent fingers.

2. Look at the metaphor in **b** of Practice B above. Write your own "Happiness is …" metaphor.

> **English and Technology**
> You can set your word processor to correct common errors as you type.

1. **a.** The <u>sun</u> was a <u>golden giant</u>.
   b. <u>Happiness</u> is a <u>chocolate ice cream cone</u>.
   c. <u>Joy</u> is the <u>morning of a first snowfall</u>.
   d. The <u>wind</u> was a <u>howling animal</u>.
   e. The ice turned the <u>tree branches</u> into <u>bent fingers</u>.
2. Answers will vary. Check to make sure that students have written a metaphor and not just a statement about happiness.

WRITING WITH STYLE
Using Figures of Speech

Figures of speech can give style to your writing. They help the reader see what you are seeing and understand exactly what you mean. Which of the sentences in each pair below creates a clearer picture? Write the correct letter on a separate sheet of paper.

1. a. Her hat had lots of colorful feathers and was very fancy.

    b. Her hat was as brilliant as a peacock's tail.

2. a. The night was as dark as the inside of a deep cave.

    b. The night was very dark.

3. a. The boy was very shy.

    b. The boy was a shy little rabbit hiding in the corner.

4. a. The wind howled like a mournful ghost searching for a place to rest.

    b. The wind howled.

5. a. Their new quarterback is built like a brick shed.

    b. Their new quarterback is very, very big.

1. b
2. a
3. b
4. a
5. a

Of course, you do not want to use figures of speech in every sentence you write. You do not even want to use them in every paragraph. Once in a while, they can really help you create a more vivid, precise picture for your reader. You probably figured out by now that the key to descriptive writing is precision, or saying exactly what a thing is.

VOCABULARY BUILDER
Using Suffixes

A suffix is a group of letters added at the end of a word. A suffix changes the meaning of a word. Often, it also changes the word's part of speech. When *-ly* is added to the end of an adjective, it makes the adjective an adverb. For example, when *-ly* is added to the adjective *weird*, it becomes the adverb *weirdly*.

1. On your own paper, use the suffix *-ly* to make the word in parentheses into the adverb that would fit into the sentence. The first one has been done as an example.

   a. The ball hit him (sudden) from behind. _suddenly_

   b. She (quick) hid the money in her purse. quickly

   c. She laughed (wicked) after she played the trick on him. wickedly

   d. There was (most) junk at the garage sale. mostly

   e. He shook his head (sad) and left the room. sadly

2. Add the suffix *-ly* to each of the following adjectives. Then, use each adverb in a sentence. Answers will vary for the sentences.

   a. swift swiftly

   b. loud loudly

   c. clear clearly

   d. strange strangely

   e. tight tightly

Summary Have students use the summary to outline the main idea and details of the chapter.

Summary

Your purpose for writing a descriptive paragraph is to give your reader exact images and ideas.

A descriptive paragraph is organized like other paragraphs. It has a topic sentence, a body of supporting sentences, and a concluding sentence.

When describing something, use sentences that appeal to sight, sound, smell, taste, and touch.

Use colorful and specific nouns, verbs, and adjectives.

Use figures of speech for clearer images. A simile is a figure of speech that compares two things by using the word *like* or *as*. A metaphor is a figure of speech that suggests one thing is another.

simile
descriptive
implies
metaphor
senses
exaggeration
figure of speech
literal

1. implies
2. senses
3. descriptive
4. literal
5. simile
6. figure of speech
7. exaggeration
8. metaphor

More Vocabulary Review is provided in the Classroom Resource Binder.

Vocabulary Review

Match each term in the box with its meaning.

1. suggests in an indirect way
2. sight, hearing, smell, taste, and touch
3. giving a picture in words
4. actual or real
5. a comparison that uses *like* or *as*
6. an expression in which the literal meaning is different from the actual meaning
7. something stretched beyond the truth
8. a figure of speech that suggests a likeness between two things

Chapter Quiz

Complete the items below on a separate sheet of paper.

1. What is the goal of writing a descriptive paragraph?

2. How does a simile help describe something?

3. Write the word in each pair below that presents the clearer picture.

   a. talk; chatter

   b. horse; stallion

   c. shattered; broken

4. Decide if each of the following sentences is a simile, a metaphor, or neither one. Write **S** if it is a simile, **M** if it is a metaphor, or **NO** if it not a figure of speech.

   a. The cat was as fat as a marshmallow.

   b. The railroad tracks were silver threads sewn into the landscape.

   c. The dark sky looked mysterious.

   d. The panther was as black as the night.

▶ **Test Tip**
Make sure you understand the directions before you begin working.

Chapter Quiz

1. The goal of a descriptive paragraph is to describe something as clearly as possible.

2. A simile helps a reader understand something unknown by saying it is like something known. It helps the reader better understand what is being described or to see something in a new way.

3. **a.** chatter

   b. stallion

   c. shattered

4. **a.** S

   b. M

   c. NO

   d. S

Critical Thinking

Why is it important to use the senses to describe things?

Critical Thinking Answers will vary. Possible answer: Senses help a reader understand what is being described. The reader can see, feel, hear, taste, or smell what the writer is describing.

Writing Activity

Write a descriptive paragraph about your school cafeteria. Write details about the things you see, hear, touch, smell, and taste there. Use colorful words and figures of speech.

Writing Activity Answers may vary. Check to make sure that students use colorful words and figures of speech.

*Comparisons can
make writing clear
and effective.*

*Amy Tan (born 1952) is
from California. Tan's first
novel,* The Joy Luck Club,
*was a best seller. It
compares the lives of four
Chinese women with the
lives of their American-born
daughters. It tells how a
young woman learns to
appreciate her Chinese
heritage. Tan also wrote*
The Kitchen God's Wife,
The Hundred Secret
Senses, *and* The
Bonesetter's Daughter.

Reading Challenge See
*Tapestry: A Multicultural
Anthology* for an excerpt from
Amy Tan's *The Joy Luck Club.*

To help students tap their prior
knowledge of the chapter topic,
see the **Chapter Project** in the
Classroom Resource Binder.

Learning Objectives

- Write a paragraph of comparison.
- Use transitional words within that paragraph.
- Identify similarities and differences in a paragraph of comparison.

Chapter 12 Writing to Compare

Words to Know

comparison	the act of noting the likenesses and differences of things
similarities	points of likeness; ways that things are alike
differences	points that are not alike; ways that things are different
characteristics	features that make something or someone special and individual

12-1 What Is a Paragraph of Comparison?

Making a **comparison** is often a good way to develop a topic. A comparison is the act of noting the likenesses and differences of things. When you have two things that are definite, you can write a paragraph of comparison. You can compare books, people, places, and animals.

The following are examples of comparisons. To *compare* means to point out how two things are alike or how they are different.

black–white

tall–short

happy–sad

fast–slow

friendly–unfriendly

A paragraph of comparison takes two subjects and points out how they are alike and how they are different.

Brush Up on the Basics

A subject names what the sentence is about. (See Grammar 3 in the Reference Guide.)

The chart below shows two subjects that can be compared. There are enough differences to make a well-developed paragraph.

Modern Automobiles	Early Automobiles
start quickly with key	crank to start
fast—up to 100 mph	slow—30 mph
reliable	broke down often
comfortable	cold, wet
purpose: transportation	purpose: transportation

A paragraph of comparison is developed the same way as any other paragraph. It has the same three main parts.

1 topic sentence

2 (a) supporting detail

(b) supporting detail ⎫ body

(c) supporting detail ⎭

3 concluding sentence

1. A topic sentence presents the subjects and sets up the comparison.

   Modern automobiles are surely an improvement over the earliest models.

2. The body of the paragraph presents details that support the topic sentence. The details prove the topic sentence is true.

   In the early days of the automobile, drivers had to spend time and energy cranking up a car just to get it going. Today, a turn of the key makes an engine roar. It certainly took longer for motorists long ago to get somewhere. Although many modern autos can

The Writing Process

How can brainstorming a list of comparisons help you write a topic sentence? (See The Writing Process, page WP5.)

easily go 100 miles per hour, the early cars were racing at 30! When today's drivers start a trip, they expect to get where they are going. However, the pioneers of motoring never knew for sure if their new invention would make it all the way. Another important feature of today's cars is comfort. Modern drivers expect heaters and air conditioners. In contrast, drivers long ago had to carry heavy blankets to keep warm. Because the cars were open to the weather, people got wet when it rained.

3. The concluding sentence restates the subjects of the comparison.

Despite the differences, both today's cars and automobiles from long ago took people where they wanted to go.

When would you write a paragraph of comparison? You will find many times when you need to write a paragraph of comparison.

You might want to compare two characters in a book.

You might want to compare two books written by the same author.

You might want to compare two friends, two cities, or two teachers.

Comparison is a good way to develop a paragraph.

Practice A

On a separate sheet of paper, write some sentences that compare. Use the topics suggested on page 166 to get you going.

(Practice A continues on next page.) ⟹

(Practice A continued.)

Do not just say one is better or worse than the other. Mention some qualities of the subjects being compared in your sentence.

Example: Compare two sports.

Basketball provides more physical exercise than golf.

Answers will vary. Check to make sure that students are comparing qualities of the subjects in their sentences.

1. Compare two animals.

2. Compare two movies.

3. Compare summer and winter.

4. Compare roller skates and ice skates.

5. Compare two brands of athletic shoes.

Sometimes in a comparison, you will want to prove that one thing is *better* than another. At other times, you will just want to show that they are different or that they are alike. You will write about their **similarities**, or likenesses, and their **differences**, or the things that are not alike.

Practice B

Which of the following topic sentences suggest that the writer is going to use comparison to develop the paragraph? On a separate sheet of paper, write the numbers of the sentences that suggest comparisons.

1, 2, 5, 6, 7, 9

1. The Greeks and the Romans had many things in common.

2. I like Saturdays better than Sundays.

3. Last summer, I saw my favorite singer in concert.

4. My favorite book is *The Twenty-One Balloons*.

5. *Call of the Wild* and *White Fang* are books about dogs in the frozen North.

6. I think that today's teenagers have to make more decisions than teenagers of the last generation.

7. A new city park is more important than a new baseball stadium.

8. Students at Westside Middle School work very hard.

9. I like apples better than pears.

10. Thousands of people are homeless.

12-2 Using Transitional Words in Comparisons

Do you remember learning about transitional words and phrases in Chapter 8? Transitional words show the connection between one sentence and another. They guide readers through a paragraph.

The following transitional words and phrases are especially useful in a paragraph of comparison.

Transitional Words and Phrases	
however	unlike
on the other hand	but
in comparison	then
although	now
on the contrary	similarly
in like manner	in the same way

Think About It

Which of these transitional words would introduce similarities? Which would introduce differences?

Read the following sentences to see how some of the transitional words and phrases from the box on page 167 can be used.

Patrick is kind. *However,* his brother can be quite mean.

Last spring was warm and dry. *In comparison,* this spring was rainy and cool.

Unlike Cecil, Mike is very friendly.

Although my dog is fun, my cat keeps me from feeling lonely.

Centerville is a crowded, noisy city, *but* Springfield is still a peaceful, sleepy town.

Practice A

1. Two amusements parks—Wonder World and The Great Getaway—are being compared.

2. but, on the other hand, but, in comparison

Read the following paragraph of comparisons.

> Wonder World and The Great Getaway are both big amusement parks, but each draws a very different crowd. Wonder World is a park built for those who love to dream and to imagine. Walking into Wonder World is like walking into another universe. It is a land full of elves and princesses and storybook characters. On the other hand, The Great Getaway is a place for the daring. Wonder World offers a boat trip through a fantasy land, but The Great Getaway offers a hair-raising trip on the world's largest roller coaster. Visitors to Wonder World come away saying, "Wasn't that cute?" In comparison, when visitors to The Great Getaway leave, they are barely able to speak at all.

On a separate sheet of paper, answer the following items.

1. Tell which two things are being compared.

2. List the transitional words and phrases used in the paragraph. You should find four of them.

Practice B

To do this Practice, first think of two people whom you know. They might be two friends, two teachers, two relatives, or two writers.

Answers will vary. Check to make sure that students have included in their lists both similarities and differences before they begin writing their paragraphs of comparison.

1. On a separate sheet of paper, make two columns. Begin each column with the name of one of the people. Under each name, list the **characteristics,** or distinguishing features, of that person. Include at least five characteristics for each person.

   Example:

My friend, Ronda Jones	My friend, Estella Perez
tall	short
smart	also smart
likes reading, music, tennis, and movies	likes the outdoors, camping, hiking, and football
is an excellent student	is a good athlete
is always cheerful	is rather moody

2. Use the information from your lists to write a paragraph of comparison. Remember that the topic sentence will introduce the comparison. You might want to reread the sample paragraph about automobiles on pages 164–165 as a model paragraph.

3. When you finish your paragraph of comparison, copy this checklist onto a separate sheet of paper. Then, put a check mark by each item you find in your paragraph.

   ❏ a topic sentence that states the subjects compared

   ❏ at least three sentences of supporting details

   ❏ some transitional words and phrases

   ❏ a concluding sentence

WRITING WITH STYLE
Making a Paragraph Stronger

The following two paragraphs were written on the same topic:
The safety of a new car called the Superbo 6000. Each paragraph
was developed in a different way.

1. Paragraph of description

The Superbo 6000 has brought great improvements to the
area of auto safety. A new, secret body material has made the
car almost crash proof. When it first came out, the Superbo
was put through some pretty amazing tests. It was crashed
head-on into a solid brick wall, and, in another test, the
Superbo was rolled over and over. In every test, both the
robot driver and the car came through without serious harm.
However, the most impressive example of the Superbo's
safety came on the open road. In a real highway accident,
a family of five riding in a Superbo was hit by a large pickup
truck. The truck was traveling at 50 miles per hour! The
Superbo 6000 had some minor damage, but the people were
unharmed. Indeed, the Superbo 6000 begins a new era
in auto safety.

2. Paragraph of comparison

The Superbo 6000 is safer than other cars on the market
today. Most cars still have steel or fiberglass bodies, but the
Superbo is built from a new, secret material. Harder than
steel and almost impossible to dent, the material absorbs
shocks. The Superbo 6000 is also equipped with wider tires
than those on most other automobiles. These wider tires
give the car a more stable ride on slick roads. Although the
Superbo 6000 costs a bit more than many other cars, its
safety record makes it today's best automobile.

Both methods (description and comparison) developed strong
paragraphs. Which method of development do you think
worked best for this topic? Why?

VOCABULARY BUILDER
Using Suffixes That Make Nouns

Adding a suffix, or word ending, to a base word can change the part of speech. The suffix *-ness* can change an adjective into a noun. When *-ness* is added, the adjective *weird* becomes the noun *weirdness*.

1. Add *-ness* to each of the following words in parentheses to change them into nouns. Rewrite the sentences on a separate sheet of paper.

a. Her (quick) saved him from drowning.
Her quickness saved him from drowning.

b. The (sudden) of the rainstorm surprised everyone.
The suddenness of the rainstorm surprised everyone.

c. He giggled and stuttered, showing his (nervous).
He giggled and stuttered, showing his nervousness.

d. A terrible (sore) spread through her muscles after the game.
A terrible soreness spread through her muscles after the game.

e. After his best friend moved away, he was left with a feeling of (sad).
After his best friend moved away, he was left with a feeling of sadness.

You can also use suffixes to make verbs into nouns. For example, if you add the suffix *-ion,* the verb *act* would become the noun *action.* If you add the suffix *-er,* the verb *write* can become the noun *writer.* Here are some of the common noun suffixes: *-ion, -ist, -or, -er, -al,* and *-ant.*

2. The following words in parentheses are missing suffixes. Decide which of the suffixes listed above to add to the words. Write the word with its proper suffix on a separate sheet of paper.

a. The doctor told her that she needed an (operate).   operation

b. The boss said that they must hire another (work).   worker

c. The traffic officer kept the cars moving in the right (direct).   direction

d. She needed help on the project, so she hired an (assist).   assistant

e. The (act) came on stage and read his part.   actor

Chapter

12 Review

Summary Have students use the summary to outline the main idea and details of the chapter.

Summary

A paragraph of comparison tells how two subjects are alike and how they are different.
A paragraph of comparison has the three basic parts: a topic sentence, a body, and a conclusion.
The topic sentence names the subjects and sets up the comparison.
The body presents details to support the topic sentence.
The concluding sentence restates the subjects of the comparison.
Transitional words and phrases help the readers understand a paragraph of comparison.

More Vocabulary Review is provided in the Classroom Resource Binder.

Vocabulary Review

characteristics

differences

comparison

similarities

1. comparison
2. similarities
3. differences
4. characteristics

Complete each sentence with a term from the box. Write your answers on a separate sheet of paper.

1. A paragraph of _____ shows how two things are the same or different.

2. When two things are alike, they have _____.

3. When things are not alike, they have _____.

4. Features that make someone or something special are _____.

Chapter Quiz

1. A paragraph of comparison tells how two subjects are alike and how they are different.

2. Answers will vary. Possible answer: Some pairs of subjects to compare in a paragraph of comparison include softball and baseball, Spanish and English, and electric guitars and acoustic guitars.

Chapter Quiz

Complete the following items. Write your answers on a separate sheet of paper.

1. What does a paragraph of comparison do?

2. List three pairs of subjects you might compare.

3. What does the topic sentence do in a paragraph?

4. What does the body of a paragraph do in a paragraph of comparison?

5. What does the concluding sentence of a paragraph do in a paragraph of comparison?

6. List three transitional words that help show similarities.

7. List three transitional words that show differences.

Critical Thinking

Suppose you had to compare two sandwiches or two games. What characteristics might you compare? Write your answer on a separate sheet of paper.

Critical Thinking Answers will vary. Check to make sure that students use transitional words when making comparisons.

▶ **Test Tip**
Make sure that your test response answers only what the question is asking.

3. The topic sentence of a paragraph of comparison states the subject and sets up the comparison.

4. The body of a paragraph of comparison presents supporting details to prove that the topic sentence is true.

5. The concluding sentence in a paragraph of comparison restates the subjects of the comparison and makes a final point of comparison.

6. Answers will vary. Possible answer: Some transitional words that show similarities are *similarly, in like manner,* and *in the same way.*

7. Answers will vary. Possible answer: Some transitional words that show differences are *but, however,* and *on the other hand.*

Writing Activity

On a separate sheet of paper, write a paragraph about yourself to practice making comparisons. Be sure to use transitional words and phrases to show similarities and differences. Use one of the topic sentences below, or create your own.

I would rather be a student than a teacher.

I would rather play football than soccer.

I would rather play the violin than the drums.

Writing Activity Answers will vary. Possible answer: Check to make sure that students have implemented the comparison techniques learned in this chapter.

Unit 3 **Review**

Read each of the following items. On a separate sheet of paper, write the letter that best answers each one.

1. A piece of writing that tells how to do or make something is called
   A. an explanatory paragraph.
   B. a narrative paragraph.
   C. an informative paragraph.
   D. an anecdote.

2. A paragraph that begins with a topic sentence that tells about something or someone is usually
   A. an explanatory paragraph.
   B. a narrative paragraph.
   C. an informative paragraph.
   D. an anecdote.

3. The topic sentence of a persuasive paragraph usually
   A. answers the *who, what, where, why,* and *when* questions.
   B. sets up a comparison between two things.
   C. states an opinion on a subject.
   D. contains a figure of speech, such as exaggeration.

4. The body of a descriptive paragraph mainly includes
   A. facts and figures.
   B. opinions about the main topic.
   C. examples from everyday life.
   D. details that involve the five senses.

5. What figure of speech is used in the following sentence? *The cloud was a soccer ball kicked by the wind.*
   A. simile
   B. metaphor
   C. exaggeration
   D. connotation

6. Which transition words would be most useful in a paragraph of comparison?
   A. *unlike* and *similarly*
   B. *first* and *later*
   C. *as a result* and *because*
   D. *before long* and *furthermore*

Critical Thinking Answers will vary. Possible answer: Knowing the purpose of what you are writing is important because it will tell you what type of paragraph to write.

Writing Activity For this activity, students are writing a paragraph that compares descriptive writing and comparison writing. Check to make sure that students' ideas are presented clearly and that they have written a well-developed paragraph.

Critical Thinking
Why is it important to know the purpose of what you are writing? Write your answer on a separate sheet of paper.
WRITING ACTIVITY Choose a paragraph of comparison and a paragraph of description from a textbook. On a separate sheet of paper, write a paragraph that compares them.

Unit 4 ▷ Writing an Essay

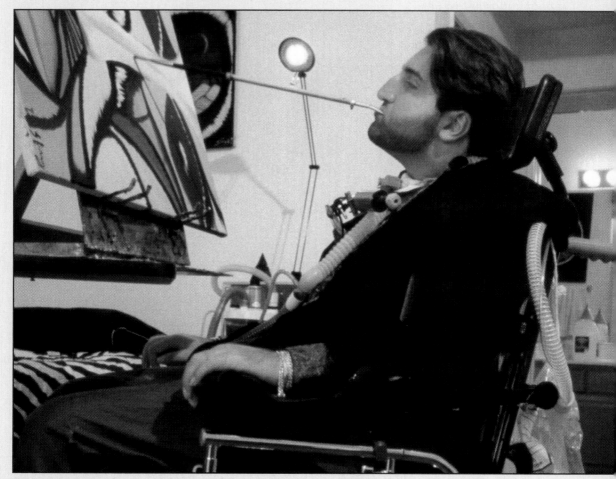

A painting uses lines, colors, and shapes to express an idea.
An essay uses words, sentences, and paragraphs to do the same
thing. What ideas might an essay express?

Caption Accept all reasonable responses. Possible answer: Essays can
express many ideas. They are used to express opinions or strong feelings
about something. They can also express ideas for change.

Essays are an important way to express ideas about important issues.

Alice Walker (born 1944) writes novels, poetry, and essays. Her novel The Color Purple *won a Pulitzer Prize for outstanding writing. Later, it was made into an award-winning movie. Walker's essays are collected in* In Search of Our Mothers' Gardens. *These essays show the damage done by racial prejudice.*

To help students tap their prior knowledge of the chapter topic, see the **Chapter Project** in the Classroom Resource Binder.

Learning Objectives

- Identify an essay as a group of paragraphs dealing with one idea.

- Identify the three basic parts of an essay: introduction, body, and conclusion.

- Tell what a thesis statement is.

- Identify a thesis statement in context.

Chapter **13** / What Is an Essay?

Words to Know

essay	a short piece of writing about a particular subject
composition	an essay
thesis statement	a sentence that presents the idea that the essay will support

13-1 / The Basic Essay

An **essay** is a short piece of writing about a particular
subject. Sometimes, an essay is called a **composition.**
In much the same way you learned to develop
a paragraph, you will learn to develop a whole essay.

An essay is also built very much like a paragraph.
A paragraph is made of sentences, and an essay is made
of paragraphs. Ideas that are too long to be covered
in one paragraph become topics for essays.

Remember the diagram of a paragraph? Study this
diagram of a paragraph again for review.

1 topic sentence

2 (a) sentence of support
   (b) sentence of support   } body
   (c) sentence of support

3 concluding sentence

Now, take a look at the diagram of an essay.

1   introductory paragraph

2   (a) paragraph of support ⎤
     (b) paragraph of support ⎬ body
     (c) paragraph of support ⎦

3   concluding paragraph

Notice that the diagram of an essay is similar to that of a paragraph. The only difference is that the parts of the essay diagram are paragraphs instead of sentences.

A basic essay includes the following elements.

1. An introductory paragraph

> Some people will not walk under ladders. Others worry if black cats cross their paths. These people act as they do because of superstitions. Superstitions are beliefs that have no basis in fact. However, many people believe that these superstitions are true.

2. A body of at least three supporting paragraphs

> Throughout the ages, there have been superstitions about salt. People once thought that salt had magic powers because it could keep things from decaying. The ancient Sumerians began the custom of throwing a pinch of salt over the left shoulder. They believed it would keep bad luck away. Several cultures considered spilled salt a sign of bad luck. Indeed, many people still toss a pinch of spilled salt over their left shoulder, just to be safe.

Even today, many people believe in signs of bad luck. Some feel they can control their futures by avoiding such signs. The superstitious never open umbrellas indoors because that is thought to bring misfortune. They never step on cracks in the sidewalk. Most avoid the number 13, believing that number is a bad luck sign. Some hotels avoid having a room numbered 13, going right from 12 to 14. Some buildings have no thirteenth floor. Even though these superstitions have no basis in fact, they certainly affect people's actions.

Just as there are signs of bad luck, so are there signs of good luck. Some people believe a four-leaf clover will bring good luck. Others look to a horseshoe or a rabbit's foot as a symbol of good fortune. Superstitions say that picking up a pin or a penny will mean a bright tomorrow. Perhaps these good luck charms have always been around because they make people feel better about the future.

3. A concluding paragraph

As people become better educated, they believe less in superstitions. However, a large number of people will still toss salt over their left shoulder or go out of their way to avoid walking under a ladder. Many people cling to superstitions because they are a bit afraid that the beliefs might, indeed, be true.

Look carefully at this essay about superstitions.

Notice that the introduction states the essay's topic. The readers know that the essay will be about people who are superstitious.

Notice the three paragraphs that make up the body of the essay.

> Paragraph 1: superstitions about salt
>
> Paragraph 2: superstitions about bad luck signs
>
> Paragraph 3: superstitions about good luck charms

Notice that each of the paragraphs in the body has a topic sentence, a body, and a concluding sentence.

Notice that the last paragraph of the essay serves as a conclusion. It is a summary that restates the topic of the entire essay.

Practice A

1. paragraphs
2. introduction
3. body
4. conclusion
5. introduction
6. body
7. three
8. five

On a separate sheet of paper, number from 1 to 8. Use the following terms to complete each sentence. Some words will be used more than once.

introduction	conclusion	three
body	paragraphs	five

An essay is a group of (1) _____ dealing with the same subject.

The three parts of the basic essay are the (2) _____, (3) _____, and (4) _____.

The topic of the essay is stated in the (5) _____.

The topic is supported in the (6) _____ of the essay.

There must be at least (7) _____ supporting paragraphs in a well-developed essay.

A basic essay would be at least (8) _____ paragraphs long.

Practice B

Read the following topics. Then, on a separate sheet of paper, number from 1 to 5. Write **P** next to the number if the topic could be covered in just one paragraph. Write **E** if you think the topic requires an essay.

1. How to iron a shirt

2. Ways to enjoy the summer

3. Famous dancers

4. Why I like ice cream

5. All about myself

1. P
2. E
3. E
4. P
5. E

13-2 ▶ The Introduction

The introductory paragraph of an essay is different from other paragraphs you have written. It has its own special pattern and purpose. The purpose is to let the readers know the topic of the essay and to interest the readers in that topic. The introductory paragraph makes a point. The rest of the essay must support that point.

One sentence in the introduction clearly states the topic. That sentence is called the **thesis statement.** The thesis statement is the most important sentence in the introduction. Everything in the essay works to support it. The thesis statement is usually the last sentence of the introductory paragraph.

The introductory paragraph in the essay on superstitions on page 178 had this thesis statement:

> However, many people believe that these superstitions are true.

Think About It

How does the thesis statement help the reader?

That statement lets the readers know what to expect from the rest of the essay. The readers will assume that the essay will support that thesis. In short, the essay will prove the thesis.

Your introductory paragraph must have a thesis statement. The thesis statement expresses the point of the essay. Once you have written a clear thesis statement, you are on your way to a good essay. You know exactly what your point is. Every sentence you write will support the thesis statement.

Read the following thesis statement.

> There are several reasons why I like being my age.

After making that statement, the writer knows exactly what to do. The writer must prove the statement by giving the reasons and discussing them. Each reason will be stated in a topic sentence and developed in a paragraph.

Practice A

1. Thanksgiving is my favorite holiday.

On a separate sheet of paper, copy the thesis statement from each of the following introductory paragraphs.

1. The turkey is on the table. It is brown and crisp and juicy. The air is filled with smells of cinnamon and cranberries and sage dressing. The family is gathered around the table. Thanksgiving is my favorite holiday.

2. Animals cannot talk. They cannot tell people what is on their mind. Their eyes, however, show feeling. They seem happy sometimes, and at other times, they seem quite sad. There is no doubt in my mind. I believe that animals, just like people, have feelings.

3. Students go to Ridgeview School every weekday for nine months of the year. They spend six hours of each day in Ridgeview's halls and classrooms. Because students spend so much time there, the school should be a better place. I think Ridgeview School could be improved in several ways.

4. The sun was shining. Soccer fans filled the stands. The two best teams were facing each other on the field. It was going to be an exciting game.

5. Not long ago, most people believed a heavy machine could never stay up in the air. Today, airplanes fly across the country in a few hours. Two brothers, Wilbur and Orville Wright, made the dream of flight come true.

2. I believe that animals, just like people, have feelings.

3. I think Ridgeview School could be improved in several ways.

4. It was going to be an exciting game.

5. Two brothers, Wilbur and Orville Wright, made the dream of flight come true.

Developing a thesis statement takes a little thought. You must look at a subject from different angles. How do you feel about the subject? Try to look at just one small part of the subject.

Given the broad subject of *movies,* one writer made this thesis statement:

The movie *The Creatures* is the most frightening film I have seen.

Given the broad subject of *your city,* another writer came up with this thesis statement:

My city needs more recreational activities for teenagers.

Practice B

Choose three of the following subjects. On a separate sheet of paper, write a sentence that could serve as a thesis statement for an essay. Do this for each subject that you choose.

automobiles	rock music
summer jobs	food
friends	pets
dislikes	loneliness

13-3 ▸ The Body

The Writing Process

Why is it important to know your audience when writing an essay? (See The Writing Process, page WP15.)

Having written the thesis statement, the writer goes on to develop the body of the essay. A strong essay should have a body of at least three paragraphs of support. Look back at the body of the essay on superstitions on pages 178–179.

What is the topic sentence of the first supporting paragraph?

> Throughout the ages, there have been superstitions about salt.

What is the topic sentence of the second paragraph?

> Even today, many people believe in signs of bad luck.

What is the topic sentence of the third supporting paragraph?

> Just as there are signs of bad luck, so are there signs of good luck.

Notice that each topic sentence supports the thesis statement that many people today are still superstitious.

Practice

Practice writing topic sentences to support a thesis statement. On a separate sheet of paper, write topic sentences that could develop each of the following thesis statements. The first topic sentence has been written for you.

1. **Thesis statement:** My favorite food is _____ .

   Topic Sentence 1: My favorite food is tacos.

   Topic Sentence 2: _____

   Topic Sentence 3: _____

2. **Thesis statement:** There are several reasons that _____ is my favorite relative.

   Topic Sentence 1: _____

   Topic Sentence 2: _____

   Topic Sentence 3: _____

3. **Thesis statement:** My life would be quite different if I had been born one hundred years ago.

   Topic Sentence 1: _____

   Topic Sentence 2: _____

   Topic Sentence 3: _____

Look at the topic sentences you have written. Think about how you would develop each of them into supporting paragraphs.

13-4 ▸ The Conclusion

The purpose of the concluding paragraph is to summarize your essay and let your readers know that the end has come. You should not introduce any new ideas in the conclusion. Restate the thesis statement, using different words.

Sometimes in the conclusion, a writer will repeat a few key points or give an opinion. The concluding paragraph, like the introductory paragraph, is not developed in the same way as other paragraphs.

Reread the concluding paragraph from the essay on superstitions on page 179.

> As people become better educated and learn more about the real world, they believe less in superstitions. However, a large number of people in the world will still toss salt over their left shoulder or go out of their way to avoid walking under a ladder. Many people cling to superstitions because they are a bit afraid that the beliefs might, indeed, be true.

Notice how the paragraph restates some of the points mentioned in the body of the essay. It uses examples, like throwing salt over the left shoulder and not walking under a ladder, as superstitions that many people still believe.

Practice

Read each of the following conclusions. On a separate sheet of paper, tell whether each conclusion is a good conclusion or a bad conclusion. Write *Effective* if it is a good conclusion. Write *Ineffective* if it is a bad conclusion, or one that introduces another idea.

1. Ineffective
2. Effective

1. Indeed, Ridgeview School must improve, or some students will stop going to class there. Changes should be made before it is too late. Next year, I will graduate and go on to college.

2. I am glad that we celebrate the day the Pilgrims feasted at Plymouth Colony. I always look forward to the sights, the smells, and the warm feelings of Thanksgiving.

WRITING WITH STYLE
Stating the Main Idea

It is most important that the introductory paragraph clearly states the main idea of the essay. The writer and the readers need to be sure just what point the essay will make. A clear thesis statement helps to keep the essay on track.

One of the introductions below has a clear thesis statement. The other introduction would leave readers wondering what the essay is about. Which introduction do you think is clearer?

1. I was nervous. I worried about my appearance, and I worried about what I would say. Would they like me? Would I do things correctly? I was right to worry because the first day of my new job was a disaster.

2. I was glad to have a job. They could have hired a lot of different people, but they chose me. My parents were really glad that I was working. It would be great to have some money to spend. Things did not go very well the first day, but I know I can learn do the job right. I get a week's vacation after I have worked for six months.

You probably chose Introduction 1 because it limits the topic and presents a clear thesis statement. Introduction 2 is less clear. You were probably wondering about the writer's topic.

What do you expect the essay following Introduction 1 will be about?

What do you think the essay following Introduction 2 might be about?

VOCABULARY BUILDER
Using Suffixes That Make Verbs

You can use some suffixes to change nouns and adjectives into verbs. Two common suffixes are *-ify* and *-ize*. For example, with these suffixes, the noun *terror* becomes the verbs *terrify* and *terrorize*. When you add a suffix, the end of the base word is often cut off. A dictionary will show you how much of the base word to keep.

harmony + ize = *harmonize*   special + ize = *specialize*

horror + ify = *horrify*   note + ify = *notify*

Choose one of the words in italic type above to fill in each blank. Rewrite the sentences on a separate sheet of paper.

1. The singers in the trio tried to _____.

2. The scary music and the special effects will _____ visitors at the Halloween haunted house.

3. If you move, be sure to _____ the post office of your new address.

4. The college students decided to _____ in foreign languages.

1. The singers in the trio tried to harmonize.

2. The scary music and the special effects will horrify visitors at the Halloween haunted house.

3. If you move, be sure to notify the post office of your new address.

4. The college students decided to specialize in foreign languages.

Chapter

13 / Review

Summary Have students use the summary to outline the main idea and details of the chapter.

Summary

An essay is a group of paragraphs that deal with one idea.
An essay has an introductory paragraph, at least three paragraphs of supporting details, and a concluding paragraph.
The introductory paragraph of an essay must have a thesis statement. The thesis statement is a sentence that tells the main point of the essay.
Everything in an essay must support the thesis statement.
Each supporting paragraph in the body of an essay must have a topic sentence, a body, and a concluding sentence.
The concluding paragraph of an essay sums up the main points. It restates the thesis, using different words.

thesis statement
essay
composition

1. essay
2. composition
3. thesis statement

More Vocabulary Review is provided in the Classroom Resource Binder.

Vocabulary Review

Match each term in the box with its meaning. Write your answers on a separate sheet of paper.

1. A piece of writing about a particular subject is called an _____.

2. Another name for an essay is a _____.

3. A sentence that presents the idea that an essay will support is a _____.

Chapter Quiz

1. The purpose of the introductory paragraph is to tell readers what the essay will be about. It also

serves as a way to grab readers' attention so they will read on.

2. A thesis statement tells the reader the main point that the essay will support.

3. Each paragraph in the body of an essay supports the thesis statement.

Chapter Quiz

Complete the following items. Write your answers on a separate sheet of paper.

1. What does the introductory paragraph of an essay do?

2. What does the thesis statement do?

3. Why is it important to have three paragraphs in the body of an essay?

4. What does the concluding paragraph of an essay do?

5. Why is it important to restate the thesis statement in the conclusion?

▶ **Test Tip**
Make sure to use complete sentences when answering questions, unless you are told otherwise.

4. The purpose of a concluding paragraph is to summarize the main points of an essay and restate the thesis statement using different words.

5. Restating the thesis statement emphasizes the main point a writer wants to make.

Critical Thinking

How are the parts of an essay similar to the parts of a paragraph? Write your answer on a separate sheet of paper.

Critical Thinking Answers may vary. Possible answer: Like a paragraph, an essay has an introduction, a body, and a conclusion.

Writing Activity

Choose one of the following topics or create your own topic. On a separate sheet of paper, write an introductory paragraph for an essay about the topic. Your paragraph needs a thesis statement to let readers know the point of the essay. It also needs to grab the readers' interest.

Dress codes in school   Playing on a sports team

Why people might visit   Using the Internet
my community

Writing Activity Answers will vary. Check students' work for the inclusion of a strong thesis statement.

A personal essay often states the writer's deepest beliefs.

James Baldwin (1924–1987) grew up in Harlem in New York City during the Great Depression. He saw the frustration and hopelessness of the people around him. These experiences gave him material for his novel, Go Tell It On the Mountain. *Baldwin's book of essays is called* The Fire Next Time. *These writings give a vivid picture of his personal beliefs.*

To help students tap their prior knowledge of the chapter topic, see the **Chapter Project** in the Classroom Resource Binder.

Learning Objectives

- Write a list of possible essay topics.
- Write a simple outline for an essay.
- Write a short essay from your outline.

Chapter 14 / Writing Your Own Essay

See the Workbook for **Extra Practice**.

Words to Know

outlining	creating a plan for a piece of writing
rough draft	the first, unpolished copy of a piece of writing

14-1 / Choosing a Topic

Some people say that the hardest part of writing is deciding what to write about. Actually, you will probably discover a lot of topics for your essays. Here are some suggestions.

Tell what happened

Have any funny, embarrassing, or frightening things happened to you? Perhaps you know about something really unusual or exciting that happened to someone else. Have you had any adventures on a job, at school, or on vacation? Sometimes, even small situations can make good essays.

Tell about people or places

People you know or people you have only heard or read about can be good subjects for essays. Do you know of someone who showed great courage? Wisdom? Artistry? Do you know about someone unusual? Someone who has an unusual career?

Have you visited, lived in, or read about any interesting places? Even ordinary places like a busy neighborhood can make exciting essay topics.

Explain how to do something or how to make something

Writing a how-to essay is very similar to writing a how-to paragraph. Do you know how to do something that might interest others? Perhaps you have a hobby that gives you experience and skills that you can share. You might, for example, tell your readers how to make a dress or how to improve their tennis skills.

After doing a little research, you could write a how-to essay on a subject that is new to you. You might explain how to fly a jet or how to make a canoe.

Give your opinion and persuade others

Everyone has opinions. You can use your ideas to convince your readers of your opinions. Do you have an opinion about problems in schools, laws involving teenagers, the way minority groups are treated where you live? You can find ideas for essays in newspapers, on television, and in movies.

Think About It

Why is it important to choose a topic that you find interesting?

Practice A

On a separate sheet of paper, copy the headings from the diagram below and that continues on page 196. Under each heading, write as many essay topics as you can. Write at least three for each heading.

Answers will vary. Accept all reasonable responses. Check to make sure that students' topic ideas relate to each heading.

Example: Things that happened

a. Six teenagers were lost in a mountain blizzard.

b. A winter storm knocked out electricity for five days.

c. I almost drowned when a storm came up on the lake.

d. My dog found its way home after being lost for a week.

e. I went to a winter survival camp in the mountains.

1. Things that happened

   a.

   b.

   c.

2. Unusual people

   a.

   b.

   c.

3. Exciting places

   a.

   b.

   c.

(Practice A continues on next page.) ⇒

(Practice A continued.)

4. How to do something

    a.

    b.

    c.

5. Things I believe in and could persuade others to believe

    a.

    b.

    c.

Choose topics that are broad enough

When you choose a topic, remember that you must have enough to say about it to fill five paragraphs. Recall from Chapter 13 that you will need to write at least three paragraphs in the body of your essay. Remember that each paragraph will discuss a different point. As you consider a topic, ask yourself, "Can I think of three important points about this topic?"

If you cannot think of three important points, choose another topic.

Do not choose a topic that is too broad

The Writing Process

How can you narrow a topic that is too broad? (See The Writing Process, page WP6.)

Very often, people choose topics that are too broad. Do not pick a topic so broad that you cannot cover it in a basic essay. For example, you would not want to write one short essay on *Trees of America*. The topic is so broad that all you would be able to do is list the trees. You could not possibly discuss all of the different kinds of trees, their uses, where they grow, how they are cared for, and so on. When you limit your topic to *How Americans Depend on Trees*, you could easily write a paper that makes a point and is the right length.

Practice B

On a separate sheet of paper, number from 1 to 10. Read each suggested essay topic below, and decide if it is suitable for a short essay. Write **too limited**, **too broad**, or **good** next to each number. Five of the listings would be good essay topics.

1. My plan to make a million dollars
2. Equal rights for all Americans
3. The history of the state of New Jersey
4. My favorite Ohio vacation spot
5. How to make shrimp and avocado salad
6. My funny Uncle Harvey
7. Romance novels
8. Pollution
9. The ugliest place I have ever visited
10. One day at a mall

1. good
2. too broad
3. too broad
4. good
5. too limited
6. good
7. too broad
8. too broad
9. good
10. good

14-2 ▸ Planning Your Essay

Some people think that the quickest and easiest way to get an essay written is just to start writing. They ask, "Why waste time outlining my plans?" They are wrong. If you begin writing without planning ahead, you may find yourself rambling. You may even get lost halfway through the essay. You may find yourself confused. If you are confused, your readers will surely be!

At this point, you may get discouraged and give up. Why let that happen? **Outlining** can give you a helping hand. Outlining is creating an outline, or a plan for writing. An outline is a plan that lays out the main part of your essay. It does not take very long to plan your essay in a simple outline.

Once that outline is complete, the task of writing the essay becomes quite manageable—even enjoyable. After all, writing can be a pleasurable and exciting activity.

Now, to plan an essay, just fill in the following basic essay format on a separate sheet of paper.

1. Introduction

Write your thesis statement. Be sure to write a complete sentence.

2. Supporting Paragraph 1

Write the topic sentence presenting your first idea of support. Be sure to write a complete sentence.

Summarize Detail 1 to support the topic sentence.

Summarize Detail 2 to support the topic sentence.

Summarize Detail 3 to support the topic sentence.

3. Supporting Paragraph 2

Write the topic sentence presenting your second idea of support. Be sure to write a complete sentence.

Summarize Detail 1 to support the topic sentence.

Summarize Detail 2 to support the topic sentence.

Summarize Detail 3 to support the topic sentence.

Brush Up on the Basics

In an outline, use capital Roman numerals to label a main idea. Use capital letters to label supporting ideas. (See Capitalization 19 in the Reference Guide.)

4. Supporting Paragraph 3

Write the topic sentence presenting your third idea of support. Be sure to write a complete sentence.

   Summarize Detail 1 to support the topic sentence.

   Summarize Detail 2 to support the topic sentence.

   Summarize Detail 3 to support the topic sentence.

5. Conclusion

You can develop the conclusion as you write your essay.

Use this basic essay diagram, or outline guide, when you plan an essay. You will find that once your outline is completed, the hardest part of your job is over.

Read the following example of an essay outline.

Topic: Some ways to spend a rainy Sunday afternoon

1. Introduction

   Thesis statement: There are several ways to put a rainy Sunday afternoon to good use.

2. Supporting Paragraph 1

Most people's homes could use some cleaning.

   a. Clean the closets. (Give old clothes to a charity.)

   b. Wash the inside windows so they sparkle when the sun shines.

   c. Clean out the refrigerator.

   d. Clean the basement or the attic.

The Writing Process

How can an outline help you to plan your essay? (See The Writing Process, page WP9.)

3. Supporting Paragraph 2

There might be an old friend or a distant relative who would be surprised and pleased by a phone call or a letter.

    a. Call someone who moved away.

    b. Write letters to relatives.

    c. Call or visit an elderly person who might be lonely.

    d. Write thank-you notes, birthday cards, or get-well wishes to people.

4. Supporting Paragraph 3

Catch up on your reading.

    a. Visit a far-off land just by opening a novel.

    b. Read a book that teaches something new.

    c. Spend a few hours reading a Sunday paper.

    d. Do a crossword puzzle, and read sections of a newspaper that you normally skip.

5. Conclusion

Practice

Answers will vary. You may wish to check students' topic ideas before they proceed. Check students' outlines for logic and organization.

Now, it is time to really get writing! On a separate sheet of paper, you will make your own outline for a basic essay.

First, choose a topic. Look back at the list of topics you wrote in Practice A on pages 195–196. You might want to use one of them. You might also choose from the topics listed on page 201. Choose something that interests you. Make sure your topic is neither too broad nor too limited.

Suggested topics

- The great (or terrible) part about having a brother (or sister)

- The great (or terrible) part about being an only child

- What I hope to be doing when I am 60

- My unusual family

- Mistakes parents often make

- Some very effective TV commercials

- A terrifying airplane flight

- A day I would like to forget

- How to prevent bicycle accidents

Write your topic at the top of your paper.

Now, complete the outline on pages 198–199.

14-3 ▸ Writing Your Complete Essay

Congratulations! If you have come this far, it means that you have completed the outline for your essay. The hardest work is done. Now, with the outline in hand, it is time to write the essay.

Practice

On a separate sheet of paper, write your own essay. Use your outline from the Practice on pages 200–201.

Answers will vary. Check to make sure that students follow their outlines and that their essays contain an introduction with a thesis statement, a body of at least three supporting paragraphs, and a concluding paragraph.

(Practice continues on next page.) ⟩

(Practice continued.)

English and Technology

You can use a word-processing program to highlight your thesis statement. Then, you can refer to it as you write.

Introduction You will need to write two or three sentences that lead up to your thesis statement. You might try a brief description or story that leads to the thesis. Here is an example.

> It was raining hard. The clouds were so thick that it was almost like night at midday. It was Sunday. I was home alone with nothing to do, and I was bored. However, I soon discovered that there are ways to put a rainy Sunday to good use.

Notice the thesis statement from the sample outline at the end of the introduction on page 199.

Supporting paragraphs As you begin writing your supporting paragraphs, recall everything you learned in Units 2 and 3 about writing good paragraphs. You can use examples for support. You can use facts and figures. You can use details. Just take it one paragraph at a time and always use your outline as your guide. This approach will ensure that you do not become confused and that your last paragraph is as strong as your first paragraph.

If you begin to have trouble, return to Units 2 and 3 and give yourself a quick review. Then, go on. It is important to keep writing and thinking. You have all of the tools that you really need. So, just keep on using what you already know.

On page 203 is an example of a completed supporting paragraph developed from the sample outline.

Like most people, I live in a house that could always use a Sunday's worth of cleaning. My closets were bulging with clothes I never wore. There are needy people who could use those old clothes. As I watched the rain, I realized that my windows as well as my closets needed attention. It was raining that Sunday, but one day the sun would shine in on all of that dirt. Last of all, I turned to a really big job: the attic. Cleaning the attic was a dusty, dirty chore, but it meant finding wonderful old treasures. I used that rainy Sunday to make my house sparkle.

Conclusion You will need to write a short paragraph of conclusion. Your job here is to summarize your points and let your readers know that your essay has come to an end. You will also restate your thesis using different words.

You can restate the main points.

Cleaning the house, renewing old friendships, and catching up on reading are all good ways to spend time. A rainy Sunday became a chance to do things that I never before found time to do.

You can find a lesson in what you have said.

Do not let time pass by without making it count. I found that a rainy Sunday afternoon does not have to be boring at all. Because I used my time wisely, that Sunday turned out to be a most worthwhile day.

With the conclusion comes the end of the **rough draft**, or the first, unpolished copy, of your essay. If you followed the outline, you should have written a well-organized, easy-to-follow essay that presents a point and supports it. You should feel that your essay is clear and well developed. Your readers should find your essay easy to understand.

WRITING WITH STYLE
Supporting a Paragraph

The two paragraphs below could both serve as supporting paragraphs in an essay with the following thesis statement. Decide which paragraph you think is stronger. Then, on a separate sheet of paper, answer the questions that follow the paragraphs.

There are often some interesting people in a bus station.

1. While I waited for my cousin to arrive on a bus from Kansas, I saw a unique family. There were four of them—a man, a woman, and two little girls. The man, a tall, thin fellow, wore a wide-brimmed, black hat. The woman and the girls wore long, black capes with tight-fitting hoods. Not only was their clothing interesting, but their faces were, too. They waited an hour for their bus. When the loudspeaker announced that the next bus to Massachusetts was leaving, the family picked up their bags. They headed for the station exit as calmly as a gentle breeze.

2. While I waited for my cousin to arrive on a bus from Kansas, I saw a unique family. There were four of them. There was a man. There was a woman. There were two little girls. They wore interesting clothing. They waited an hour for their bus. They stood very still. I had to wait at the bus station for my cousin because my dad had to work. When the loudspeaker announced the next bus, the family left.

You probably thought Paragraph 1 was the better paragraph. Why?

a. Which paragraph uses description and detail?

b. Can you find any similes in Paragraphs 1 or 2?

c. Do the sentences vary in difficulty and length in Paragraph 1?

d. Are there any sentences that do not stick to the topic in Paragraph 2?

a. Paragraph 1 uses more detail and description than Paragraph 2.

b. Paragraph 1 uses the simile, "They headed for the station exit as calmly as a gentle breeze." Paragraph 2 does not have any similes.

c. Paragraph 1 uses sentences of varying complexity and length. Most sentences in Paragraph 2 are short, simple sentences.

d. All the sentences in Paragraph 1 stick to the topic. One sentence in Paragraph 2 does not ("I had to wait at the bus station for my cousin because my dad had to work.").

VOCABULARY BUILDER
Having Fun with Illustrated Words

On a separate sheet of paper, write a synonym for each of the following words. Then, either draw a picture that illustrates the meaning of the word or cut out a picture from a newspaper or magazine. Advertisements will be a good source of pictures.

1. scowl
2. blissful
3. forlorn
4. daring
5. hilarious
6. gigantic
7. boulevard
8. banquet
9. delicate
10. cinema

Answers will vary.
Possible answers:
1. frown
2. peaceful
3. unhappy
4. brave
5. funny
6. huge
7. avenue
8. feast
9. fragile
10. movie theater

14 ▷ Review

Summary Have students use the summary to outline the main idea and details of the chapter.

Summary
Choose a clear essay topic that is neither too broad nor too limited.
Understand your own purpose. Decide if you intend to tell what happened, tell about a person or a place, explain how to do something, or persuade your readers that your opinion is correct.
Always make an outline before you write your essay.
Follow your outline to write each paragraph. Doing so will help you write a clear, well-organized essay.

outlining
rough draft

1. false, outlining
2. false, rough draft

More Vocabulary Review is provided in the Classroom Resource Binder.

Vocabulary Review

Write *true* or *false* after each sentence. If the sentence is false, change the underlined word to make it true. Choose a term from the box. Write your answers on a separate sheet of paper.

1. A rough draft is creating a plan for a piece of writing.

2. The first, unpolished copy of a piece of writing is called the outlining.

Chapter Quiz

1. An essay topic can come from something that happened, tell

about a person or place, tell how to make something, or share an opinion.

2. If you write an essay without an outline, you might begin to ramble or get confused.

Chapter Quiz

Complete the following items. Write your answers on a separate sheet of paper.

1. What are two ways you can find essay topics?

2. What might happen if you began to write an essay without an outline?

3. What might you include in an outline for an essay?

4. What should the first few sentences in the introduction of an essay do?

5. What do you need to do in the conclusion of an essay?

Critical Thinking

How can you decide if a topic is broad enough for an essay? Write your answer on a separate sheet of paper.

Critical Thinking Answers will vary. Possible answer: You can tell if a topic is broad enough for an essay by developing an outline and seeing if there are enough main ideas for a three-paragraph essay.

▶ **Test Tip**
You can use a separate sheet of paper to make notes as you work through a question.

3. An outline for an essay includes the thesis statement, topic sentences for the body paragraphs, and the supporting details for each.

4. The first few sentences in the introduction lead up to the thesis statement. They also serve as a way to grab readers' attention.

5. The conclusion of an essay summarizes the points and lets the reader know that the essay has ended. It also restates the thesis statement in other words.

Writing Activity

Choose one of the following thesis statements or write your own. On a separate sheet of paper, make an outline for your essay. Follow the directions on pages 198–199.

- We all must work to save our planet.

- Many people seem to be superstitious.

- My pet _____ was one of the best friends I ever had.

- Computers continue to change our lives.

Writing Activity Answers will vary. Encourage students to do this activity independently. Check to make sure that students have all the parts of an essay and that their essays prove or explain their thesis statement.

A well-written essay can help to bring changes in society.

Lorraine Hansberry (1930–1965) was a gifted playwright and essayist. She wrote the award-winning play, A Raisin in the Sun. *It describes an African American family's struggle to make a better life. It was the first play by an African American woman to be performed on Broadway in New York City. Hansberry's essays are collected in* To Be Young, Gifted, and Black. *These essays discuss racism, the need for world peace, and other social problems she hoped to change.*

Reading Challenge See the Adapted Classics series for Lorraine Hansberry's *A Raisin the Sun.*

To help students tap their prior knowledge of the chapter topic, see the **Chapter Project** in the Classroom Resource Binder.

Learning Objectives

- Revise a draft of an essay.
- Edit a draft of an essay.
- Identify past and present verb tenses.
- Identify transitional words that link paragraphs.
- Write a final copy of an essay.

Chapter 15 ▷ Writing Better Essays

Words to Know

edit	to prepare a piece of writing for the final copy by correcting any mistakes in facts, grammar, usage, and mechanics
content	the ideas in a piece of writing
proofread	to mark errors in a piece of writing
mechanics	the spelling and punctuation of a piece of writing

15-1 ▷ The Final Copy

In this chapter, you will write the final copy of the essay you began in Chapter 14. You will have a chance to revise and **edit** your draft. To edit means to prepare a piece of writing for the final copy by correcting any mistakes in facts, grammar, usage, and mechanics. Once you complete these two steps, your final copy should be a clear, well-developed piece of writing.

Think back to "The Writing Process" at the beginning of this book. In Chapter C of "The Writing Process," you learned how to revise a piece of writing. In Chapter D of "The Writing Process," you learned how to edit a piece of writing.

Revising Your Draft

Think back to what you learned about revising on pages WP22–WP27 in Chapter C. What should you look for when you revise your draft? Ask yourself, *Did I communicate my ideas clearly? Did I say everything I wanted to say? Do my readers have the information they need to understand my topic?*

When you revise, you make sure that your draft is clearly written. This is the time to check the **content**, or ideas, in your writing. It is the time to think about the reason that you wrote your draft and to make sure it is clear who your readers are.

Introduction

❏ Does my essay have a thesis sentence?

❏ Is my thesis sentence clear?

Supporting paragraphs

❏ Are there at least three supporting paragraphs in my essay?

❏ Does each topic sentence have a supporting paragraph?

❏ Does each sentence in the paragraph support the topic sentence?

❏ Are there at least three sentences of detail in each paragraph?

❏ Are there any sentences that do not relate to the topic sentence that should be removed?

❏ Are transitional words used to help the writing flow?

Conclusion

❏ Does my essay have a conclusion?

❏ Does my conclusion restate my thesis?

Now, reread your essay. How do you think it sounds? You can use this Revision Checklist from page WP27 in Chapter C to make sure that you checked all the important points.

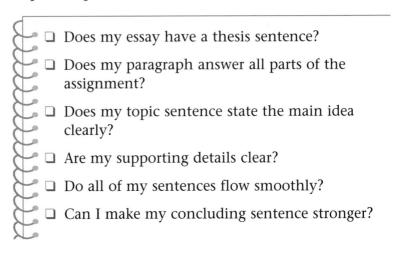

❏ Does my essay have a thesis sentence?

❏ Does my paragraph answer all parts of the assignment?

❏ Does my topic sentence state the main idea clearly?

❏ Are my supporting details clear?

❏ Do all of my sentences flow smoothly?

❏ Can I make my concluding sentence stronger?

Practice A

Answers will vary. Check to make sure that students are finding their errors and marking the places where corrections need to be made.

Use the Revision Checklist above to revise the essay you wrote for the Practice on page 201. Mark the places on your draft that need to be corrected.

Practice B

Answers will vary. Check to make sure that students corrected the errors they marked in Practice A.

Now that you have reviewed your draft using the Revision Checklist, look back at the kinds of things that you would like to correct. On a separate sheet of paper, make the corrections to your draft. Then, rewrite your draft and include the new corrections from Practice A on this page.

15-2 ▶ Editing Your Draft

When you edit, you find and correct any mistakes in facts and style. When you **proofread**, you mark any mistakes in **mechanics**, or the spelling and punctuation of a piece of writing. You also check for misspelled words, missing punctuation, and unrelated details. Such problems will make your essay unclear to your readers.

When you proofread, look for the following kinds of mechanical mistakes.

English and Technology

You can usually use a word-processing program to check the spelling in your writing.

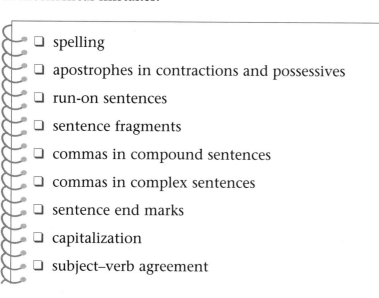

- ❑ spelling
- ❑ apostrophes in contractions and possessives
- ❑ run-on sentences
- ❑ sentence fragments
- ❑ commas in compound sentences
- ❑ commas in complex sentences
- ❑ sentence end marks
- ❑ capitalization
- ❑ subject–verb agreement

Proofreading is only one part of editing. Think back to what you learned about editing on pages WP30–WP35 in Chapter D. What should you look for when you edit your draft? Ask yourself, *Did I choose the correct words to help me to communicate my ideas clearly? Did I spell everything correctly? Do all of my subjects agree with their verbs? Did I use the correct verb tenses? Did I use punctuation marks correctly?*

Now, reread your essay. You can use this Editing Checklist from page WP35 in Chapter D to make sure that you checked all the important points.

❑ Do all the sentences state a complete thought?

❑ Are any words missing?

❑ Are all the words spelled correctly?

❑ Do all of the sentences begin with a capital letter?

❑ Do all the sentences end with a punctuation mark?

Read the following example of an edited paragraph. Notice the corrections in blue.

Brush Up on the Basics

A subject should always agree with its verb. (See Grammar 21 in the Reference Guide.)

The penguin is an unusuel animal from the icy antarctic. Some people say penguins look like little men wearing tuxedos. Penguins stand up on short legs. They walk with a waddle. Although they are birds, they can't fly. A bird called the albatross lives in the antarctic, two. Their strange walk and unusuel appearance make penguins fun to watch.

Practice A

Read the following paragraph. On a separate sheet of paper, list any changes and corrections you think are necessary. Look for spelling errors, missing commas, capitalization errors, sentence fragments, and sentences that do not belong in the paragraph.

There is a new house on elm street. It is surrounded by beautiful trees. The trees are tall and have white flowers in the Spring. They look like they have been there for a hundred years. Fall is my favorite season. During the day, you can see the sun shining thrugh the branches of the trees. And hear the birds chirping. The house has big windows. the Sunlight comes in through the windows and makes the house very bright. At sundown, the sun turn bright orange. And It makes the sky orange two. Just before it gets dark, you can see a squirrels or too runing across the branches. The beautful house on Elm street is like a piture out of a book.

Practice B

Use the Editing Checklist on page 213 to edit the essay you wrote for the Practice on page 201. Mark the places on your draft that need to be corrected.

Answers will vary. Check to make sure that students are finding their errors and marking the places where corrections need to be made.

Practice C

Now that you have reviewed your draft using the Editing Checklist, look back at the kinds of things that you would like to correct. On a separate sheet of paper, make the corrections to your draft. Then, rewrite your draft and include the new corrections from Practice B on this page.

Answers will vary. Check to make sure that students corrected the errors they marked in Practice B.

(Practice C continues on next page.) ➠

The Writing Process

How can proofreading marks help you to edit your writing? (See The Writing Process, page WP35.)

Using Proofreading Marks

When you proofread your writing, you can use proofreading marks to note corrections you would like to make. Proofreading marks provide a quick and simple tool to use when you edit. Think back to what you learned about proofreading marks on page WP35 in Chapter D. Then, take a look at the following list of symbols and their meanings.

Insert letters or words here.	∧	Make this letter lowercase.	/
Capitalize this letter.	≡	Delete or replace this.	ℒ
Indent a new paragraph	⫪	Check spelling.	◯

Practice D

On a separate sheet of paper, copy the following paragraph. Use proofreading marks to correct the paragraph.

i just read a book about the road to the white house. this book begins by asking, "what makes a person want to be president?" The book gives many reasons that people get into politics. For example, the Feeling of of power and the desire to be famous. People should remember that being president is hard you may be famous, but and you never have any time to youself.

Checking Verb Tenses

Read the following two paragraphs. Can you tell what the major difference is between Paragraph 1 and Paragraph 2?

1. The sun set, and I began my night in the wilderness. I snuggled down in my sleeping bag and watched the stars twinkle in the black sky. Then, I heard the long howl of a wolf somewhere in the darkness. I pulled the sleeping bag around my head. It was going to be a long night.

2. The sun sets, and I begin my night in the wilderness. I snuggle down in my sleeping bag and watch the stars twinkle in the black sky. Then, I hear the long howl of a wolf somewhere in the darkness. I pull the sleeping bag around my head. It is going to be a long night.

Paragraph 1 is written in the past tense. It is describing something that has already happened. Past-tense verbs like *snuggled*, *watched*, and *heard* are used. The writer uses past-tense verbs throughout the paragraph.

Paragraph 2 is written in the present tense. It is describing something as it happens. Present-tense verbs like *snuggle*, *watch*, and *hear* are used. The writer uses present-tense verbs throughout the paragraph.

The Writing Process
Why is it important to edit for grammar? (See The Writing Process, page WP33.)

You should avoid shifting tenses within an essay. Decide if you will write in the past tense or present tense, and then stick to that choice.

Notice that the paragraph below changes verb tenses.

> The elevator *stopped* between the second and third floors. The three people inside the elevator *looked* worried. One man <u>pushes</u> the buttons nervously. The other man <u>tries</u> to open the elevator door. The woman on the elevator *banged* on the door. Then the trapped trio *yelled* for help.

The verbs in italic type are past-tense verbs. The underlined verbs are present-tense verbs. All of the verbs should be in either past tense or present tense so that the readers know *when* the events are happening.

Practice A

On a separate sheet of paper, rewrite the paragraph above so that all the verbs are in either past tense or present tense.

The elevator stopped between the second and third floors. The three people inside the elevator looked worried. One man pushed the buttons nervously. The other man tried to open the elevator door. The woman on the elevator banged on the door. Then the trapped trio yelled for help.

or

The elevator stops between the second and third floors. The three people inside the elevator look worried. One man pushes the buttons nervously. The other man tries to open the elevator door. The woman on the elevator bangs on the door. Then the trapped trio yells for help.

Practice B

Review the essay you wrote for the practice on page 201. On a separate sheet of paper, correct any errors in verb tense. Ask yourself the following questions.

Is the essay written in the past or present tense?

Is that verb tense used throughout the essay?

Answers will vary. Check to make sure that students have used verb tenses consistently in their essays.

15-4 ▸ Linking Paragraphs with Transitional Words

You have already learned how transitional words link sentences within a paragraph. You should also use transitional words to show the links *between* your paragraphs. For example, transitional words that show time can guide your readers through your essay. Read the following example.

The parade began early in the morning. The air was still cool, and the marchers were in good spirits. The bands played loudly, and the baton twirlers threw their batons high into the air. The flowers on the horse-drawn floats were fresh and colorful. It was a beautiful sight.

Several hours later, the mood of the parade changed. The temperature soared to 98 degrees, and the marchers were hot. The band members had to unbutton their high collars, and the dancers dragged their feet. The flowers on the floats wilted and faded. Even the horses seemed hot, tired, and in need of water. Luckily, the end of the parade route was near.

The transitional words are in italic type. They show the relationship between the second paragraph and the first paragraph. They help readers to recognize the passage of time. Such transitional words are often used at the beginning of a paragraph.

Review the transitional words listed in Chapter 8 on pages 111–112. The same transitional words can be used at the beginning of a paragraph to link the paragraphs themselves.

Notice in the following paragraph how the transitional words *For example* take the readers from one idea to the next.

> The mountain lion is a large, wild animal. It belongs to the cat family. Throughout the history of the Americas, the mountain lion has given people cause for alarm. *For example*, the early settlers of North America hated to hear the wail of the mountain lion. They thought it sounded like a person in terrible pain. They knew that the cry meant the lion was hunting. They knew that their sheep, their calves, and their ponies were not safe.

When you write, you already know the steps you will be taking to develop your ideas. Your readers, though, do not have your writing outline in front of them. If your writing is not clear, you will confuse your readers.

Use transitional words to guide your readers. That way, they will understand your ideas.

Transitional words can also tell your readers that the conclusion has come. You might begin a concluding paragraph with a transitional expression such as *In conclusion, Thus, or Therefore.*

Transitions act as bridges between ideas. Use them to bridge the ideas between sentences and then between whole paragraphs.

Practice A

Read the rough draft of your essay. Have you used any transitional words or phrases to begin your paragraphs? Try adding some transitions to show connections between paragraphs.

Answers will vary. Check to make sure that students have correctly and effectively inserted transitional words in their essays.

WRITING WITH STYLE
Writing a Draft

Writing both a rough draft and a final copy is a necessary part of developing your essay. Do not try to save time by skipping a step in the essay-writing process.

Your edited work will be clearer to your readers than the first draft. Even the most experienced writers find mistakes in their first drafts.

Look at the following two paragraphs. Paragraph 1 is a first draft. Paragraph 2 is a final copy. On a separate sheet of paper, tell what changes the writer made.

1. The planet mars is more like earth than any other planet. Mars has polar caps that probably are of ice and snow. The caps get larger in the winter and slowly melt in the summer. Scientists thinks that Mars has an atmosphere. It is denser than Earth's atmosphere. The planet Venus has an atmosphere, too. During the day, the surface of Mars would be comfortably warm, but at night it became bitterly cold. There are no oceans! There is much less water on Mars than on Earth. The humidity of Mars is about the same as that of a desert on Earth. Living beings exactly like humans could not live on Mars. However, scientist believe there is plant life on the planet.

2. The planet Mars is more like Earth than any other planet. Like Earth, Mars has polar caps that probably are of ice and snow. Those caps get larger in the winter and slowly melt in the summer. Scientists think that Mars has an atmosphere. However, that atmosphere is denser than Earth's. During the day, the surface of Mars becomes comfortably warm, but at night it becomes bitterly cold. There are no oceans on Mars. In fact, there is much less water on Mars than on Earth. The humidity of Mars is about the same as that of a desert on Earth. Although living beings exactly like humans could not live on Mars, scientists believe there is plant life on the planet.

VOCABULARY BUILDER
Deciding Between Commonly Confused Words

Writers often confuse certain words because those words look or sound so much alike. When you use these words in your writing, be careful. Make sure you are writing the words you mean to use.

Decide which word in parentheses would correctly complete each of the following sentences. Use a dictionary if you need help. Write your answers on a separate sheet of paper.

1. Everyone came to the meeting (except, accept) Jill.

2. The bus (past, passed) him by without stopping.

3. I really (wonder, wander) if the sun will ever shine again.

4. Which team do you think will (loose, lose) Saturday's game?

5. Mr. Clemson (quiet, quite, quit) his job as a chicken plucker.

6. He loves to eat chocolate-covered bananas for (desert, dessert).

7. He can eat more apples (then, than) anyone I know.

8. She broke the (led, lead) on her pencil by pressing too hard.

9. The teacher insisted on Sylvia's (presence, presents) in English class.

10. (They're, Their, There) tickets were being held at the box office.

1. except
2. passed
3. wonder
4. lose
5. quit
6. dessert
7. than
8. lead
9. presence
10. Their

Chapter

15 Review

Summary Have students use the summary to outline the main idea and details of the chapter.

Summary

When you revise a draft, you make sure that everything is clearly written.
When you edit a draft, you correct mistakes in facts, grammar, usage, and mechanics.
Proofreading helps you mark mistakes in a piece of writing.
You can use proofreading marks to indicate where corrections need to be made.
Verb tenses should be consistent in writing.
Transitional words link paragraphs and make the relationships between paragraphs clear.

proofread

edit

content

mechanics

1. proofread
2. content
3. mechanics
4. edit

More Vocabulary Review is provided in the Classroom Resource Binder.

Vocabulary Review

Match each term in the box with its meaning.
Write your answers on a separate sheet of paper.

1. to mark errors in a piece of writing

2. the ideas in a piece of writing

3. spelling and punctuation in writing

4. to prepare a piece of writing by correcting mistakes in facts, grammar, usage, and mechanics

Chapter Quiz

1. Revising helps make sure that your ideas are clear.

2. Editing will correct mechanical errors and help make an essay easier for readers to understand.

3. When editing, look for mistakes in spelling and punctuation.

Chapter Quiz

Complete the following items. Write your answers on a separate sheet of paper.

1. What is the purpose of revising your essays?

2. What is the purpose of editing your essays?

3. What are two types of mistakes to look for when you edit?

4. What are three types of mistakes to look for when you proofread?

5. Why is it a good idea to avoid shifting verb tenses within an essay?

6. What are two ways transitions can be used in an essay?

▶ **Test Tip**
Keep a positive attitude. Tell yourself that you will do well.

4. Answers will vary. Possible responses: spelling errors, missing punctuation, and capitalization errors.

5. Shifts in verb tenses in an essay are confusing. Readers cannot follow the order of events.

6. In an essay, transitional words are used to link sentences and to link paragraphs.

Critical Thinking

What are three questions to ask yourself about your essay when you edit it? Write your answer on a separate sheet of paper.

Critical Thinking Answers will vary. Possible response: Check to make sure that students understand that they should ask themselves if they have spelled words correctly, resolved fragments and run-ons, and used the proper punctuation marks.

Writing Activity

On a separate sheet of paper, write the final copy of your essay. By now, you will have a revised and edited rough draft. In the final copy, be sure to include any changes and corrections that you think need to be made. Write the title of your essay at the top of the first page.

Writing Activity Answers will vary. You may wish to give students two grades for their essays: one on content and the other on grammar and mechanics.

Unit 4 Review

Standardized Test Preparation This unit review follows the format of many standardized tests. A Scantron® sheet is provided in the Classroom Resource Binder.

Read each of the following items. On a separate sheet of paper, write the letter that best answers each one.

1. An essay must have at least
   A. three paragraphs.
   B. four paragraphs.
   C. five paragraphs.
   D. six paragraphs.

2. The main point of an essay is first stated in
   A. the first paragraph of the body.
   B. the topic sentence.
   C. the supporting details.
   D. the concluding paragraph.

3. Which of the following could be used as the topic for a whole essay?
   A. staying out too late
   B. watching too much TV
   C. ways teens talk with their parents
   D. eating junk food instead of meals

4. When you revise an essay, you should
   A. make sure your ideas are clear.
   B. check the content of your writing.
   C. make sure you included supporting details.
   D. all of the above

5. Which question should you ask when checking the mechanics of an essay?
   A. Is there a thesis statement?
   B. Do the sentences in each paragraph support the topic sentence?
   C. Do the sentence subjects agree with the verbs?
   D. Does the conclusion restate the thesis?

6. To show the links between paragraphs in an essay,
   A. shift verb tenses.
   B. use transitional words.
   C. change the point of view of the narrator.
   D. edit for mistakes in style.

Writing Activity Answers will vary. Check students' work for organization and logical support for their thesis statements.

Critical Thinking

How is an essay like a paragraph? On a separate sheet of paper, make a list of the similarities and differences.

WRITING ACTIVITY On a separate sheet of paper, make an outline for an essay that you might write about a topic that interests you. Pick a topic that you already know a lot about. In your outline include at least three paragraphs that would support your thesis statement.

Critical Thinking Answers will vary. Possible response:

Essay	Paragraph
long, thesis statement, introduction, body, conclusion, supporting details	short, topic sentence, introduction, body, conclusion, supporting details

Unit 5 ▷ Practical Writing

People from all over the world send letters to one another. Post offices handle millions of pieces of mail every day. What types of everyday writing do people send through the regular mail and e-mail?

Caption Accept all reasonable responses. Possible answer: Everyday writing that people send through the mail and through e-mail include advertisements, catalogs, memos, bills, reminders, and so on.

Letters can be a record of a person's experiences, thoughts, and feelings.

Virginia Woolf (1882–1941) wrote many novels, essays, and letters. Woolf's novel To the Lighthouse *is about her own childhood.* Three Guineas *and the essay* "A Room of One's Own" *show her strong interest in women's issues. Most of Woolf's novels are set in London, where she lived and worked.*

To help students tap their prior knowledge of the chapter topic, see the **Chapter Project** in the Classroom Resource Binder.

Learning Objectives

- Write a friendly letter.
- Write a formal business letter.
- Properly address an envelope.

Chapter 16 ➤ Writing Letters

Words to Know

format	the plan, style, or layout of a piece of writing
ZIP code	a postal code designed to speed up mail service by assigning special numbers to each area of the country
abbreviation	a shortened form of a word

16-1 ➤ Writing a Friendly Letter

Perhaps you have friends or relatives who live far away. One way to keep in touch with them is by writing a letter. A friendly letter is a letter written to someone you know. A friendly letter does the following things.

1. It lets the person know you are thinking of him or her.

2. It allows you to tell the person what has been happening to you.

3. It lets the person know that you would like to hear from him or her, too.

As with any other form of writing, a letter should express your thoughts clearly to your readers.

People expect letters to be written in a certain way. Even friendly letters have a proper **format**, or plan or style, that should be followed.

The Parts of a Friendly Letter

215 S.E. 49th Street
Portland, OR 97201
September 8, 2002

} Heading

Dear Terry,

} Salutation

Let your friends and relatives know you are thinking of them.

I hope you're happy with your new job in California. You certainly sounded excited in your last letter. We all miss you here, but we're glad you like your new home.

Tell them what has been happening to you.

I have some news for you. I finally got my driver's license. Yes, I know I had to take the test five times, but I passed it last week. Those driving lessons that you suggested really paid off. Believe it or not, I can even back out of the driveway without hitting anything. When you come for a visit, I'll take you for a ride.

I'm still working at the Burger Barn. Last week they made all the employees dress up in animal costumes. Did I ever feel silly! You should've seen me dressed up like a chicken.

} Body

Encourage your friends and relatives to write.

I would love to hear all about your new home and your new job. Have you met any interesting people? Don't forget to write.

Your friend,

} Closing

Carol

} Signature

When you look at the sample of the friendly letter, you can see it has five parts.

The Heading
The heading tells where you are and when you are writing. It usually appears in the upper right corner of the page and has three lines. The first two lines give your address, and the third gives the date. Notice the correct capitalization and punctuation in the sample.

Sometimes, if your letter is very informal, you can leave off the address in the heading. Always be sure to include the date.

The Salutation
The salutation is a greeting. It begins on the left side of the paper. In a friendly letter, the salutation is followed by a comma. Be sure to capitalize the first letter of the salutation.

"Dear _____," is the most common greeting. However, in a friendly letter, you can use any greeting you wish. For example, you can use, *My dear Susan* or *Hi Jill.*

The Body
In this part of the letter, you talk to your friend or relative. Remember your paragraphing skills here. Just like any other time, you should be writing in clear paragraphs.

The Closing
The closing is the way you sign off. It is written in the lower right of the page below the body of your letter. It begins with a capital letter and is followed by a comma.

The Writing Process

How can writing a draft of your letter help you write the final version? (See The Writing Process, pages WP14–WP19.)

You may use any closing you like in a friendly letter. These are some commonly used closings.

Sincerely,	Love,
Sincerely yours,	As always,
Yours truly,	Your friend,

The Signature

The signature ends your letter. It is written below the closing. Use only your first name if it is a letter to a close friend or relative. Otherwise, it is best to write both your first and last names so that there is no question about who wrote the letter.

Practice A

Brush Up on the Basics

The names of streets, highways, cities, states, and countries begin with a capital letter. (See Capitalization 9–11 in the Reference Guide.)

1. a
2. a
3. b
4. b
5. a

Each of the following pairs shows the same part of a friendly letter. One item has been written correctly. The other item has errors. On a separate sheet of paper, write the letter of the correct item.

1. **a.** 555 Elm Street
   Lakeview, WA 98003
   August 1, 2002

   b. 555 Elm Street
   Lakeview Wa 98003
   August 1, 2002

2. **a.** Sincerely yours,
   Lynn

   b. sincerely yours!
   Lynn

3. **a.** dear Uncle Elmer:

   b. Dear Uncle Elmer,

4. **a.** February 5, 2002
   4141 Hawk Drive
   Sunnyside, AZ 85201

   b. 4141 Hawk Drive
   Sunnyside, AZ 85201
   February 5, 2002

5. **a.** Yours truly,
   Jan

   b. Yours Truly, Jan

Practice B

Show that you know the format of a friendly letter. On a separate sheet of paper, write a letter to Aunt Ruth. Use the following items as a guide.

1. the heading

2. the salutation

3. the body (You do not have to write the letter now. Just draw lines to represent the body.)

4. the closing

5. the signature

Sample responses:

1. 555 Elm Street
   Lakeview, WA 98003
   August 1, 2001

2. Dear Aunt Ruth,

3. (Students draw lines on their paper where the body of the letter would be written.)

4. Love,

5. (Students sign their names.)

Answers will vary. Check to make sure that students have written a well-developed letter that follows the friendly letter format.

Portfolio Project

Write the body of the letter to Aunt Ruth. Explain that you just started a new job at the Wonderworld Amusement Park. Tell her about the things you do, an interesting person you work with, and how you like your job. Be sure to write in paragraphs, and follow the format of the sample letter.

16-2 ▶ Writing a Business Letter

You will probably do business by mail many times. Perhaps you will order a product or complain about a product to a manufacturer. Perhaps you will write to a business as a part of your job or write to request information.

A business letter should be businesslike. That means it should be neatly typed, if possible. A business letter is formal, and so it must follow a specific format.

English and Technology

Many word-processing programs will format a letter for you. All you need to do is insert your information.

See *Pacemaker® Computer Literacy* for more information about desktop publishing.

When writing a business letter, follow these guidelines.

1. Use standard-sized ($8\frac{1}{2}$" x 11") paper.

2. Type the letter on a computer, if possible. If not possible, write neatly in blue or black ink.

3. Write on only one side of the paper.

4. Follow the format shown below.

The Six Parts of a Business Letter

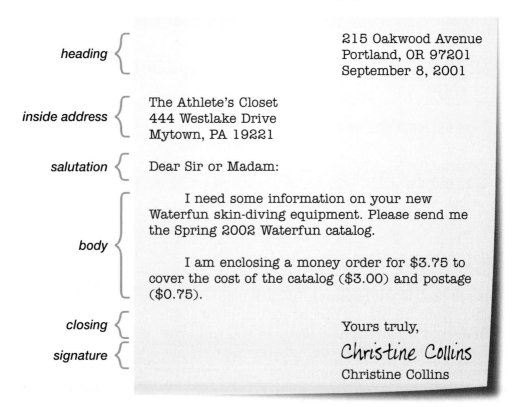

heading {
215 Oakwood Avenue
Portland, OR 97201
September 8, 2001

inside address {
The Athlete's Closet
444 Westlake Drive
Mytown, PA 19221

salutation {
Dear Sir or Madam:

body {
I need some information on your new Waterfun skin-diving equipment. Please send me the Spring 2002 Waterfun catalog.

I am enclosing a money order for $3.75 to cover the cost of the catalog ($3.00) and postage ($0.75).

closing {
Yours truly,

signature {
Christine Collins
Christine Collins

A business letter can also be done in block style, as shown below. Use block style only when the letter is typed. In block style, all parts of the business letter begin at the left margin. The paragraphs are not indented. There are two spaces between paragraphs.

Block-Style Business Letter

The Athlete's Closet
444 Westlake Drive
Mytown, PA 19221
September 15, 2001

Ms. Christine Collins
215 Oakwood Avenue
Portland, OR 97201

Dear Ms. Collins:

We are happy to send you the Spring 2002 Waterfun catalog. We are also enclosing an order blank so you can order more products.

You will also be receiving, free of charge, a copy of the new book for skin divers called <u>Underwater Adventures</u>. Enjoy the book and remember us when you need equipment.

Very truly yours,

Sonia Miller

Sonia Miller
Sales Manager

SM:mj

The salutation of a business letter includes the title and the last name of the person to whom you are writing. It is followed by a colon. Here are some examples.

Dear Mr. West:

Dear Ms. Johnson:

If the name of the person or persons to whom you are writing is unknown, you have several choices. Here are some examples.

Dear Sir:

Dear Madam:

Gentlemen:

Ladies:

Dear Sir or Madam:

To whom it may concern:

Another choice is to use the person's title, as in the following example.

Dear Sales Manager:

Notice that the salutation in a business letter is followed by a colon (:).

The signature in a business letter is usually typed four spaces below the closing. This method leaves room for a written signature directly under the closing. The signature should always be written by hand, even in a typed letter. Do not use a title such as *Mr.*, *Ms.*, or *Mrs.* in a signature.

Here is an example.

Yours truly,

Barbara Bixley

Barbara Bixley

You will notice some added letters at the bottom of the sample business letter from Sonia Miller on page 235. The letters read *SM:mj.* Notations like these are used when the letter is typed by someone other than the writer. In this case, Sonia Miller (SM) had her secretary Mark Jones (mj) type the letter.

Practice A

On a separate sheet of paper, use the block-style business letter on page 235 to answer the following questions. The first question has been done for you as an example.

1. Who wrote the letter?   *Sonia Miller*

2. What is the name of her company?

3. To whom was the letter written?

4. When was the letter written?

5. What was the inside address?

6. What closing was used?

7. What position does the letter writer have with the company?

8. Did the letter writer type her own letter?

2. The Athlete's Closet

3. Christine Collins

4. September 15, 2001

5. Ms. Christine Collins
   215 Oakwood Avenue
   Portland, OR 97201

6. Very truly yours,

7. Sales Manager

8. no

Practice B

Read the following advertisement. On a separate sheet of paper, write a business letter ordering an item described in the ad. Save the letter.

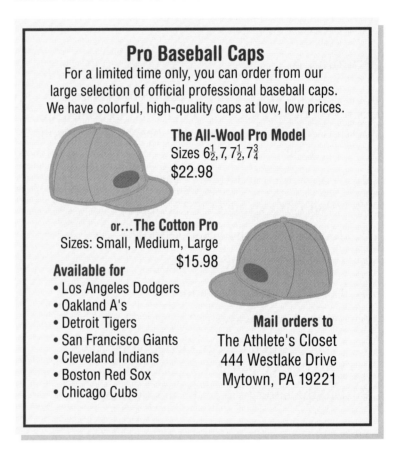

Pro Baseball Caps

For a limited time only, you can order from our large selection of official professional baseball caps. We have colorful, high-quality caps at low, low prices.

The All-Wool Pro Model
Sizes $6\frac{1}{2}, 7, 7\frac{1}{2}, 7\frac{3}{4}$
$22.98

or...**The Cotton Pro**
Sizes: Small, Medium, Large
$15.98

Available for
- Los Angeles Dodgers
- Oakland A's
- Detroit Tigers
- San Francisco Giants
- Cleveland Indians
- Boston Red Sox
- Chicago Cubs

Mail orders to
The Athlete's Closet
444 Westlake Drive
Mytown, PA 19221

Be sure to include all of the necessary information in your letter so that you will get the product you want.

16-3 ▸ Addressing the Envelope

It is important that you correctly address the envelope for your letter. Notice the format of the addressed envelope on the next page.

return address {
Mark Lee
2929 Lincoln Avenue
Westmont, NY 10013

main address {
Mr. Bill West
140 Maywood Road
Boise, ID 83701

1. The return address is your address. It goes in the upper left corner. This part is important in case the mail has to be returned to you.

2. The main address is the name and address of the person to whom you are writing. It goes in the lower-right quarter of the envelope.

   Be sure to include the **ZIP code**. The ZIP code is the postal code designed to speed up mail service in the United States. Without a ZIP code, the letter will be returned to you. If you do not know the ZIP code, call the post office and ask or look it up on the U.S. Postal Service's website.

Also, use the post office's **abbreviation** for a state's name. An abbreviation is a shortened form of a word. A list of U.S. Postal Service abbreviations is listed on page 240. Notice that they are written in capital letters and do not need periods.

3. Put a postage stamp in the upper right corner of the envelope. Be sure you have the correct amount of postage.

Use waterproof ink on the outside of your envelope.

Think About It

Why is it important to include the return address on an envelope?

States and Their Postal Abbreviations		
Alabama AL	Kentucky KY	North Dakota ND
Alaska AK	Louisiana LA	Ohio OH
Arizona AZ	Maine ME	Oklahoma OK
Arkansas AR	Maryland MD	Oregon OR
California CA	Massachusetts MA	Pennsylvania PA
Colorado CO	Michigan MI	Rhode Island RI
Connecticut CT	Minnesota MN	South Carolina SC
Delaware DE	Mississippi MS	South Dakota SD
District of Columbia DC	Missouri MO	Tennessee TN
	Montana MT	Texas TX
Florida FL	Nebraska NE	Utah UT
Georgia GA	Nevada NV	Vermont VT
Hawaii HI	New Hampshire NH	Virginia VA
Idaho ID	New Jersey NJ	Washington WA
Illinois IL	New Mexico NM	West Virginia WV
Indiana IN	New York NY	Wisconsin WI
Iowa IA	North Carolina NC	Wyoming WY
Kansas KS		

What is the postal abbreviation for your state?

Practice A

(Students write their name and address in the upper left-hand corner of the envelope.)

Miss Wanda Webster

444 Wexler Way

Williams, WY 83001

(Students draw a picture of a stamp in the upper right corner of the envelope.)

Place a sheet of paper on your desk. Draw a rectangle the size of a business envelope, which is about 4" x $9\frac{1}{4}$". Address the envelope as if it contained a letter to Miss Wanda Webster, who lives at 444 Wexler Way, in Williams, Wyoming. The ZIP code there is 83001. Use your own name and address for a return address, and draw a picture of a postage stamp. Use the chart above to find the correct state abbreviation.

Folding the business letter.
Fold your letter in thirds, following these steps.

1. Lay the letter on a desk, face up.

2. Fold the bottom of the sheet up about one-third of the way, and crease it.

3. Then, fold the top down to within one-half inch of the bottom crease, and crease it again.

4. Holding the letter at the top crease, put it in a business envelope.

Folding a friendly letter.
You may fold a friendly letter the same way as a business letter, or you may fold it in this way.

1. Lay the letter on a desk, face up.

2. Fold the bottom of the sheet up to within one-half inch of the top, and crease it.

3. Then, fold the letter in thirds, folding the sides in toward the middle.

4. Put the letter in a small envelope so that the receiver can start reading the letter as soon as it unfolds.

Practice B

Fold the business letter you wrote in Practice B on page 238. Address a business envelope for the letter, and place the folded letter in the envelope.

Check to make sure that students have accurately addressed their envelopes.

WRITING WITH STYLE
Writing a Business Letter

Which letter below would someone be more likely to answer? Why? Point out the problems with the letter you did not choose.

Letter A

Dear Pacific Comic Book Company,

I read that you were going to have a comic book show here. Do you know how I can get tickets? I have been collecting comic books since I was 12. Will there be any old Superman comics at the show?

From Jack Turner

Letter B

1000 West Elm Street
Lansing, MI 48901
June 4, 2001

Pacific Comic Book Company
P.O. Box 771
Seattle, WA 98101

Dear Sir or Madam:

According to your advertisement in the May issue of *Collectors' World* magazine, you will be sponsoring a comic book show in Lansing this summer. I would appreciate more information on that show. When and where will it be held? How much will tickets cost? Where might I purchase the tickets?

Please send me any information about your show. If possible, include a list of the comic books you will be showing.

Very truly yours,

Jack Turner

Jack Turner

VOCABULARY BUILDER
Using Words in the World of Finance

The words in italic type in the sentences below are commonly used when talking about business and finance.

Read each word as it is used in a sentence. On a separate sheet of paper, match each word with its definition. Use a dictionary if you need help.

1. The Markam Shoe Company sent me an *invoice* after I received the shoes.

2. We planned to *rent* a house at the beach for the weekend.

3. Before they moved into the apartment, they signed a *lease*.

4. The company sent out a *catalog* showing the spring line.

5. Harold sent a $10 *money order* to pay for a new pair of pants.

6. Hannah decided the car was too *expensive*.

1. invoice = b
2. rent = c
3. lease = e
4. catalog = f
5. money order = d
6. expensive = a

Definitions

a. costly

b. a detailed bill giving the prices of goods sent

c. payment made for use of something that belongs to another person

d. a written order that a certain sum of money be paid to a certain person

e. a contract allowing someone to use property in return for rent

f. a book or list of items for sale

Summary Have students use the summary to outline the main idea and details of the chapter.

Summary

A friendly letter has five parts: heading, salutation, body, closing, and signature.
A business letter has six parts: heading, inside address, salutation, body, closing, and signature.
The salutation in a business letter is always followed by a colon (:).
The main address is written or typed in the lower right quarter of an envelope. The return address is in the upper left corner. The stamp is placed in the upper right corner.
Use state postal abbreviations and ZIP codes when addressing envelopes.
Fold a business letter in thirds and put it in a business envelope for mailing.

ZIP code
format
abbreviation

1. format
2. ZIP code
3. abbreviation

More Vocabulary Review is provided in the Classroom Resource Binder.

Vocabulary Review

Complete each sentence with a term from the box. Write your answers on a separate sheet of paper.

1. One _____ for a business letter is the block style.

2. The part of an address that helps the post office deliver a letter is the _____.

3. The post office uses an _____, or shortened form, for each state's name.

Chapter Quiz

Complete the following items. Write your answers on a separate sheet of paper.

1. What are the five parts of a friendly letter?

2. What two things does the heading of a friendly letter tell?

3. What punctuation would you use in the salutation of a friendly letter?

4. What punctuation would you use in the salutation of a business letter?

5. List two ways in which a business letter is different from a friendly letter.

6. What is the format of a block style business letter?

7. What is the return address? Where does it go on an envelope?

Critical Thinking

When would you write a friendly letter? When would you write a business letter? Write your answer on a separate sheet of paper.

Critical Thinking Answers will vary. Possible response: You would write a friendly letter to thank someone for a gift or to tell someone about what has been happening to you recently. You would write a business letter to order a product or complain about a product.

▶ **Test Tip**
When you are asked to remember the parts of something, try to picture the whole thing as well as the parts.

Chapter Quiz

1. The five parts of a friendly letter are the heading, salutation, body, closing, and signature.

2. The heading of a friendly letter tells where you are and when you are writing.

3. A comma is used with the salutation of a friendly letter.

4. A colon is used with the salutation of a business letter.

5. A business letter is more formal than a friendly letter; it also has an inside address.

6. In block style, all parts of a business letter begin at the left margin.

7. The return address is the sender's address and appears in the upper left-hand corner of an envelope.

Writing Activity

On a separate sheet of paper, write a friendly letter to someone who would like to hear from you. Perhaps you have a friend who moved away. Maybe you have a relative you have not talked to in a while.

Writing Activity For this activity, check to make sure that students have included all the parts of a friendly letter and that they have a well-written and well-developed letter.

The same skills you use for writing essays in school can help you get a job.

Studs Terkel (born 1912) was a Chicago newspaper reporter. He also wrote exciting and informative books based on his interviews with people. Hundreds of people told him their memories of having no job during the Great Depression for his book Hard Times. *In* Working, *he wrote about the everyday working lives of all different kinds of people.*

To help students tap their prior knowledge of the chapter topic, see the **Chapter Project** in the Classroom Resource Binder.

Learning Objectives

- Write a letter of application.
- Write a résumé.
- Fill out a job application.

Chapter 17 / Writing to Get a Job

Words to Know

inquire	to ask about something
qualify	to be suited; to have the necessary training
application	a form with questions that a person must answer when applying for a job
reference	a person who can give information about someone else
interview	a meeting between a job seeker and an employer during which questions are asked and answered
résumé	an account of a person's education, experience, and qualifications

17-1 / Writing a Letter of Application

Sooner or later, almost everyone applies for a job. Job hunting most often means having a personal interview with a employer. Job hunting also usually calls for some writing. Your goal in job hunting, of course, is landing a job. Therefore, you will want to put your best foot forward, in both your interview and in any written items.

In Chapter 16, you worked on writing letters. You wrote friendly letters and business letters. Sometimes, applying for a job means writing a letter to an employer. Perhaps you have seen a job ad in a newspaper that explains that anyone interested in the job should **inquire**, or ask about the job, by mail. Perhaps you know you would like to work at a certain beach resort this summer. You would probably write a letter asking if there will be any jobs available for which you **qualify**, or are suited.

When you write a letter of **application**, you will use the business letter format. An application is a form with questions you must answer when applying for a job. Read the following sample letter of application. Notice the type of information that is included.

350 West Beach Drive
Juniper Beach, CA 97001
April 24, 2001

Kelly Long
Forest Glen Kennel
83 Lake Street
Juniper Beach, CA 97001

Dear Ms. Long:

Name the position that interests you.

  I am interested in applying for a job as a dog groomer and kennel assistant.

Indicate your educational background and availability.

  I will be graduating from Mission High School in June, and I will then be available for full-time work. Until then, I could work after school and on weekends.

Give a short summary of your experience and qualifications.

  I have had a dog of my own since I was ten, and I have always taken full responsibility for its care. My dog is a long-coated husky, so I am experienced at brushing, bathing, and general grooming. In addition, I have taken care of other people's pets when the owners were away on vacation. I would be happy to provide you with references. I do love animals and enjoy caring for them.

Ask for an interview.

  May I call you to arrange an interview?

Sincerely,

Diane Elliot

Diane Elliot

Notice the information provided and the questions asked in the letter.

- In the first paragraph, Diane asked about a specific job.

- In the second paragraph, she let the employer know what kind of work schedule she could handle.

- In the third paragraph, she sold herself just a little. Do not be afraid to tell about your good points. She described her experience and qualifications and offered references. A **reference** is a person who can give information about someone else.

- In the fourth paragraph, she requested an **interview**. An interview is a meeting between a job seeker and an employer during which questions are asked and answered.

Brush Up on the Basics

Make sure to use a comma after the closing in a letter. (See Punctuation 13 in the Reference Guide.)

The tone of the letter was friendly, yet businesslike. The letter gave a brief explanation of Diane's qualifications. Letters of application should not be long. An interested employer will contact the writer for more information. If the letter is too long, a potential employer may not take the time to read it.

Practice

Read the job ads on page 250. On a separate sheet of paper, write a letter expressing interest in one of the jobs. Be sure to give a brief explanation of your qualifications.

Answers will vary. Check to make sure that students present qualifications that would match the ad.

(Practice continues on next page.) ⇒

Playground Activities Director

Must be good with children of all ages. Should be creative and interested in games and sports. Job involves organizing summer activities. No experience is necessary, but previous work with children is preferred. Contact: Sue Hall, Elk Public Parks, P.O. Box 222, Elk, VT 05600.

Think About It

How can brainstorming about your interests and talents help you answer a job ad?

Video Store Clerk

Must be interested in films and be good at handling money and dealing with the public. Should have some experience setting up video equipment and should understand basic video recorders. Send letter of application to: William Palmeri, Star Video, 752 Roseway Blvd., Sherwood, NH 03988.

Cashier

Crestview Cinema needs a box-office cashier for evenings and weekends. Must be good with numbers and at handling money. Previous experience working with the public preferred. Contact: Mr. Welch, Crestview Cinema, 300 Main St., Crestview, WA 98771.

17-2 Writing a Résumé

A **résumé** is an important tool when you begin job-hunting. A résumé is a short account of a person's education, experience, and skills. It gives an employer a look at a job applicant's qualifications.

Résumés follow a specific format. Look at the sample résumé on page 251.

Kate Gilbert
4323 Old Orchard Road
Seattle, WA 98101
(206) 555-2213
kgilbert@email.com

Education   Pacific High School
                   Seattle, WA
                   Graduated June 2001

Work Experience

5/01–9/01   Lifeguard. Bowman Park Pool, Seattle. Supervised
             children and adults in park pool. Operated cash
             register to collect swim fees. Managed locker room,
             towels, and pool equipment.

6/00–9/01   Record Store Clerk. New Day Record Store,
             14 River Mall, Seattle. General salesperson.
             Operated cash register and handled money.

6/99–9/00   Babysitter. Provided part-time summer child care
             for Mrs. Barbara Moss, 302 Canyon Dr., Seattle.

Community Activities

1/01–   Volunteer. Meals for the Homeless Program,
present   Seattle. Spend three to five hours each week
             serving meals at community center.

6/99–9/00   Volunteer Guide. Seattle City Zoo. Led tour groups
             and explained zoo exhibits.

Skills   Type 45 WPM
                   Hold Red Cross Lifesaving Certificate

References   Available upon request

There are certain things you should notice about the résumé.

❏ The applicant's name, address, phone number, and e-mail address are provided at the top of the résumé.

❏ Categories are listed on the left, and information is given on the right.

❏ The applicant's most recent experiences are listed first.

❏ All job experiences and volunteer work are listed. Even unpaid jobs can be impressive credits.

❏ References may or may not be listed on the résumé. If you decide to list references, give two or three and provide a name, a position, and an address for each one. For example, a reference listing might look like this.

> Ms. Sara Wade
> General Manager
> New Day Record Store
> 14 River Mall
> Seattle, WA 98101

Former employers, volunteer supervisors, fellow workers, coaches, and teachers all make good references. You should always get permission from a person before you use his or her name as a reference.

English and Technology
Make sure you include your computer skills on your résumé.

See *Pacemaker® Computer Literacy* for more information about developing computer skills.

Practice A

Answers will vary. Check to make sure that students have listed all the required information for their references.

Think of at least three people you know whom you could use as references. On a separate sheet of paper, list their names, positions, and addresses.

Practice B

On a separate sheet of paper, write a résumé for yourself. This résumé will be a useful tool when you look for a job. Use the résumé on page 251 as a guide. Because your experience is different from Kate Gilbert's, your résumé will have different information but a similar format.

Answers will vary. Check students' résumés for accuracy of information presented.

17-3 ▶ Filling Out a Job Application

When you apply for a job, you will probably have to fill out an application. Job applications vary. Some ask for more information than others. Some are quite long and others are very brief. It is important to read all of the questions on a job application carefully. It is a good idea to look at all of them quickly before you even begin to answer. Fill out applications in ink. Make sure you understand the questions before you begin writing so that your application will be neat. Take special care with spelling, punctuation, and capitalization. Take a list of information with you so that you will not have to look up addresses or try to remember dates. Remember that you are trying to make a good impression. You want the employer to notice your application. Your application should stand out because it shows care and effort—not because it is messy or incomplete.

Fill in every item on an application. If an item does not apply to you, write NA. This means that the item is "not applicable" to you.

The Writing Process

Why is it important for the spelling, punctuation, and capitalization on a job application to be correct? (See The Writing Process, pages WP32–WP35.)

The amount of room to write on a job application is often limited. Write within the space given. Print information, except where a signature is required, so that it is easy to read. There may not be room to list all of your job experiences. List more recent experiences and those you think are related to the job you are seeking.

Answer honestly, but do not forget anything that might be in your favor. This is not the time to be overly modest.

Practice A

Answers will vary. Check students' lists for inclusion of all pertinent information that they would need for filling out a job application.

Read the sample job application on page 255. On a separate sheet of paper, make a list of all the information you would take with you if you were going job hunting. This list should include previous paid and volunteer jobs with dates, addresses, phone numbers, and supervisors' names. Do not forget postal ZIP codes and telephone area codes. Also, include the address of the last school you attended. Some applications will ask for your Social Security number, so include that on your list. Write the names and addresses of at least three people whom you can list as references. Remember that you should always get permission from a person before using his or her name as a reference.

Practice B

Answers will vary. Check students' work for accuracy and for inclusion of reasons why they would be good candidates for the positions.

Think of a job that you would like to have. Reread the last part of the sample job application on page 255. On a separate sheet of paper, write the last part of a sample application explaining in two or three sentences why you think you would be good at the job you would really like to have.

Job Application
Lake of the Woods Summer Camp

Position: _Camp Cook_

Date: _4/24/01_

Name: _Jean_   _M._   _Perez_
    (First)   (Initial)   (Last)

Address: _201 Webster St._   _3A_
    (Number and Street)   (Apt. no.)

San Pedro   _CA_   _90731_
    (City)   (State)   (ZIP)

Phone Number: _(310) 555-8265_

Social Security #: _555-21-7810_

Date available for work: _6/14/01_

Previous jobs (paid and volunteer):

(Employer)	(Position held)	(Dates of employment)	(Reason for leaving)
Fred's Burgers	fry cook	6/99–present	NA
Long Hot Dogs	cook/clerk	6/98–9/98	school
Mrs. H. Wilson	babysitter	9/97–6/98	employer moved
Point Fermin Park	volunteer guide	6/97–9/97	school

Last year of education completed:

San Pedro High School, 1001 W. 15th St., San Pedro, CA 2001
(School)   (Address)   (Year completed)

Write two or three sentences explaining why you think you would be good at the job.

I like the outdoors and would be an enthusiastic member of the camp staff. My experience at Fred's Burgers and at Long Hot Dogs taught me to cook for large groups. I have also taken some classes in diet and nutrition at Harbor College.

WRITING WITH STYLE
Writing a Letter of Application

If you were an employer, which of the following people would you be more likely to call for an interview? Give the reasons for your choice.

1. Dear Mr. Chin,

I would like a job in your restaurant. I am trying to save enuf money to buy a car, and I think working in a restaurant would be fun. My friend Todd worked in your restaurant, and he liked the job a lot. I have never worked in a restaurant before, but I am sure I could do a good job. You can call me at 555-7562.

Thanks. Tim Tyler

2.
427 East Lincoln Drive
Denver, CO 80220
May 14, 2001

Oscar Chin
Snow Cap Café
602 Mountain Crest Road
Denver, CO 80220

Dear Mr. Chin:

Do you have a summer opening for a busboy at the Snow Cap Café? If you do, I would like to apply for the position.

I have worked with the public before as a clerk at Martin's Minute Market. I have a 3.6 grade-point average. I am very interested in the restaurant business to learn all I can.

Please let me know if we might schedule an interview. I can be reached by phone at 555-6210.

Sincerely,

Matt Woods

Matt Woods

VOCABULARY BUILDER
Using Words in the Job Market

A. On a separate sheet of paper, match each of the following terms with the correct definition.

1. application
2. career
3. employee
4. employer
5. interview

a. a face-to-face meeting
b. a chosen occupation
c. a person with a paid job
d. a written request for a job
e. a person who pays others to do a job

A. 1. d
2. b
3. c
4. e
5. a

B. 1. application
2. interview
3. employer
4. employee
5. career

B. Now, use the terms listed above to fill in the following blanks. Write your answers on a separate sheet of paper.

1. Sandy filled out an _____ for a job as a camp counselor.

2. Three days later, the camp director called Sandy for an _____.

3. The director asked Sandy for the name of a former _____ as a reference.

4. Sandy hoped that she would soon be an _____ of the Lake of the Woods Summer Camp.

5. Sandy is thinking about a future _____ in which she works with children.

C. 1. A botanist studies plants.
2. A cosmetologist gives beauty treatments.
3. A zoologist studies animals.
4. A journalist works on a newspaper or magazine staff.
5. A pharmacist prepares and sells medicines.

C. Many careers are described by words ending with the suffix *-ist*. For example, a person can become a *scientist* or a *dentist*. Use a dictionary to find out what work each of the following people do: (1) botanist, (2) cosmetologist, (3) zoologist, (4) journalist, and (5) pharmacist. Write your answers on a separate sheet of paper.

Chapter

17 ▷ Review

Summary Have students use the summary to outline the main idea and details of the chapter.

Summary

A letter for a job application follows the form of a business letter. It expresses your interest in a specific job. It also asks about openings and briefly describes your qualifications.

A résumé is an outline giving a short account of a person's background. A résumé includes a name, address, phone number, and e-mail address. It also lists a person's education, work experience, community activities, skills, and an offer of references.

Most job interviews require you to fill out a job application. Applications will differ, but they need to be filled out completely and neatly.

More Vocabulary Review is provided in the Classroom Resource Binder.

Vocabulary Review

Match each term in the box with its meaning. Write your answers on a separate sheet of paper.

qualify

résumé

application

interview

inquire

references

1. résumé
2. inquire
3. references
4. qualify
5. application
6. interview

1. an account of a person's education, experience, and qualifications

2. to ask about something

3. people who can give information about someone else

4. to be suited for

5. a form with questions to answer when applying for a job

6. the meeting of a job seeker and an employer when questions are asked

Chapter Quiz

Complete the following items. Write your answers on a separate sheet of paper.

1. What is a letter of application?

2. What are three things you might mention in a letter of application?

3. Why does a letter of application need to be brief?

4. What is the purpose of putting your work experience on a résumé?

5. Why might an employer want to talk to your references?

Critical Thinking

How can you make a good impression when you fill out a job application? Write your answer on a separate sheet of paper.

Critical Thinking Answers may vary. Possible answer: You can make a good impression on a job application by filling it out neatly and completely. It also needs to be well written, without any errors in spelling, etc.

Chapter Quiz

1. A letter of application indicates an applicant's interest in a job.

2. A letter of application names the job that interests you, your educational background, and a summary of your experience.

3. A letter of application needs to be short and to the point because an employer might not bother to read a letter that is too long.

4. Your work experience shows an employer whether you are qualified for a job.

5. References give additional information about your work experience and your potential as an employee.

Writing Activity

Choose a workplace where you would like to work. On a separate sheet of paper, write a letter of application and a résumé to help you get a job there. Use real information from your own life.

Writing Activity Encourage students to complete this exercise independently. Check students' work for content and writing errors.

Writers put all of their thoughts on paper.

Booker T. Washington *(1856–1915) was a leading African American teacher and writer. He founded the Tuskegee Institute, a college in Alabama. Washington spent his life working for civil rights for African Americans. He used his skills as a writer to put his thoughts on paper. He described his life and views in his autobiography,* Up From Slavery.

Extra Reading See the Pacemaker® Classics series for Booker T. Washington's *Up from Slavery.*

To help students tap their prior knowledge of the chapter topic, see the **Chapter Project** in the Classroom Resource Binder.

Learning Objectives

- Write a thank-you note.
- Write get-well wishes and express sympathy in notes.
- Write an invitation.
- Write complete, clear messages.
- Write effective bulletin board ads and classified ads.

Chapter 18 / Everyday Writing

Words to Know

communication	sending and receiving messages
sympathy	the act of sharing another's feelings; feeling sorry for another's suffering
acceptance	answering "yes" to an invitation
regrets	the polite refusal of an invitation
classified ad	a short newspaper advertisement arranged in a group, or class, with similar ads

18-1 / Writing Notes and Invitations

Communication is sending and receiving message's from someone. A note is an example of a short communication from one person to another. A note is usually informal. However, it has the same purpose as any other writing. Its purpose is to communicate the writer's message as clearly as possible.

At certain times, you will want to write a note. If someone gives you a present, it is appropriate to show your appreciation with a thank-you note. If someone invites you to an event, you may want to answer the invitation with a note. When friends are ill, notes can cheer them up. If someone you know has a death in the family, a sympathy note is appropriate.

Stores sell greeting cards that have messages. However, writing a few words of your own will make each card more personal. You can add your own touch to a greeting card as the writer did on page 262.

Date { February 5, 2001

Greeting { Dear Bev,

Happy Birthday { **HAPPY BIRTHDAY**

Personal message { I wish I could spend your birthday with you, but I'll be thinking of you.

Closing { Your friend,

Signature { Stan

Thank-You Notes

A thank-you note is, of course, a way of saying *Thanks!* You should thank someone for a gift or for doing something especially kind and thoughtful. If you are a guest in someone's home, it is thoughtful to say *Thank you.*

When someone sends or gives you a gift, it is very important to respond right away with a thank-you note. If the present came in the mail, a note is one way of letting the sender know that you received the gift. If you have been a guest in someone's home, you should respond with a thank-you note within a week of the visit.

When writing a note, remember your purpose. You want to say *Thank you* and let the person know that you appreciate his or her thoughtfulness. Aunt Rose sent Jill a sweater for her birthday. Read Jill's thank-you note on page 263. Notice that it looks similar to a friendly letter.

Think About It

How would a thank-you note to a friend differ from a thank-you note to a grandparent?

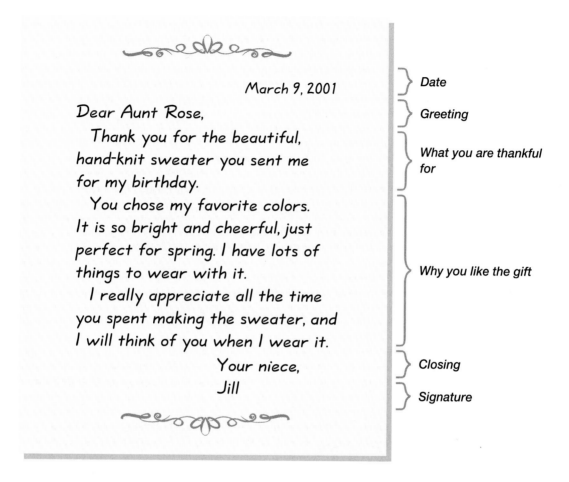

March 9, 2001 — Date

Dear Aunt Rose, — Greeting

Thank you for the beautiful, hand-knit sweater you sent me for my birthday. — What you are thankful for

You chose my favorite colors. It is so bright and cheerful, just perfect for spring. I have lots of things to wear with it.

I really appreciate all the time you spent making the sweater, and I will think of you when I wear it. — Why you like the gift

Your niece, — Closing

Jill — Signature

Notice that Jill did not only say *Thanks*. She also told her aunt how much she liked the present and what she liked about it.

A thank-you note after a visit would be similar. Always be specific. Pick out at least one thing that you especially enjoyed about your visit, and mention it to your host or hostess.

Practice A

On a separate sheet of paper, list three specific things that Jeff thanks Mrs. Wilson for in the note on page 264.

(Practice A continues on next page.) ⫸

(Practice A continued.)

Answers will vary. Students should mention three of the following: Jeff thanks Mrs. Wilson for inviting him to spend the holiday weekend with her family; for the wonderful meal she cooked; for an evening of traditions and songs; for the snow; and for making him feel at home.

December 28, 2001

Dear Mrs. Wilson,

Thank you so much for inviting me to spend the holiday weekend with your family. It would have been a rather lonely time in my apartment alone.

I have told all my friends about the wonderful meal you cooked. That was the biggest turkey I have ever seen! I am also glad I had a chance to be a part of some of your family's holiday traditions. It was especially fun singing with you.

You even arranged for snow to make my holiday visit complete! Thanks for everything. You know how to make a guest feel at home.

Sincerely yours,
Jeff Roth

Practice B

Answers will vary. Check students' work for inclusion of specific reasons and for following the format for writing thank-you notes.

Each of the following items on page 265 describes a situation that calls for a thank-you note. On a separate sheet of paper, choose one, and write the note. Remember to be specific about why you are thankful. Use the sample thank-you notes in this lesson as guides. Create any names and details you need to complete the note.

- You receive two tickets to a professional baseball game from your Uncle Harry. You take your friend with you to the game, and you are lucky enough to catch a foul ball.

- Your friend's family includes you on a trip to the beach. You spend the weekend in a cabin by the sea.

- For your birthday, your friend Jack gave you a compact disc you had been wanting. It was expensive and hard to find.

- Perhaps you really do owe someone a thank-you note for a gift or for a visit. You may write that person a note to complete this assignment.

Get-Well Notes and Sympathy Notes

People who are sick or injured usually spend a lot of time resting. They probably miss seeing their friends. You can cheer people up with notes. Most of all, you can let them know you are thinking of them.

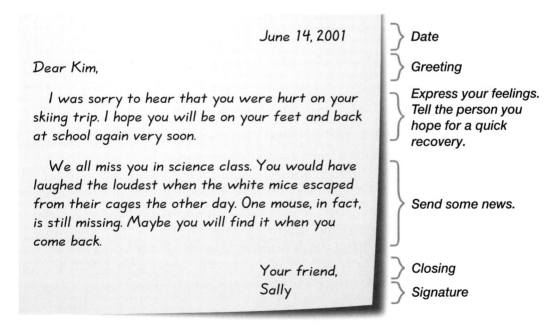

June 14, 2001 — Date

Dear Kim, — Greeting

I was sorry to hear that you were hurt on your skiing trip. I hope you will be on your feet and back at school again very soon. — Express your feelings. Tell the person you hope for a quick recovery.

We all miss you in science class. You would have laughed the loudest when the white mice escaped from their cages the other day. One mouse, in fact, is still missing. Maybe you will find it when you come back. — Send some news.

Your friend, — Closing
Sally — Signature

Sometimes, it is hard to know what to say when someone's friend or relative dies. However, it is important to let the person know that you care. The act of sharing feelings is called **sympathy**. A simple sympathy note can express your concern.

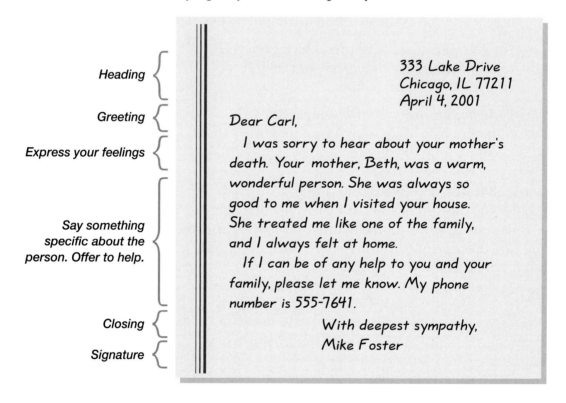

Heading

Greeting

Express your feelings

Say something specific about the person. Offer to help.

Closing

Signature

333 Lake Drive
Chicago, IL 77211
April 4, 2001

Dear Carl,

    I was sorry to hear about your mother's death. Your mother, Beth, was a warm, wonderful person. She was always so good to me when I visited your house. She treated me like one of the family, and I always felt at home.

    If I can be of any help to you and your family, please let me know. My phone number is 555-7641.

        With deepest sympathy,
        Mike Foster

Mike had not seen Carl for quite a while, but he wanted to let him know he cared. Mike included his address and phone number in the note so that Carl could contact him if he needed any help. There are three parts to this sympathy note: (1) Mike expressed his feelings, (2) he said something specific about why he liked Carl's mother, and (3) he offered to help.

Practice C

On a separate sheet of paper, choose one of the following situations, and write a note about it that expresses your feelings. Let your imagination supply any necessary details. Use the model get-well and sympathy notes in this lesson as guides.

- Your teacher, Mrs. Ward, is in the hospital after breaking her leg.

- Your friend's older brother was killed in an automobile accident. You have already talked to your friend and expressed your sympathy. Now, you want to write a note to his parents.

- Do you know anyone who is sick and would be cheered by a get-well note? Write that note for this assignment.

Answers will vary. Check students' get-well and sympathy notes for content and format.

Invitations

Are you planning a party? You might call people on the phone and invite them to your get-together. You can also invite people to your party by sending invitations. It is important to include all the details of the event in your invitation.

What do you need to let people know?

1. the kind of party it will be (Sometimes, it is a good idea to use the word *casual* or *formal* so that people know how to dress.)

2. the time and date of the party

3. where the party will take place

4. whether the guests should bring anything

5. write *RSVP* at the bottom of the invitation if you want people to tell you if they will come

The Writing Process

Why is it important to know your purpose for writing? Why is it important to know your audience? (See The Writing Process, pages WP14–WP15.)

The letters *RSVP* mean that people should respond with **acceptance** or **regrets**. When you reply with an acceptance, you are answering "yes" to an invitation. When you reply with regrets, you are politely refusing an invitation. Write your phone number after the RSVP. To cut down on the number of responses, you can write "RSVP—regrets only." Then, you can assume that anyone who does not call is coming to your party.

The letters RSVP are the first letters of the words in the French expression: *Repondez s'il vous plait.* In English this means "Respond, if you please."

You can buy printed invitations in a store. These usually have spaces for time, date, and place. Then, all you have to do is fill in the blanks. Make sure to add any other necessary information at the bottom of the invitation.

If you write your own invitations, you will use the same form as you did for the other notes in this lesson.

English and Technology

You can use a word-processing program to create unique invitations.

Date invitation is sent

Greeting

When and where

Other details

Phone number for acceptance or regrets

June 25, 2001

Dear Linda and Ted,

Joe and I are having our Fourth of July Celebration again this year. We hope you can come and join the group.

The party will be on Wednesday, July 4, from 4:00 P.M. until 10:00 P.M. at our house (431 Mill Street). We will provide the meats to barbeque. Please bring a salad or dessert to share with others. Dress casually and plan to stay late enough to see the fireworks display.

Your friend,
Kate Oliver

RSVP 555-1259

Kind of party

What to bring

Closing

Signature

Practice D

On a separate sheet of paper, use the model Fourth of July party invitation on page 268 to answer the following questions.

1. Who is giving the party?

2. When will the party be held?

3. Where will the party be held?

4. What kind of party is it?

5. What should Linda and Ted bring?

6. Should Linda wear a formal dress? Why or why not?

7. What phone number should Ted or Linda call with acceptance or regrets?

1. Joe and Kate Oliver
2. Wednesday, July 4, from 4:00 P.M. until 10:00 P.M.
3. At the Oliver's house, 431 Mill Street
4. Fourth of July barbeque
5. A salad or dessert
6. No. The invitation says to dress casually.
7. 555-1259

18-2 Making Sure Others Get Your Message

Fran is babysitting for Mrs. Betty Charles. At 7:00 P.M., her sister Anne calls with an important message. "Tell Betty," she says, "that I will not be able to pick her up tomorrow morning. Tell her that my car needs to go into the repair shop. I want her to pick me up at the Fourth Street Auto Garage at 10:00 A.M. If she has any questions, she can call me at 555-2291 before 8:00 tomorrow morning. If I do not hear from her, I will expect her at the garage."

Fran cannot depend on her memory to keep track of all that information. She will have to give Mrs. Charles a written message.

While her sister Anne talks, Fran takes brief notes, as you can see in the example on page 270.

> Can't pick you up, car in repair shop, pick her up—Fourth St. Auto Garage—10:00 A.M.—any questions, call 555-2291 before 8:00 A.M.

After Fran hangs up, she should write out the message to give to Mrs. Charles.

February 14   7:00 P.M.

Mrs. Charles,
Your sister Anne called. She cannot pick you up tomorrow morning as planned. Her car is in the repair shop. She needs you to pick her up at the Fourth Street Auto Garage at 10:00 A.M. If there is a problem with that, call her at 555-2291 before 8:00 A.M. tomorrow.

                                          Fran

Notice that the message includes the following items:

- the time and date of the message
- the name of the person who called
- what the caller wanted
- a number to call back
- Fran's name signed at the bottom

Practice A

On a separate sheet of paper, tell what information is missing from each of the messages on page 271.

1.

January 5
7:00 A.M.

Tom,

Your friend called. He said he needed to talk to you. Call him back.

Gina

1. The name of the person who called, a number to call back
2. The time and date of the message, a number to call back, the place of the meeting
3. To whom the note is written, a name signed at the bottom, a number to call back

2.

Dad,

Mr. Carlton said he would meet you at 8:00. He said it was important and that he needed to talk to you.

Chris

3.

March 5
4:00

I won't be home for dinner.

You may need to give someone a message that includes directions. Have you ever tried to tell someone how to get to your house? Sometimes, it is difficult to draw a map, or the directions must be given over the phone or in writing. It is important that the directions be clear and simple. Otherwise, you could cause someone to be completely lost.

Read these sample directions. Notice that

- they are short and simple.

- the directions for each turn are written on a new line.

- they are neat and easy to read.

> *Directions from school to 215 Oak Street.*
> *Go north two blocks on Maple Street*
> *to Stevens Avenue.*
> *Turn left on Stevens and go half a block*
> *to Oak Street.*
> *Turn right on Oak and go three blocks*
> *to 215 Oak Street.*

Practice B

On a separate sheet of paper, write directions telling someone how to get to your house from school or from some other place. Remember to keep the directions neat and simple, and write directions for each new turn on a separate line. It might help to jot down some notes or draw a simple map for reference before you begin to write the directions.

18-3 Writing an Advertisement

There may be times when you will have something to sell—perhaps something you no longer need or perhaps services for certain jobs. You can write ads to let people know that you have something to sell.

Many stores, restaurants, schools, and other public places have bulletin boards on which people place ads. A **classified ad** is a short newspaper advertisement arranged in a group, or class, with similar ads. Newspapers offer classified ad sections for which people pay to place their ads.

Practice A

Suppose that you have a 12-speed bicycle to sell. On a separate sheet of paper, list all of the details you think you should include in an advertisement. Create any details that you need.

Answers will vary. Check to make sure students' details would be appropriate for placing in an ad.

> Example: red color, boy's bike

Now that you have finished making the list, check to see if you included all of the details necessary to make a sale. Compare your list to the following one.

- Name the item (bike).

- Give important facts that will attract buyers (type, brand name, color, condition, extras, price).

- Tell how buyers can reach you (phone number).

Look at the ads below and on page 274. The first is a bulletin board ad for a bicycle. The second is a classified ad that is ready to be placed in a newspaper.

Bike for Sale

Boy's Smith 12-speed
Red frame, wide all-surface tires
Excellent condition
$125
Call Joe at 555-6201

Headline that catches attention and names item

Details

Condition
Price
Phone number

(Practice A continues on next page.) ⇢

Bike. Boy's Smith 12-speed, red, wide
tires, excl. cond., $125. 555-6201

People usually pay for classified ads by the line,
so they make their ads as short as possible. They use
abbreviations for some words. Notice the abbreviation
excl is used for *excellent*, and *cond* is used for *condition*.
That shortens the ad and saves money. The following
two ads offer a service rather than an item for sale.

Bulletin board ad:

Yardwork
Experienced yard care offered by two
high-school seniors.
Lawns mowed, shrubs trimmed,
flowers planted and maintained.
References
$15.00 per hour
Call Rick at 555-1387 or Dave at 555-9971

Classified ad:

Yardwork. Lawns, shrubs, flowers.
3 yrs. exp., references. $15/hr.
Rick, 555-1387, or Dave, 555-9971

What kind of work do Rick and Dave do? Have they ever done this kind of work before? How can people be sure they are good workers? How much do they charge? Where can they be reached? What abbreviations were used in the classified ad?

Practice B

On a separate sheet of paper, write your own ads. Write both a bulletin board ad and a classified ad. Sell either an item or your services for a certain job. Use the sample ads in this lesson as guides, and remember to include all of the necessary information.

Some suggested items:

> record or CD collection, scooter, computer, puppies, sports equipment

Some suggested services:

> babysitting, car washing, dog walking

Answers will vary. Check to make sure students' ads follow the format for either a bulletin board ad or a classified ad.

WRITING WITH STYLE
Choosing a Classified Ad

Which of the following classified ads would probably get a better response? Why?

1.

> Canoe. 16', fiberglass, with 2 life jackets and paddles. Like new. $200. 555-8711

Ad 1 is better. It lists a price. People would have a hard time calling about the canoe advertised in Ad 2 because it does not give a phone number.

2.

> Canoe. 16', fiberglass, with 2 life jackets and paddles. A great buy.

VOCABULARY BUILDER
Using Words in a Newspaper

Read the following paragraph. Then, use the newspaper terms in italic type to fill in the blanks.

> Our local newspaper just won an award for its fine *journalism*. The award came soon after the paper printed an exciting *feature* about the volunteers in our city. "Most Active Volunteers in 50 Years," the *headline* read. An *editorial* in the same *edition* of the paper praised the volunteers for their years of service.

1. An _____ is a piece of writing in a newspaper or magazine. It gives an opinion.

2. The work of gathering and reporting the news is called _____.

3. A _____ is a special article in a newspaper or magazine.

4. An _____ includes all the copies of a newspaper or magazine printed at one time.

5. The title of an article printed in large, bold type is the _____.

1. editorial
2. journalism
3. feature
4. edition
5. headline

Chapter

18 ▷ Review

Summary

Send a thank-you note if someone gives you a gift or does something thoughtful.

Be specific in a thank-you note. Tell what you liked or appreciated.

A thank-you note follows the same format as that of a friendly letter. Notes can also express get-well wishes or sympathy.

Written invitations must provide all necessary information.

Written messages need to be clear and simple. They should always include the date and the time.

Write directions simply and clearly. Start each new step of the directions on a new line.

Written ads let people know you have something to sell. You can put ads on bulletin boards, or you can place them in the classified section of a newspaper.

More Vocabulary Review is provided in the Classroom Resource Binder.

Vocabulary Review

Match each term in the box with its meaning.
Write your answers on a separate sheet of paper.

| classified ads |
| sympathy |
| acceptance |
| communication |
| regrets |

1. sending and receiving messages
2. polite refusal of an invitation
3. feeling sorry for another's suffering
4. short newspaper ads arranged in groups or classes
5. answering "yes" to an invitation

1. communication
2. regrets
3. sympathy
4. classified ads
5. acceptance

Chapter Quiz

1. You might send notes to say thank you, to invite someone to an event, or to send get-well wishes.

2. First, Carlo would thank his aunt for the thoughtful gift. He might also tell her that he has wanted that game for a long time and how much fun he and his friends have playing the game.

3. You would send a get-well note to someone who is sick or who is in a hospital.

Chapter Quiz

Complete the following items. Write your answers on a separate sheet of paper.

1. What are three situations in which you might send a note?

2. Carlo's aunt sent him an exciting computer game. What are two things that Carlo might include in his thank-you note?

3. When might you send a get-well note?

4. When might you send a note of sympathy?

5. What are four things to include on an invitation?

6. What does RSVP mean?

7. How is a classified ad different from a bulletin board ad?

▶ **Test Tip**
Look for key words in each question to help you find the answer. These key words tell you what to do.

4. You would send a note of sympathy to someone whose friend or relative has passed away.

5. An invitation includes the kind of party being given, the time and date of the party, where the party will be held, and whether guests should bring anything.

6. RSVP means that the people giving the party want to know whether you can come. You have to send your acceptance or regrets.

7. A classified ad is shorter than a bulletin board ad. It includes abbreviations because people pay for the ad by the number of lines in the ad. Bulletin board ads can usually be posted for free.

Critical Thinking

How can you write directions that will be easy to follow? Write your answer on a separate sheet of paper.

Critical Thinking Answers may vary. Possible answer: Directions can be easy to follow if they are clear and simple. Also each new step should start on a new line so they are easier to follow.

Writing Activity

Suppose you are having a birthday party. On a separate sheet of paper, write an invitation that tells your guests what they need to know. Then, write a thank-you note to one of the guests for the present you received.

Writing Activity Answers will vary. Check students' letters for both content and format for invitations and thank-you notes.

Unit 5 **Review**

Read each of the following items. On a separate sheet of paper, write the letter that best answers each one.

1. Unlike a friendly letter, a business letter has

   A. a heading.
   B. an inside address.
   C. a closing.
   D. a signature.

2. Which of the following letter parts is correct?

   A. Dear Sirs,
   B. Sincerely yours:
   C. My dear Aunt Mary,
   D. Yours truly;

3. Which of the following would *not* usually be listed on a résumé?

   A. work experience
   B. education
   C. skills
   D. friends

4. When you go for a job interview, you will probably have to fill out

   A. a letter of application.
   B. a reference.
   C. a résumé.
   D. an application.

5. Your friend's parents take you camping for the weekend. To show your appreciation, you might send them

   A. a thank-you note.
   B. a sympathy note.
   C. a get-well note.
   D. an invitation.

6. The purpose of a résumé is to

   A. take the place of a job application.
   B. request an interview for a job.
   C. tell an employer about your skills.
   D. ask about available jobs at a workplace.

Critical Thinking Answers will vary. Possible answer: Writing skills are helpful when you are applying for a job because an employer will see that you are well educated and that you take care and pride in your work. Good writing skills will make a good impression.

> **Critical Thinking**
> Why are good writing skills helpful when you are applying for a job? Write your answer on a separate sheet of paper.
> **WRITING ACTIVITY** On a separate sheet of paper, write a short essay describing some of the writing you might do when applying for a job. Explain why writing neatly and accurately will help you in your job search.

Writing Activity Answers will vary. Check students' essays for content and mechanics.

Unit 6 ▷ Writing in School

Think about the types of writing you do for school. Some of that writing probably starts in your school library. How might you use a library when you have a writing assignment?

Caption Accept all reasonable responses. Possible answer: You can use a library to help you find topics for writing. It will also help you to find information to support your report.

Good book reports tell enough about the story to interest the reader in the book.

Sandra Cisneros (born 1954) grew up in Chicago, Illinois. She was the only daughter in a family with six sons. As a child, she was shy and often escaped into a world of books. Later, she wrote about her Spanish-speaking neighborhood. In Cisneros's first book, The House on Mango Street, *the narrator wishes for a home of her own.*

Reading Challenge See *Tapestry: A Multicultural Anthology* for an excerpt from Sandra Cisneros's *The House on Mango Street.*

To help students tap their prior knowledge of the chapter topic, see the **Chapter Project** in the Classroom Resource Binder.

Learning Objectives

- Write a book report.
- Describe the setting of a novel.
- Describe a main character.
- Identify the conflict in a story and explain how it is resolved.
- Write your opinion of a novel and support it with examples.

Chapter 19 Writing a Book Report

Words to Know

report	an account of a particular subject
novel	a long work of fiction
element	a basic part or feature of the whole
setting	the time and place of an event, story, or play
character	a person in a story or play
plot	the main story of a novel or play
conflict	a problem or struggle that is at the center of the story
incident	an event
resolution of the conflict	a solution; an end to the conflict

19-1 The Basic Book Report

Discussing a book can add to your enjoyment of it. Sometimes, it is interesting to stop and think about why you liked a book so much.

Your teacher may ask you to write a **report**, or an account, about a **novel** you have read. A novel is a long work of fiction. There are many ways to write a report about a novel. This chapter will look closely at one common book report format.

As you begin a book report, remember the following important fact: You cannot tell everything that happened in a novel. It is not important to tell the story itself. It is important, however, that you show an understanding of the **elements** of the story.

An element is a basic part or feature of the whole. The following items are the basic elements of a novel.

setting when and where a story takes place

characters the people in a story. At least one character will have a problem that needs to be solved.

plot a story line; what happens

conflict the main problem of a story

incident an event that affects the conflict

resolution of the conflict how the conflict is resolved

A description of the above elements makes a complete book report. You should conclude your report by giving your opinion of the book.

Look at the following book report carefully. The next section in this chapter will take you through each part of the book report.

English and Technology

You can use a word-processing program to put the title of a book, a play, or a newspaper in italic type when you write.

Book Report
Title: <u>Dark Waters</u>
Author: Jack Summers

Setting: The story takes place aboard an ocean liner on the Atlantic Ocean. The time is during World War I—probably around 1915.

Main characters and plot: One of the main characters is a boy named David Starr. David is a handsome, red-haired, 17-year-old American traveling alone to England. At the beginning of the book, he is nervous about the trip. However, he overcomes his fears and turns out to be very brave. He shows his bravery by warning the ship's captain that a spy is on board and by finding a hidden bomb. David does this even though he knows the spy might catch him and kill him. David never gives up. "They just have to believe me," he tells his friend Anna. "Their lives depend on it. I must make them believe me." Although others on the ship say he is imagining things, David trusts his own feelings and keeps looking for the spy and the bomb.

Conflict: There is a spy and a bomb aboard a luxury liner. Will David Starr find them in time and save the ship?

Incident: One exciting incident occurs when David and his friend Anna try to sneak into the spy's cabin. They want to find proof of the spy's evil plans and take that proof to the captain. They have to pick the lock of the cabin with Anna's hairpin. While they are inside the cabin, they find what they need—a book of secret codes and some letters from the Germans who are involved. The spy, Arnold Stone, returns while they are in the cabin. They hide in a closet, hoping they will not be discovered. Luckily, they escape and take the book and letters to the captain.

Resolution of conflict: Only minutes before the bomb is set to go off, David convinces the captain to search the ship. Because David and Anna would not give up, the bomb is discovered and disarmed, and the ship and all its passengers are saved.

Opinion: This book was very exciting. I worried that if no one believed David and Anna, the ship would have been blown up, and everyone on board would have been killed. I liked the main characters, David and Anna, because they never gave up. I hated the evil Arnold Stone because he did not care about anyone but himself. The book taught me some interesting facts about World War I. I had not known that German submarines attacked nonmilitary boats. In all, Dark Waters was easy to read and was packed with suspense.

The Writing Process

How does this book report answer the *wh-* questions? (See the Writing Process, page WP8.)

Practice

1. Jack Summers wrote *Dark Waters*.
2. The story takes place during World War I, probably around 1915.
3. The story takes place aboard an ocean liner on the Atlantic Ocean.
4. David Starr is a main character.
5. David is handsome and red-haired. (He is also brave, persistent, and confident.)
6. David has to prove that a spy and a bomb are on the ship.
7. David and Anna find a book of secret codes and some letters.
8. The spy, Arnold Stone, is the villain.
9. Yes, David and Anna save the ship.
10. The person who wrote the report liked the novel because it was exciting and suspenseful.

Use the report about the book *Dark Waters* to answer the following questions on a separate sheet of paper.

1. Who wrote *Dark Waters*?

2. When does the story take place?

3. Where does the story take place?

4. Name a main character in the story.

5. Write two adjectives that describe David Starr.

6. What problem does David have to solve?

7. What two items do David and Anna find in the spy's cabin?

8. If David and Anna are the heroes in the novel, who is the villain?

9. Are David and Anna able to save the ship?

10. Did the person who wrote the book report enjoy the novel or not? Why?

19-2 Setting

When you report on the setting of a novel, you must describe where the story takes place and when the story takes place. These elements are important because they affect how the story is told. For example, imagine a story about a bank robbery set in the West in 1850. Now, imagine a bank robbery story set in modern New York City. They would probably be very different stories.

Sometimes, an author will tell you exactly when and where the story takes place. Somewhere in the early pages, he or she might mention, for example, the city of Tombstone, Arizona, and the year 1890. Then, it is easy to describe the setting in your report.

However, sometimes an author does not tell exactly when and where the story is set. In such cases, you must look for clues, and they are usually easy to find. How do the people dress? Do they ride horses or drive automobiles? How do they talk? Does it seem as if they are in a big city or a small town? Sometimes, you may not be able to give the place a specific name. However, you should be able to say something to identify the place: a small American town, a big city in the East, a tropical island, and so on. Likewise, you should be able to identify the time, even if you cannot give a specific date: modern times, long ago, the days of the Western frontier, colonial days, the future, and so on.

Practice

The following paragraphs do not tell the setting in specific words. However, you can use clues to decide when and where the stories take place. What is the setting of each paragraph? On a separate sheet of paper, list the clues you used to arrive at your answer.

1. Big Jim pushed his ten-gallon hat back and wiped the sweat off of his forehead. He took a long drink of water from his canteen. Then, he patted his horse and whispered under his breath, "We will catch those train robbers yet! If I have to ride 50 miles across this desert, I will have them in my jail by sundown."

2. Sharon held the briefcase full of money tightly against her body. She knew the two men were still after her. She waited nervously for the subway train to arrive. The subway station was crowded, and people pushed against her. She was glad. She could hide in the crowd. At last, the train arrived.

Answers will vary a bit, but they should be similar to the following:

1. The setting is the Old West during frontier days. Clues given are the character's dress (ten-gallon hat), type of transportation (horses), and the train robbery.

2. The setting is a big, modern city. Clues given are type of transportation (subway), one character's dress and style (leather jacket and spiked pink hair).

(Practice continues on next page.) ⮕

"Hey, move it!" someone yelled to her. She hurried aboard the subway train. She took a seat next to a frowning young man with a black leather jacket and spiked, pink hair.

19-3 ▸ Characters

It is better to give a clear description of one main character in a story or novel than to merely list all of the characters. Choose a main character who really interests you from a story or novel—someone you especially like or dislike. Then, write a paragraph or two describing that character.

Remember the following tips and questions when describing a main character:

- Describe the character's physical appearance.

- Describe the character's personality.

- Tell about one thing the character did that made you like or dislike him or her.

- Tell about any difficulties or hardships the main character overcomes.

- Tell about any changes in the main character. What caused the changes?

- What problem, or conflict, did the main character face?

Think About It

How would you describe your favorite TV character to someone who does not watch the show?

When you write about a character, remember the following guidelines.

- Use specific examples.

For instance, when you say that a character is brave, give an example of something brave that he or she did. If you say you liked a character, tell why.

Then, give an example of something he or she did that impressed you.

Notice how specific examples are used in the main character section of the book report on pages 284–285. The statement that David is brave is supported by an example of something brave that he did.

- Use direct quotations from the book that you are reporting on to support your points.

If you say that the character you are describing is cruel, copy a quotation from the book to prove your point. Find something cruel that the character says. Copy the words directly from the book, and remember to put them in quotation marks.

Notice the direct quotation in the main character section of the book report on pages 284–285. The quotation supports the idea that David is determined and never gives up.

Practice

Choose a main character from a story or novel that you have recently read. On a separate sheet of paper, write a one-paragraph character description. Use the following headings and topic sentence for your report.

Answers will vary. Check to make sure students adequately and accurately present details that support why the character they chose was an interesting person.

Book:

Character's name:

Character description:

Topic Sentence: The character ___name___ in ___title___ was a very interesting person.

19-4 Plot

When students start describing the plot of a story or novel, they often run into trouble. They find themselves telling many little details and soon discover they cannot include everything. Their discussion can become confusing. It is best to begin by looking at the separate elements that make up the plot. Then, you can briefly describe how they were handled in the book.

Every story must have a conflict. The conflict makes a story. It is what makes people want to read to the end. They want to find out how the conflict is resolved. The conflict is simply a problem. Will the lost boys find their way out of the woods? Will the police detective find the person who murdered her partner? Will the family be able to explain the creature from another planet living in their house? A story could be written around each of those conflicts.

Notice how the book report on pages 284–285 describes the conflict in the book *Dark Waters*.

Practice A

Answers will vary. Check to make sure students address the conflict in the television show or movie and not just the plot.

Think about the plot of a television show or movie you saw recently. On a separate sheet of paper, write one or two sentences describing the conflict in that show or movie.

Stories are made up of many incidents that work toward a resolution of the conflict. In certain stories, the incidents may lead to the solution of the problem. In other stories, the incidents may make matters worse, increase the problem, and heighten the suspense.

The incident described in the book report takes the conflict one step closer to a resolution. By finding the code book and the letters, David and Anna can convince the captain that there is a spy on board and save the ship.

It is very difficult to describe everything that happens in a story or novel. It is better to describe the major elements very clearly.

Practice B

On a separate sheet of paper, write one paragraph describing an interesting incident you either saw in a movie or television show or read in a story or novel. Tell how that incident affected the conflict in the story. Did it make matters worse, or did it lead to a resolution of the problem?

Answers will vary. This exercise may be challenging for some students. Explain to students that every incident or event in a story helps to move the plot and affects the conflict.

For every conflict, there is a resolution. The events of a story take the readers toward that resolution. The plot of a story is built around that conflict and its resolution. Your book report should answer the question *How is the conflict, or problem, resolved*?

The last part of your report involves giving your opinion of the story or novel. Again, the key is to be specific. Do not merely say that you liked the book. Tell why you liked it. Give reasons for your opinion. Do not say you liked it because it was exciting. Give a specific example of something exciting that happened. Reread the opinion section of the *Dark Waters* book report on page 285. Notice how the person who wrote the report used specific details to back up the statement that the novel was exciting.

Use the paragraphing skills that you learned in earlier pages of this book to write a well-developed opinion paragraph.

Think About It

Why is it important to give a specific example of something exciting that happened?

WRITING WITH STYLE
Giving an Opinion

The following paragraphs give two readers' opinions of Jack London's novel *Call of the Wild*. Which paragraph gives a clearer picture of what the novel is about? Why?

1. I liked Jack London's *Call of the Wild* very much. I thought that it was a very good book. It was exciting and interesting, and I could hardly put it down. It was very well written. In fact, *Call of the Wild* was one of the best books I have ever read. I think that people would really enjoy reading *Call of the Wild*.

2. I thought Jack London's *Call of the Wild* was an excellent book. London made me understand the feelings of the main character, a big dog named Buck. I wanted Buck to survive. I worried about him when he fought other dogs and fell into the hands of cruel masters. London also described the setting, the frozen Arctic, so clearly that I could see it in my mind. *Call of the Wild* was an exciting adventure I would recommend to most readers.

Paragraph 2 is better because the writer backs up his or her opinion with specific details. Paragraph 1 is too vague and does not demonstrate an understanding of the book.

VOCABULARY BUILDER
Defining New Words

Read the paragraph below. Find at least three words that are new to you. Perhaps you do not know their meanings. Perhaps you think other people might not know their meanings. Look up each of the three new words in a dictionary. Write a definition for each word, and use each word in a sentence.

For example, if you read the word *rave* and did not know its meaning, you would first write a definition.

> *rave*—to talk wildly

Then, you would use it in a sentence.

> The man *raved* about the new car he had bought.

Now, find at least three new words in the following paragraph.

> The prisoners were planning their escape. Dangerous Dan and California Slim had been in jail for ten long years. Now, they were digging a tunnel to freedom. The only implement they had was a rusty old spoon. The men took turns digging with that spoon. Every night for six months, Dan and Slim burrowed through the hard, dry earth. At last, Dan called to Slim one night just before midnight. His voice was hoarse with anticipation. He whispered that he saw a light at the end of their tunnel. Dan believed that light meant freedom.

Answers will vary. Check to make sure that students' definitions and sentences reflect the meaning of the words as they are used in the paragraph.

Summary Have students use the summary to outline the main idea and details of the chapter.

Summary

Do not tell the whole story in a book report. Instead, choose the major elements and write about them in detail.

Describe the setting of a book. If the exact setting is not given, use clues to decide where and when a story takes place.

Describe the appearance and personality of the main character in a book.

Do not give away the whole plot of a book. Instead, point out the main conflict. Describe the important events and tell how they are resolved.

Give your opinion of the book. Use specific examples to support your opinion.

More Vocabulary Review is provided in the Classroom Resource Binder.

Vocabulary Review

Complete each sentence with a term from the box. Write your answers on a separate sheet of paper.

novel	
report	
element	
setting	
character	
plot	
resolution of the conflict	
incident	
conflict	

1. a long work of fiction

2. the main events of a novel or play

3. the time and place of an event, story, or play

4. a person in a story or play

5. an account of a particular subject

6. an event

7. a basic part or feature of a whole

8. a clash of two opposing forces

9. a solution to a conflict

1. novel   6. incident
2. plot   7. element
3. setting   8. conflict
4. character   9. resolution
5. report   of the conflict

Chapter Quiz

Complete the following items. Write your answers on a separate sheet of paper.

1. Which four elements of a novel should you describe in a book report?

2. What details should you include when you describe a character?

3. How can you tell what the setting of a story is if an author does not state it?

4. Why is it important to understand the setting of a story?

5. Why does a story need a conflict?

6. When you give your opinion of a book, how do you support what you say?

Critical Thinking

What kinds of things should you include in a book report? Write your answer on a separate sheet of paper.

Critical Thinking Answers will vary. Possible answer: A book report should show a basic understanding of the elements of the story. These elements are the setting, characters, plot, conflict, incident, and resolution of the conflict.

Chapter Quiz

1. A book report describes the setting, characters, plot, conflict, main incident, and the resolution of the conflict.

2. You can include details about the character's physical appearance, the character's personality, any difficulties the character overcame, and problems the character faced.

3. Readers can figure out the setting of a story by looking for clues that show where and when the story is set.

4. It is important to understand the setting of a story because it affects how the story is told.

5. A story needs a conflict because the conflict is what makes the story interesting for the reader.

6. You need to back up all opinions with specific examples from the story.

Writing Activity

Think about a novel or story that you have read recently. Which details told what the main character was like? On a separate sheet of paper, describe how these details helped you to understand why the character is important to the story.

Writing Activity Answers will vary. Encourage students to look at their character from as many different angles as possible.

Effective writers use their writing skills to answer important questions.

Richard Wright
(1908–1960) was the first person to use the phrase "Black power." He was raised in poverty in the South. After a hard childhood in Mississippi, Wright moved to Chicago. There, he began to write in order to answer questions he had about racial injustice. His best-known novel is Native Son. *Wright also wrote a successful autobiography,* Black Boy.

Reading Challenge See *Tapestry: A Multicultural Anthology* for an excerpt from Richard Wright's *Black Boy.*

To help students tap their prior knowledge of the chapter topic, see the **Chapter Project** in the Classroom Resource Binder.

Learning Objectives

- Write answers to questions in complete sentences.
- Begin answers by restating the subject of the question.
- Write essay answers in well-developed paragraphs.
- Read essay questions carefully and answer the specific question that is asked.

Chapter 20 — Writing Answers on Tests

See the Workbook for **Extra Practice**.

Words to Know

restating	saying something again or in a different way
identify	to show to be a particular person, place, or thing

20-1 — Short-Answer Questions

Some test questions ask for short written answers. When you are asked this type of question, strong writing skills will help you create clear answers.

Here is a question that calls for a short answer.

Question: Why is Paul Revere famous?

Answer: Paul Revere is most famous for his midnight ride to Concord. He warned the American patriots that the British soldiers were coming.

The answer is written in complete sentences. Each sentence has a subject and a predicate and expresses a complete thought. The first sentence of the answer begins by **restating** the question, or saying the question in a different way.

Question: Why is Paul Revere famous?

Answer: Paul Revere is famous for...

It is important to restate the question. This helps you stick to the point.

Think About It

Why are writing skills important in a science class or a social studies class?

Here is an example of a science question and its answer.

Question: What is a barometer?

Answer: A barometer is an instrument that measures the pressure in the atmosphere.

Notice that the answer begins by restating the subject of the question.

Practice A

On a separate sheet of paper, answer each of the following questions with one or two sentences. Make sure that you answer in complete sentences. The first two items have been started for you. Use them as a model.

Answers will vary a bit but should be similar to the following.

1. Students should complete the phrase using the name of their principal.

2. My favorite food is pizza.

3. A tricycle is a cycle with three wheels.

4. On the Fourth of July, we celebrate the anniversary of America's independence from Great Britain.

5. A group of words is a complete sentence if it has a subject and predicate and expresses a complete thought.

1. Who is the principal of your school?
The principal of my school is…

2. What is your favorite food?
My favorite food is…

3. What is a tricycle?

4. Why do we celebrate the Fourth of July?

5. What makes a group of words a complete sentence?

You are often asked to **identify** some person, place, or thing in test questions. When you identify, you show that someone is a particular person or that something is a particular place or thing. To identify something means to name its characteristics. What makes a thing what it is? Which of its features are different from others of its type? Why is it special? These are characteristics.

Example:

> Question: Who was Jackie Robinson?
>
> Answer: Jackie Robinson was the first African American baseball player to play in the major leagues.

Notice that the answer restates the question. Then, it tells why Robinson is famous. It tells what makes him different from other people.

Also, notice that the answer is written in a complete sentence. It restates the subject of the question.

Practice B

1. Read each of the following questions and answers. On a separate sheet of paper, write **CS** if the answer is a complete sentence. Write **NS** if it is not a complete sentence.

    a. Question: What is the smallest state in the United States?

    Answer: Rhode Island

    b. Question: What happened at the Boston Tea Party?

    Answer: At the Boston Tea Party, a band of American patriots disguised themselves as Native Americans. Then, they dumped tea into Boston harbor. They were protesting against the tax on tea.

    c. Question: Identify Wyatt Earp.

    Answer: a gunfighter and law officer of the Old West

    d. Question: Identify Thomas Jefferson.

    Answer: Thomas Jefferson wrote the Declaration of Independence. He was also the third president of the United States.

    e. Question: What is Jupiter?

    Answer: the largest planet

1. a. NS
   b. CS
   c. NS
   d. CS
   e. NS

(Practice B continues on next page.) ⟹

2. a. Rhode Island is the smallest state in the United States.

c. Wyatt Earp was a gunfighter and law officer of the Old West.

e. Jupiter is the largest planet.

(Practice B continued.)

2. You should have found three answers that were not complete sentences. Now, rewrite those answers as complete sentences.

Always restate the subject of the question in the first sentence. Do not use a pronoun to replace the subject.

Here is an example.

> **Question: Identify Abraham Lincoln.**
>
> **Unclear Answer: He was the sixteenth president of the United States.**
>
> **Clear answer: Abraham Lincoln was the sixteenth president of the United States.**

Notice that the first answer used the pronoun *he* instead of stating the subject. The clearer answer named the subject of the question.

Brush Up on the Basics

Remember that a complete sentence has a subject and a predicate and expresses a complete thought. (See Grammar 1 in the Reference Guide.)

Practice C

On a separate sheet of paper, choose and write the best answer for the following question. Be ready to explain your choice.

Question: Identify Topeka.

Answer 1: It is the capital of Kansas.

Answer 2: capital of Kansas

Answer 3: Topeka is the capital of Kansas.

Answer 3 is the best choice. It is a complete sentence and restates the subject of the question.

Answers will vary a bit but should be similar to the following. Each answer should be a complete sentence and should restate the subject of the question.

1. Sally Ride was the first U.S. woman astronaut.

2. Benjamin Franklin was one of this country's founding fathers.

3. Davy Crockett fought for the independence of Texas at the Alamo.

4. John Adams was the second president of the United States.

5. Harriet Tubman was an African American slave who escaped to freedom. She helped other slaves escape on the "Underground Railroad."

20-2 ▸ Answering Essay Questions

An essay question asks for a longer answer. It asks you to discuss a topic in detail. Your answer will be a short essay of one or more paragraphs. Some essay questions can be answered quite briefly. Others require more detail. You must decide how much detail to include. Use the essay question or the directions to help you decide on a length for your answer.

Here is an example of an essay question and its answer.

Question: How would you describe the Hawaiian island of Kauai?

Answer: The island of Kauai is often described as the most beautiful of the Hawaiian Islands. Kauai's Waimea Canyon is very colorful. Some people compare it to the Grand Canyon. The smooth rocks of Waipahee Falls make a natural slide for swimmers. Most of the island is sunny. Kauai's Mount Waialeale, however, is the rainiest spot in the world. Because of its lush plant life, beautiful Kauai is sometimes called the *Garden Island*.

- Notice that this essay answer is written in the form of a paragraph.

- Remember that a well-developed paragraph has a topic sentence. Notice how the topic sentence restates the subject of the question. *The island of Kauai is often described as the most beautiful of the Hawaiian Islands.*

- A well-developed paragraph has at least three sentences of supporting details. *Waimea Canyon sentences, Waipahee Falls sentence, Mount Waialeale sentence.*

- A well-developed paragraph has a concluding sentence. *Because of its lush plant life, beautiful Kauai is sometimes called the "Garden Island."*

As in the short-answer questions, you should not refer to the subject with a pronoun. The writer did not say, "*It* is often described as the most beautiful of the Hawaiian islands." Rather, the subject, *Kauai,* was restated.

Practice A

On a separate sheet of paper, write a topic sentence that could begin a one-paragraph essay answer for each of the following questions. You will not be presenting any details in this exercise. Just write a topic sentence.

Example

Question: How would you describe Alaska's natural resources?

Topic sentence: The state of Alaska is rich in natural resources.

Notice that the topic sentence restates the question as a statement and adds the descriptive word *rich*. A strong topic sentence shows how a paragraph will develop.

The Writing Process

How can brainstorming before you write help you to answer the question? (See The Writing Process, page WP5.)

1. Question: How could the food in the cafeteria be improved?
    Topic sentence:

2. Question: Describe how Americans celebrate the Fourth of July.
    Topic sentence:

3. Question: Discuss how television can be educational.
    Topic sentence:

Answers will vary but should be similar to the following. Make sure students restate the subject of the question.

1. The food in the cafeteria could be improved in two ways.
2. Americans celebrate the Fourth of July in different ways.
3. Television can be educational in several ways.

Always read essay questions carefully. Read the question two or three times to be sure you understand it. Then, begin your essay. Make sure that the information you are writing really answers the question.

What is wrong with the answer to the following essay question?

Question: Describe three uses of the helicopter.

Answer: Helicopters are very useful. Helicopters are often used as ambulances. They carry injured people from an accident to the hospital. They can get people to the hospital much faster than regular ambulances. Helicopters do not have to depend on roads, as cars do, or on landing strips, as regular airplanes do. Helicopters save lives.

The answer above contains useful information. However, it does not answer the question. The question asked for three uses of the helicopter. Read the answer to the same question on page 304. Is it a clearer answer? Why?

Helicopters are very useful. For example, helicopters are used as ambulances to carry injured people from an accident to the hospital. Forest firefighters use helicopters to search for fires in the mountains. The Army uses helicopters, too. Helicopters carry troops directly into battle and move wounded soldiers from the battlefields to hospitals. Helicopters do jobs no other vehicles can do.

The second answer about helicopters could also have been written in three paragraphs. One paragraph might have discussed how helicopters are used as ambulances. A second paragraph might have discussed how forest firefighters use helicopters. A third paragraph could say how helicopters are used in battle. With three paragraphs, the writer could have given many more details. You must determine how long and detailed an answer your teacher expects.

Watch for key words in essay questions. Here are a few examples.

- Describe: tell about; make a picture with words

- Explain: make clear; give the details

- Discuss: tell about; give good and bad points; share your opinion

Watch for numbers: Does the question ask you to give three reasons, to discuss two points, and so on?

Think About It

How can finding the key word in an essay question help you to answer the question?

Practice B

Choose one of the following numbered items. On a separate sheet of paper, write a one-paragraph answer. It is often a good idea to make some notes before you begin writing your answer. For example, if you choose the first question, your notes might look like the following.

great-grandfather

came from Poland

traveled to America alone at 13

could not speak English until he was 19

saved enough money to open a small fruit stand

eventually owned a large supermarket

1. Describe your great-grandfather or great-grandmother.

2. Describe two major industries in your state.

3. Explain how the holiday of Thanksgiving began.

4. Discuss three ways a person can stay healthy.

5. Discuss cats as pets.

6. Explain this quotation by Thomas Jefferson: "All men are created equal."

7. Explain the saying: "You can catch more flies with honey than with vinegar."

8. Identify a famous person from your state.

9. Describe two ways bees help people.

10. Explain how tennis is played.

WRITING WITH STYLE
Writing Answers

Students in a science class were given the following essay question. Which do you think is stronger, Answer 1 or Answer 2? Why?

Question: Describe three ways frogs are valuable.

Answer 1:
They eat insects. They are also a good source of food for people. In France, they are a popular food. In the United States, some people eat their legs. In Germany, people often cook and eat the entire frog.

Answer 2:
Frogs are valuable creatures. First, they eat many harmful insects. Second, they are a source of food for some people. Frogs are considered delicious foods in France and Germany. Third, frogs serve as food for other animals. Snakes and birds living near water eat frogs. Even some fish eat frogs. Frogs, indeed, have some important uses.

Answer 2 is the better answer. Answer 1 does not give three ways frogs are valuable, as the question asks.

VOCABULARY BUILDER
Checking Your Dictionary Skills

Words in a dictionary are arranged in alphabetical order. If the first letter of two words is the same, you decide their order by looking at the second letter. If the second letter is also the same, you look at the third letter.

1. Alphabetize the following words:
   coffee, eye, fire, freeze, control, fan, arrow, art

2. Look at the following dictionary entry for the word *snake*. Use the entry to answer the questions below.

The pronunciation shows how to say the entry word.

Some definitions use examples to make meanings clear.

Some words have more than one meaning. Each meaning is numbered.

snake (snāk) *n.* 1. a crawling reptile with a long, thin body covered with scales and with no legs. 2. a person who cannot be trusted: *The snake cheated me out of my money.* 3. a long, flexible rod used to clear blocked pipes. *v.* to move, twist, wind, or curve like a snake.—snaked, snaking

The dictionary may show other forms of the word.

The part of speech is often abbreviated.
n = noun   adj = adjective
v = verb   adv = adverb

a. Can *snake* be used as a noun?

b. Can *snake* be used as a verb?

c. Can *snake* be used as an adverb?

d. How many definitions are given for *snake* as a noun?

e. What does *snake* mean when it is used as a verb?

f. Write your own sentences using *snake* as a noun and then as a verb.

1. arrow, art, coffee, control, eye, fan, fire, freeze

2. a. yes
   b. yes
   c. no
   d. three
   e. to move, twist, wind, or curve like a snake
   f. Answers will vary. Possible answers: The snake moved gracefully across the road. (noun) We snaked our way slowly up the mountain. (verb)

20 ╱ Review

Summary Have students use the summary to outline the main idea and details of the chapter.

Summary

Some test questions ask for short written answers. Always write the answers in complete sentences.
When you answer a question, restate the subject of the question.
When you answer essay questions, write one or more well-developed paragraphs.
The topic sentence of an essay question answer restates the subject of the question.
Read essay questions carefully. Make sure that the paragraph you write answers the question.

identify
restating

1. restating
2. identify

More Vocabulary Review is provided in the Classroom Resource Binder.

Vocabulary Review

Complete each sentence with a term from the box. Write your answers on a separate sheet of paper.

1. The first sentence of a short-answer question starts by _____ the subject of the question.

2. Many test questions ask you to _____ a person, place, or thing.

Chapter Quiz

1. It is important to restate the question because this helps you stick to the point of the question.

2. A short answer question requires a one- or two-sentence answer. An essay question asks you to define, explain, describe, or prove something. Writing an essay requires you to write in-depth about the topic.

Chapter Quiz

Complete the following items. Write your answers on a separate sheet of paper.

1. Why should you restate the question when you begin a short written answer?

2. How is a short answer question different from an essay question?

3. How can you decide how long an answer to an essay question should be?

4. Write a topic sentence to set up the answers to this essay question. *What are three ways that the computer has changed everyday life?*

5. What are two reasons to read an essay question several times?

▶ **Test Tip**
Make sure to include a topic sentence when you answer an essay question.

3. You can use the key words in a question to decide the length of the answer.

4. The computer has changed everyday life in three important ways.

5. It is important to read an essay question several times so that you really understand it and are able to answer it fully.

Critical Thinking

How can the writing process help you answer an essay question? Write your answer on a separate sheet of paper.

Critical Thinking Answers will vary. Possible answer: The writing process contains the steps that can be used to develop the answer to an essay question.

Writing Activity

Choose one of the essay choices listed below. On a separate sheet of paper, write a one-paragraph essay answer.

- Identify _____ (any famous person you choose).

- Describe _____ (a well-known tourist attraction).

- Explain why people celebrate _____ (any holiday).

- Discuss the good and bad points of having _____ (any animal) as a pet.

Writing Activity Answers will vary. Check to make sure that students have a strong topic sentence and that they support that topic sentence with details or examples.

A lively imagination can be one of a writer's important tools in report writing.

Ray Bradbury (1920–2000) was a popular science-fiction writer. He wrote very imaginative novels and short stories. One of his best-known fiction works is The Martian Chronicles. *It is a series of reports from Mars to Earth. He also wrote* Dandelion Wine. *Many of his stories are set in fantastic "other worlds."*

To help students tap their prior knowledge of the chapter topic, see the **Chapter Project** in the Classroom Resource Binder.

Learning Objectives

- Identify good report topics.
- Identify the card catalog and other reference books.
- Use index cards for selective note taking.
- Organize notes and write an outline for a report.
- Identify the introduction, the body, and the conclusion of a report.
- Write a bibliography.

Chapter 21 Writing a Report

Words to Know

research	the gathering of facts and other information
source	any book, place, person, or material from which you gather information
periodical	a publication, such as a newspaper or a magazine, that is published at regular intervals
card catalog	a file in a library that contains information for every book
cross-reference	a reference to another part of a book or to another source of information on the same subject
Dewey Decimal system	a system used in libraries to put books in order; the specific number assigned to each book, pamphlet, and so on that classifies the item according to subject
reference book	a source of information
bibliography	a list of books or sources for a particular topic
quote	to repeat or copy exactly the writing or speech of another

21-1 Choosing the Topic of a Report

When a teacher first assigns a report, it can seem like
a big task. However, if you approach the job step-by-step,
the task is much simpler.

Look at the following steps to take when you write a research report.

1. Choose a topic.

2. Do the **research**, or gather facts and other information that you need. Then, take notes.

3. Write an outline.

4. Write the report. Write a rough draft. Then, proofread, revise, and write a final copy.

5. Write a bibliography.

Each section in this chapter will help you through one of the steps. This section begins with the first step, choosing a topic.

If possible, choose a topic you like.
Sometimes, a teacher will assign your report topic. At other times, you will be free to choose your own topic. A report usually takes quite a bit of time and effort. It is certainly best if you choose a topic that interests you. A report assignment is often a chance to learn new things and to meet new people.

Make sure your topic is narrow enough.
Many students have trouble with reports because they try to research a topic that is too broad. For example, what would happen if you tried to write a three-page report on the country of Peru? Where would you begin? You could not possibly cover the entire subject or sort through all the available material. It would be much better for you to limit your topic. Perhaps, you might write about the people of Peru, discuss Peru's history, or how the country is governed.

Writing a report can be confusing if your topic is too broad. Make it easy on yourself. Narrow your topic to a size you can manage.

The Writing Process

How can you use the *wh-* questions to help you narrow your topic? (See The Writing Process, pages WP6–WP8.)

Practice A

In each of the following pairs, choose the topic that
would be narrow enough for a three-page report.
On a separate sheet of paper, write your answers.

1. **a.** Automobiles
   b. Henry Ford and the Model T

2. **a.** Native Americans
   b. Educational opportunities for Native Americans

3. **a.** The invention of the telephone
   b. Inventions

4. **a.** Fighter planes of World War I
   b. Airplanes

5. **a.** Fashion
   b. How people will dress in the 2000s

1. b
2. b
3. a
4. a
5. b

Practice B

On a separate sheet of paper, write three different
narrower topics for each of the following broad topics.
Choose topics you feel would be appropriate for
a three- to five-page report.

1. Rock music

2. The Olympics

Once you have chosen a topic, make sure you have
enough sources for a good report. A **source** is any
book, place, person, or material from which you gather
information.

Answers will vary. Possible answers:
1. Rock music
   a. Pros and cons for advisory labels
   b. The changing face of rap music
   c. Protest songs of the 1960s
2. The Olympics
   a. New Olympic events
   b. Drug testing for Olympic athletes
   c. Pros and cons of professional athletes competing in the Olympics

(Practice B continues on next page.) ⟫

(Practice B continued.)

Always make sure you can find enough information on your topic. One source is usually not enough. You should try to find three sources that can give you information about your topic. For example, perhaps you heard about a woman named Holly Hanson who was a big game hunter in Africa. You decide she would be an interesting topic for a research paper. However, when you go to the library, you find only one half-page magazine article on Hanson. If that happens to you, find a new topic.

Before you actually begin gathering information and taking notes, check to see if enough information is available. Be willing to change your topic if you cannot find enough information.

21-2 ▶ Finding Information and Taking Notes

Your school library or public library is the place to begin your research. Books and **periodicals**, like newspapers and magazines, can usually provide the information you need. Sometimes, you might consult a person for information about your topic. For example, if you are writing about a scientific topic, you might want to use your science teacher as one source.

21-3 ▶ The Card Catalog

The library's **card catalog** is the place to begin looking for books with information on your topic. The card catalog contains information cards for every book in the library.

In the card catalog, there are three cards for every book. There is a subject card, an author card, and a title card. The same information appears on each card, but it is arranged differently. The cards are in alphabetical order and are cross-referenced. When cards are used as a **cross-reference**, they refer to another part of the book or to another source of information on the same subject. Author cards are alphabetized by the author's last name.

For example, if you want information on the midnight ride of Paul Revere, you could look under *Revere, Paul* or *American Revolution*. These would be subject cards.

If you knew you wanted a specific book on Paul Revere called *Brave Silversmith*, you could look in the "B" drawer of the card catalog under *Brave Silversmith*. This would be a title card.

If you knew that Walter Smith wrote the book *Brave Silversmith*, you could also look in the "S" drawer under *Smith, Walter*. This would be an author card.

For a nonfiction book, the cards are organized using the **Dewey Decimal system** of the book. That system will tell you where to find the book on the shelf. Once you have that number, a librarian can also help you. For a work of fiction, the book will be listed on the shelf alphabetically by the author's last name.

Many libraries keep this information on a computer. The computer has the same information as the card catalog. To use the computerized card catalog, you enter information, and the computer finds what you are looking for on a book's subject, author, or title.

Practice

On a separate sheet of paper, answer the following questions as if you were using the card catalog.

1. Under which letter would you look to find a book called *Scary Stories to Read in the Dark*? Would you be looking for a title card, an author card, or a subject card?

(Practice continues on next page.) ⟹

English and Technology

You can find many sources by typing a key word into a library's computerized card file.

See *Pacemaker® Computer Literacy* for more information about databases.

1. You would look under the letter *S*. You would be looking for a title card.

2. You would look under
G or *M.*

You would be looking
for a subject card.

3. You would look under *W.* You
would be looking
for an author card.

2. Under which letter would you look to find a book
about Greek mythology? Would you be looking
for a title card, an author card, or a subject card?

3. You really enjoy reading novels by an author
named Alice Wald. Under which letter would you
look to see if her books are available in your
library? Would you be looking for a title card,
an author card, or a subject card?

Answers will vary in terms
of whether your school's library
has the books listed.

A. 1. *The Pigman,* Paul Zindel

2. *Jane Eyre,* Charlotte
Brontë

3. *The Fox Steals Home,*
Matt Christopher

4. *Where the Red Fern
Grows,* Wilson Rawls

5. No

B. Answers will vary. Possible
answers:

1. Yes, *Skateboard Tough,
At the Plate* series,
Snowboard Maverick

2. Yes, *Villette*

3. *Free at Last! The Story
of Martin Luther King, Jr.,*
Angela Bull; *The
Autobiography of Martin
Luther King, Jr.,*
Clayborne Carson

Portfolio Project

A. Go to a library and see if it has the following books. If it
has the book, write the author's name. If it does not have
the book, write *No.*

1. *The Pigman*
2. *Jane Eyre*
3. *The Fox Steals Home*
4. *Where the Red Fern Grows*
5. *Mystery on White Pine Lane*

B. Then, use the card catalog to answer these questions.

1. Did the author of *The Fox Steals Home* write any books
besides that one? If so, list two.
2. Did the author of *Jane Eyre* write any other books
besides that one? If so, name one.
3. You are writing a report about Martin Luther King, Jr.
Write the title and author of two books that might
contain information you need.

21-4 ▷ Reference Books

You can also find information in the library by looking in **reference books**. You do not need to read an entire reference book, or source of information. You can look up the topic you need either in the index or the table of contents. Usually, you cannot check reference books out of the library. You must use them while you are at the library.

Most libraries have a reference shelf. You can find these books and others like them on the reference shelf.

Encyclopedia: This research tool is divided into volumes and contains alphabetized entries on many subjects.

Almanac: This book contains facts, statistics, records, and information for current and past years. It is a good place to look for quick information.

Atlas: This book contains maps and facts about places.

Who's Who in America, Current Biography: These books contain alphabetized entries with information about famous people. *Current Biography* is divided into volumes.

English and Technology
You can find maps and facts about places on the Internet.

21-5 ▷ Periodicals

Up-to-date information can often be found in periodicals like magazines and newspapers. How can you find an article about your topic? You certainly cannot look through every magazine in the library!

A publication called the *Readers' Guide to Periodical Literature* can help you find your article. The *Readers' Guide* lists articles from major magazines.

Suppose you were writing a report on the science fiction writer, Ray Bradbury. Suppose you looked under science fiction writers in the *Readers' Guide*. You might find this entry.

Title of article —— Writing Sci Fi Stories. J. Cook. —— author
magazine —— Newsday 81:120 N 17 '70

volume   page   date

Practice

1. "Ray Bradbury's Science Fiction Novels" is the title of the article.
2. B. Taylor wrote the article.
3. The article can be found in *Science Fiction Digest*.
4. The article can be found on pages 24–26 of the magazine.
5. The date of the magazine is January 6, 1969.

Use the following entry. On a separate sheet of paper, answer the following questions.

Ray Bradbury's Science Fiction Novels. B. Taylor. *Science Fiction Digest* 78:24–26 Ja 6 '69.

1. What is the name of the magazine article?

2. Who wrote the article?

3. In what magazine will the article be found?

4. On what pages can the article be found?

5. What is the date of the magazine issue?

21-6 Taking Notes

Once you have found your sources, you will need to read them and take notes. Use the tables of contents and indexes in books to help locate the information you need.

Take your notes on index cards, not on regular paper. If you use cards, you can easily organize your material by moving the cards around and arranging them according to subtopics.

Each note card will have two headings, the subtopic and the source. Suppose that your paper is on

World War I airplanes, and you are taking notes on the British Sopwith. You would write, "Types of planes—British Sopwith," at the top of your card. This is your subtopic.

The second heading will indicate your source. Perhaps you found the information in the *American Encyclopedia*. Write <u>American Encyclopedia</u> at the top of the card. Also note the volume and page number in case you need to look up the material again. Always keep a complete listing of all sources you use on separate cards. Write the title of the book, the author or editor, the volume number, the publisher, the place of publication, and the copyright date. You will need this information later for your **bibliography**. A bibliography is a list of the books and sources you used to write your report.

Study the following note card.

> *Subtopic: Types of planes-British Sopwith*
> *Source: <u>American Encyclopedia</u>, vol. A, pg. 122*
> *British Sopwith Triplane-nicknamed Tripe-1st*
> *used in battle in 1916*
> *British Sopwith Camel-two machine guns-one*
> *above wing, one behind propeller*
> *"The British Sopwith engaged in dogfights, or*
> *battles in the air, with the enemy planes."*

In the note card above, notice that the notes are not written in complete sentences. If a source contains information you want to use word-for-word, you must **quote**, or copy that information exactly, and put quotation marks around the quote. Do not copy any other information word-for-word from the source. Summarize main points found in the source. Be brief but accurate.

Brush Up on the Basics

Make sure you use quotation marks at the beginning and the end of a direct quotation. (See Punctuation 14 in the Reference Guide.)

Practice

Assume that you are writing a report on the dodo bird. Read the following selection. On a separate sheet of paper or using note cards, take notes on information that you think you could use in the report. Remember that the notes should be brief. They should not be in complete sentences unless you are copying a direct quotation.

The Dodo Bird

The dodo bird was a rather strange creature. The last dodo bird was seen around 1681. It was about the size of a turkey, but it had very short legs, a gigantic beak, and stubby wings. A short tail of curly feathers added to the dodo's odd appearance. The dodo was quite a large bird, often almost three feet high. Because it was so heavy and because its wings were so small, the dodo could not fly.

21-7 Organizing Notes and Writing an Outline

When you have finished taking notes, you will have many note cards. Separate them according to their headings. Put all the notes on one subtopic together.

Then, look at your piles of note cards. You can see how much you have to say on each subtopic. If one pile is very small, you might want to omit that subtopic. If a pile is very large, you might want to divide that one subtopic into two or more parts.

Think about the report on World War I fighter planes. The person writing this report might have ended up with four piles of notes: one on different types of planes, one on special features of the World War I plane, one on famous air squadrons of World War I, and one on famous pilots of World War I. Each of the piles of notes would represent a section of the report. As the writer organizes the note cards, the report begins to take shape.

Practice

A student is writing a report on the famous magician, Harry Houdini. Look at the following facts. On a separate sheet of paper, organize those facts into subtopic groups. Match each numbered fact with a lettered subtopic.

Facts

1. Houdini could free himself after being handcuffed, nailed in a box, and thrown into deep water.

2. His real name was Ehrich Weiss.

3. He once was a trapeze performer in a circus.

4. He considered magic a skill that could be learned.

5. He did not believe in the supernatural.

6. He could escape from prison cells.

1. B
2. A
3. A
4. C
5. C
6. B

Subtopics

A. A description of Houdini's early life

B. Houdini's magic tricks

C. Houdini's attitude toward magic

Once your note cards are divided into groups, it is time to write an outline. You may remember working with essay outlines in Chapter 14. Your report outline should be done in much the same way. Look at the outline on page 322 for a report on World War I airplanes. You should have a pile of note cards for each main section of the outline.

The Writing Process

How can an outline help you organize your notes? (See The Writing Process, page WP9.)

World War I Airplanes

I.   Introduction
II.   Different types of World War I planes
     A. British planes
         1. Sopwith
         2. Vickers
         3. Handley-Page twin-engine
     B. German Fokker
     C. French Spad
III.   Special features of World War I planes
     A. Attack features
         1. First use of machine guns on planes
         2. Bombing devices
             a. First threw bombs by hand
             b. Later developed electrical bombing device
     B. Safety features
         1. Telephones in oxygen masks
         2. Armored pilot seat
     C. Engines
IV.   Famous air squadrons of World War I
     A. French squadrons
     B. British squadrons
     C. U.S. squadrons
V.   Famous pilots of World War I
     A. Roland Garros
         1. French pilot who carried pistols and rifles
         2. First fighter pilot
     B. Quentin Roosevelt
         1. Youngest son of President Theodore Roosevelt
         2. Shot down behind enemy lines
     C. Eddie Rickenbacker
         1. U.S. race-car driver
         2. Leading U.S. "ace"
VI.   Conclusion

Writing the Report

You learned how to write a good paragraph. You learned how to organize an essay. Now, you will use the same skills to write your report. Like an essay, a report has an introduction, a body of supporting paragraphs, and a conclusion. Just be sure to follow your outline and write a clear topic sentence for each paragraph.

Think About It

How can the skills you use to organize and write an essay help you to write a report?

Your Introduction: The First Paragraph

Your introduction does not need to be long. Keep it simple and direct. The introduction should define your topic and explain the purpose of your research.

Read the following example.

> In recent wars, the skies have been a battlefield. However, World War I was the first war in which soldiers took to the air. Today, computers fire missiles. Those earliest pilots shot pistols at each other from their open cockpits. It is amazing how much military planes have advanced from early war planes, the fighter planes of World War I.

Direct Quotations in the Body

Most of your report will be written in your own words. However, you may want to quote a source directly once or twice. When you use a direct quotation, you must put the words in quotation marks and identify the source.

Read the following example.

> Many U.S. World War I pilots wanted adventure. According to the *American Encyclopedia,* "Many of the daring pilots in the slow-flying planes of World War I looked upon war as a game." U.S. race car driver Eddie Rickenbacker became one such pilot.

Your Conclusion: The Last Paragraph

At the end of your report, you will need a conclusion. Like the introduction, it should be short and simple. It should refer back to the introduction. Look at this conclusion. Then, reread the introduction on page 323. Notice how they are alike.

> During my research, I read fascinating stories of the earliest fighter planes and the men who flew them. I was amazed to find that such a short time ago planes were so different. The war planes of World War I may have been slow and primitive compared to today's aircraft, but they were exciting. They were the first fighters in the sky.

Of course, you will proofread and edit the rough draft of your report before writing the final copy. The final copy should be written in ink or typed.

Practice

On a separate sheet of paper, number from 1 to 5. Write **true** if the statement is true. Write **false** if the statement is false.

1. True
2. True
3. False

1. A report has an introduction, a body, and a conclusion.

2. The introduction tells what the report is about.

3. The body is only one paragraph long.

4. The conclusion is very much like the introduction.

4. True

5. True

5. Anything copied word-for-word from a source must be put in quotation marks, and the source must be identified.

21-9 ▸ Writing the Bibliography

A bibliography is a list of the sources you used in your research. Your sources will include any books, reference books, or periodicals that you used.

Bibliographies must be written in a special way. The sources must be listed in alphabetical order. Look at the bibliography that follows. Notice how each entry is written.

Bibliography

Arnold, William T. *The History of American Aircraft.* New York: Smith Publishing Co., 1985.

"Airplanes." *The American Encyclopedia,* Vol. 1. Chicago: Ace Education Inc., 1982, pp. 34–52.

Hart, C.L. "Flying Aces." *Newsday* (May 1987), Vol. 21, p. 22.

Write down bibliographical information as you use each source. You do not want to make an extra trip to the library just to find bibliographical information.

Practice

On a separate sheet of paper, write a bibliography with at least four entries. Use the bibliography on this page as a guide. Be sure to alphabetize the entries.

Answers will vary. Check to make sure that students have followed the correct format for each type of entry.

A research report takes a lot of work and time. You will want to present it in a way that reflects all your effort. Staple your papers together in the top left corner. Your report should include a title page, the report itself, and a bibliography.

The title page is the first thing your readers will see. Use the following title page as a guide, and present your paper with style.

Airplanes

of World War I

By

Ann Roth

May 4, 2001

VOCABULARY BUILDER
Using Library Words

The paragraph below contains words that are often used to discuss books. Read the paragraph. On a separate sheet of paper, write each of the words in italic type. Next to each word, write the number of its definition. Definitions of the words follow the paragraph. Use context clues to help you.

librarian–4,
biography–1,
table of contents–2,
index–3,
publisher–5,
illustration–7,
copyright date–6

My teacher assigned a report on a famous person, so I went to the library to look for information. The *librarian* suggested that I read a *biography.* At last, I decided to write my report on Emmett Kelly, the famous clown. I found a book on circus clowns right away. I looked in the *table of contents* and saw that the book had a whole chapter on Kelly. The *index* of the book told me he was mentioned on other pages, too. The *publisher* had included a large *illustration* showing Emmett Kelly in a colorful clown suit. The book on clowns was rather old. The *copyright date* was 1950. However, the information was still interesting.

Definitions

1. a book about a person

2. a list of chapters in a book that is found in the front of the book

3. a list at the end of the book telling subjects the book covers

4. a person who works in a library

5. a person or company who prints books, magazines, newspapers, and so on for distribution to the public

6. the year a book was published

7. a picture

Summary Have students use the summary to outline the main idea and details of the chapter.

Summary

When you write a report, limit your report topic so you can discuss it fully.
Make sure there is enough information available on your topic.
Use a card catalog and the Internet to find book and magazine articles on your topic.
Take notes on index cards. Label the cards with subtopic and source headings.
Summarize the main points in a brief, clear way.
Organize the note cards according to subtopics.
Write an outline that shows the parts of your report.
Write a rough draft, using your outline as a guide. Proofread your draft.
Write a bibliography that lists your sources.

card catalog

cross-reference

research

quote

source

reference book

periodical

bibliography

Dewey Decimal system

More Vocabulary Review is provided in the Classroom Resource Binder.

Vocabulary Review

**Match each term in the box with its meaning.
Write your answers on a separate sheet of paper.**

1. to repeat someone's exact words

2. the gathering of facts and information

3. a list of books for a particular topic

4. a library system for organizing books

5. a library file that has information for every book

6. newspaper or magazine

7. a reference to another part of a book or another source

8. any book, material, or person from which you get information

9. a source of information

1. quote

2. research

3. bibliography

4. Dewey Decimal system

5. card catalog

6. periodical

7. cross-reference

8. source

9. reference book

Chapter Quiz

Complete the following items. Write your answers on a separate sheet of paper.

1. What is the purpose of focusing a report topic?

2. What two sources, other than books and periodicals, might have information for your report?

3. What three types of cards are in a card catalog?

4. Name three types of reference books found in most libraries.

5. When you take notes, what two headings should you place on each card?

6. How do your notes help you to write an outline for a report?

Critical Thinking

How is a report like an essay? Write your answer on a separate sheet of paper.

Critical Thinking Answers will vary. Possible answer: Like an essay, a report has an introduction, a body, and a conclusion. Both an essay and a report are also in-depth looks into a topic.

▶ **Test Tip**
Close your eyes and take a deep breath before you begin a test.

4. Answers will vary. Possible answer: Most libraries have encyclopedias, almanacs, and atlases in their reference sections.

5. The first heading names the subtopic the information covers; the second heading shows the source.

6. Answers will vary. Possible answer: The subtopics or main ideas can be arranged in a logical order in an outline. You can then follow this order when writing your report.

Writing Activity

Suppose you are writing a report about the writing process. Write an introduction that clearly states your topic and would interest your readers. Review the introduction on page 323 of this chapter before you write. Write your introduction on a separate sheet of paper.

Writing Activity Answers will vary. Check to make sure that students have clear, well-written topic sentences and that the introductions grab readers' attention.

Unit 6 **Review**

Standardized Test Preparation This unit review follows the format of many standardized tests. A Scantron® sheet is provided in the Classroom Resource Binder.

Read each of the following items. On a separate sheet of paper, write the letter that best answers each one.

1. The main problem the character in a novel faces is called the
   A. plot.
   B. resolution.
   C. conflict.
   D. incident.

2. Which of the following would *not* be included in a book report?
   A. a description of the main character
   B. a description of the whole story
   C. when and where the story takes place
   D. the reader's opinion of the book

3. A library card catalog contains
   A. one card for every book.
   B. two cards for every book.
   C. three cards for every book.
   D. four cards for every book.

4. Writing a three-page report on Argentina would be a problem because
   A. not enough sources are available on this topic.
   B. the topic is too broad.
   C. the card catalog would not list books on this topic.
   D. the topic is too narrow.

5. Which reference book has entries on almost any subject?
   A. almanac
   B. atlas
   C. encyclopedia
   D. *Who's Who in America*

6. The answer to a short-answer question usually
   A. includes a topic sentence.
   B. restates the question.
   C. includes as many details as possible.
   D. has a concluding paragraph.

Critical Thinking It is important to use a topic sentence in an essay question and in a report for two reasons. First, it tells the readers what they will be reading about. Second, it helps keep the writer on track.

Writing Activity Answers will vary. Students' answers should include reports, essays, and short-answer test questions. Knowing how to write each of these is important for students' success in school because they are the primary means for evaluating students' knowledge and progress.

Critical Thinking

Why is it important to use a topic sentence in an essay question and in a report? Write your answer on a separate sheet of paper.

WRITING ACTIVITY On a separate sheet of paper, write a short answer to this question. Which three types of writing do students use in school? Tell why it is important for a student to know each of these to succeed in school.

Unit 7 ▷ Imaginative Writing

Thousands of authors publish new books every year. Hundreds of thousands of books are in print. Where do you think these authors get ideas for their books?

Caption Accept all reasonable responses. Possible answer: Many writers get story ideas from their own lives and experiences. Others get ideas from history and current events.

Writers use vivid descriptions to bring fictional characters to life.

Charles Dickens *(1812–1870) is one of the world's most popular writers. His descriptions of life in nineteenth-century England have delighted readers for over 150 years. Dickens observed people carefully. He used the details he noticed to create amazing characters. Three of his best known works are* Great Expectations, David Copperfield, *and* A Christmas Carol. *In these books, Dickens created such characters as David Copperfield, Scrooge, and Tiny Tim.*

Extra Reading See the Pacemaker® Classics series for Charles Dickens's *Great Expectations, David Copperfield, A Christmas Carol, A Tale of Two Cities,* and *Oliver Twist.*

To help students tap their prior knowledge of the chapter topic, see the **Chapter Project** in the Classroom Resource Binder.

Learning Objectives

- Write character descriptions based on real people.
- Write character descriptions that appeal to all the senses.
- Write about characters who are interesting.
- Write effective dialogue.
- Write correctly punctuated dialogue.

Chapter 22 / Creating Characters

Words to Know

trait	a special quality
unique	being the only one of its kind
habit	a thing that a person does regularly without thinking about it
imaginary	not real; existing only in one's mind
point of view	who is telling a story
villain	an evil or wicked character in a story
hero	the main character in a story; he or she is usually good
dialogue	a conversation between characters
indirect quotation	repeating what a character says but not in the exact words

22-1 / Drawing on Real Life

Have you ever read a book and felt as if you really knew a character? Are there some characters that you just cannot forget? Authors who create such characters have done their job well. An effective writer can make characters seem to come alive.

The world is full of characters—people with interesting looks and personalities. When writers create fictional characters, they often draw on some of the **traits**, or special qualities, of real people they have known.

Think about some *real people*, beginning with yourself. It can be hard to describe yourself. It is often easier to see unusual traits in other people. Practice A will give you a chance to look closely at yourself.

Practice A

1.– 4. Answers will vary.

1. On a separate sheet of paper, copy any adjectives from the following list that describe you. Then, write five more adjectives of your own that describe you.

friendly	shy	serious	energetic
quiet	funny	kind	lazy
happy	tough	clumsy	sad
lonely	attractive	slim	artistic
smart	athletic	intelligent	nervous

Brush Up on the Basics

An adjective is a word that adds to the meaning of a noun or a pronoun. (See Grammar 34 in the Reference Guide.)

2. On a separate sheet of paper, complete each of the following sentences.

My favorite food is _____.

My favorite season is _____.

If I could be doing anything I wanted, I would be _____.

I hated the time that _____.

Other people say that I am _____.

The thing that I treasure most is _____.

I admire people who _____.

The strangest thing about me is _____.

Now, write two more sentences about yourself.

3. On a separate sheet of paper, draw a picture of yourself. You do not have to be a real artist. Any little sketch will do.

Now, complete these sentences.

My best physical feature is my _____ .

My best personality feature is my _____ .

4. Use the information above. On a separate sheet of paper, write one paragraph describing how you look. Then, write a second paragraph describing your personality. Be sure to tell what makes you special or different from other people.

Have you ever heard the expression, "What a character!"? A person who is called a character is generally someone who is unusual. A character is special. A character stands out in a group. They have **unique**, one-of-a-kind traits that make them interesting. Consider the people you know, perhaps the people in your classroom. Try to identify their special traits and **habits**, or things that they do regularly.

Practice B

On a separate sheet of paper, complete each of the following sentences with the name of someone you know.

1. _____ has a most unusual way of laughing.

2. _____ is the smartest person I know.

3. _____ has the neatest handwriting.

4. _____ has a beautiful smile.

5. _____ is the funniest person I know.

Answers will vary. Encourage students to use all of the senses in their descriptions.

(Practice B continues on next page.) ⮕

(Practice B continued.)

6. _____ is the most serious person I know.

7. _____ takes a lot of risks.

8. _____ has a great personality.

9. _____ is the friendliest person I know.

10. _____ is the most generous person I know.

Now, write a paragraph of description based on one of the sentences above. Describe the unique trait of the person you have named. For example, describe how and why Sally Wilson takes a lot of risks or why Joe Brown's smile seems so beautiful.

Can you write a whole paragraph on just one trait? You can if you pay attention to detail. Try to make your readers see what you describe. Use examples. You might write about how Sally joined the track team. Use comparisons: *Joe's smile is like a sunny day.*

Use all your senses. You might describe how Sally's face looks when she has decided to do something. Perhaps her mouth snaps shut and she bites her lips. Stretch your imagination and creativity. Then, you will find that you can write a whole paragraph about that one trait.

The person you just described was a real person. Often, authors draw on real people to create **imaginary** characters. Imaginary characters are characters that are not real.

Think About It

How can details help you create a character?

You have lots of freedom when you are creating a character. You can combine the unique traits of many people to make an interesting character. You might use one person's walk and another's hairstyle. The real people that you draw upon for ideas can be people you know.

On the other hand, they can be people you only saw once but remember well. Perhaps a man waiting for the bus caught your eye because he looked so happy. Perhaps you remember a couple that you overheard in a restaurant. That conversation may inspire you to write dialogue.

Writers can exaggerate characteristics to make a character unforgettable. Use what you know from real life and real people. Then, add your imagination to create a unique fictional character.

Practice C

On a separate sheet of paper, write two paragraphs that describe a fictional character. Use characteristics from people you really know or have seen. The first paragraph should describe how the character looks. The second paragraph should describe his or her personality. Give your character a name, and bring him or her to life.

Answers will vary. Check to make sure students have described their character in terms of their physical appearance and their personality.

Begin your description by completing the following sentence.

_____ is a unique person.

Answers will vary.

Portfolio Project

Draw a picture of your character, or find a picture in a magazine or newspaper that shows how you picture your character.

Look at the description you wrote for Practice C on page 337. What senses did you call upon to describe your character? Did you describe the way the character looked? Did you describe how the character sounded?

Read the following character description. To what senses does the writer appeal?

Think About It

How can the senses help you to describe a character?

> The girl entered the room with a jangle of bracelets and a strange tinkling of bells. I watched her. She was different from anyone I had ever seen. Other people were looking at her, too. She wanted to be noticed. She had dyed her hair a bright pink color and wore matching pink eye shadow that was bold and shiny on her eyelids. The tinkling sound came from her shoes. She had tied tiny silver bells on each yellow shoelace. She was in the room only a moment. Then she was gone, leaving the sweet smell of perfume hanging heavy in the air.

Notice that the writer described the way the girl looked, sounded, and smelled. All those senses were used to create a character. Also notice the writer's reaction to the girl. Do you feel you know something about this girl? Do you know anything about the writer? When you write, you not only create characters, but you also reveal something about yourself. Writing can be a powerful act.

Portfolio Project

Use the character described on page 338 for this activity. Picture the girl in your mind. You know a little about her now. Create a more complete character by describing what you think she would be wearing. Describe her outfit in detail. Can you write more about why she wants to be noticed? Does she say anything? Creating a character begins with saying how someone looks, but beyond that, it also tells us about personality and emotion.

Answers will vary.

Practice

On a separate sheet of paper, choose one of the following, and write your description.

Answers will vary. Evaluate students' paragraphs on the clarity of their descriptions.

1. Rewrite your paragraph from Practice C on page 337, adding description that appeals to a sense other than sight.

   or

2. Suppose that you are sitting alone in a room with your eyes closed. Then, imagine that a stranger walks in. Write a one-paragraph description of that stranger without using the sense of sight.

22-3 ▶ Winning Sympathy for Your Characters

You have finished reading a book. You feel as if you have lived the story that you have just read. "That was a good book!" you exclaim.

One of the reasons you feel that way is that the author won your sympathy for the characters. You really cared about what happened to them. Whenever you create a character, one of your goals should be to make the readers care about that person.

How do you make your readers sympathize with your characters? One way is to use a lot of detail. Let the readers know the characters. Show the characters doing things and saying things that the readers will believe are real. The readers will usually sympathize with the characters that they know best.

22-4 Become the Character

You can create a believable character by putting yourself in that character's place. Become the character as you write. You may not be a 15-year-old boy from the country who has suddenly moved to San Francisco. However, if that boy is your character, try to think as he would. Try to picture things through his eyes. How would he react to a trolley ride? How would he see the Golden Gate Bridge?

Practice

Answers will vary. Encourage students to be creative and to add humor to their descriptions.

Practice putting yourself in the place of a character who is very different from yourself. Choose an object that is not alive. Maybe you will pick a doorknob, a rollerblade, a football, a flag, or a computer. Bring that object to life as a character. Be that character! On a separate sheet of paper, write one or two paragraphs. Describe yourself as the object, and describe your feelings.

Point of View

A story is often told from one character's **point of view**. When you identify the point of view, you know who is telling the story. If the story is told in the first-person point of view, the narrator uses the word *I* to describe the events.

For example, suppose there is a war between two imaginary countries: Lumboland and the Kingdom of Woo. If a story is written about a fellow from Woo, who leaves his beloved wife and 14 children to fight for his country, the readers would probably see Lumbolanders as enemies.

However, the same tale of war could be told by someone from Lumboland. A story told in the first-person point of view by this character would be quite different. The Lumboland people would probably be described as kind and gentle.

A story told by *I* is written from the first-person point of view. When a story is told in terms of the pronouns *she*, *he* or *they*, it is told from a third-person point of view.

> **The Writing Process**
>
> How can revising help you describe characters more clearly? (See The Writing Process, page WP24.)

Practice

Practice describing things from different points of view. On a separate sheet of paper, choose one of the following writing assignments, and write your paragraph.

Answers will vary. Evaluate students on their ability to write from a variety of perspectives. Remind students to use language that would reflect each perspective.

  1. Describe a mud puddle. First, write one paragraph describing a mud puddle from a five-year-old child's point of view. Then, write a paragraph describing the same mud puddle from the child's father's point of view.

(Practice continues on next page.) ⟾

2. Mr. Peters, the math teacher, wanted to surprise his students. One day, he brought apples to school. Before class, he put one apple on each student's desk. When the students walked in, they all smiled. Write a paragraph describing the incident from the point of view of one of the students. Then, write a paragraph describing the incident from Mr. Peters' point of view.

3. Describe an automobile accident. First, write a paragraph describing the accident from the point of view of the driver of one car. Then, write a paragraph describing the accident from the point of view of the driver of the other car.

 22-6 **The Bad Guy**

Just as you can win your readers' sympathy for the good characters, you can make your readers dislike the bad characters. A **villain** is an evil or wicked character in a story. A **hero** is the good character, or the main character, in a story. Create an evil villain just as you would create a hero. However, when you describe a villain, you will point out the bad things the character has done, not the good. You might make the villain *whine* and *snarl* and *growl* instead of *speak*. Your readers should hope that the villain loses in the end.

22-7 **Make Your Characters Speak— Writing Dialogue**

Dialogue is a conversation between characters. Read the following two examples of dialogue.

A. "Excuse me, sir," the woman said, "but I believe that you are standing on my toe."

B. "Hey, buddy," the woman said, "get your foot off my toe!"

As you can see, dialogue can say a lot about a character. By writing dialogue, you can build a character's personality. How is the woman in Sentence A different from the woman in Sentence B? You could say that the woman in Sentence A is too polite. You could say that the woman in Sentence B is probably angry.

Practice A

On a separate sheet of paper, write an adjective or a phrase that describes the speaker in each of the following groups of sentences.

1. "What a beautiful day!" Sarah exclaimed. "The sun is shining, the flowers are blooming, and the air is warm."

2. "It's too hot!" George complained. "That sun is beating down on me, and those stupid flowers are making me sneeze."

3. "I can hardly wait until the tryouts for the spring play," said Amy. "I'm going to try out for the leading role."

4. "Are the tryouts for the spring play really tomorrow?" asked Seth. "I don't know my lines very well. Maybe I'm catching a cold and should stay home."

Answers will vary but should be similar to the following.

1. Sarah is cheerful and happy.
2. George is a complainer and a whiner.
3. Amy is excited and confident.
4. Seth is nervous, self-conscious, and worried.

When you use dialogue, you must be sure that it sounds like the characters you have created. You must also be sure that you follow these rules so that your dialogue is clear.

1. Put quotation marks around a direct quotation, or a speaker's exact words.

    Example: "Stop teasing that kitten," shouted Jean.

2. Only the exact words are put inside the quotation marks. Explaining words are outside the quotation marks.

> Example: "I didn't mean to hurt the cat," said Wilma.

3. Separate the direct quotation from the explaining words with a comma, a question mark, or an exclamation point. The punctuation mark at the end of a quotation generally goes within the quotation marks.

> Examples: "I will cook a fine dinner," said the chef.
>
> "What's in the stew?" asked Molly.
>
> "Help me!" screamed the man on the raft.

4. Capitalize the first word of a quotation.

> Example: The waiter said, "The cook is very sorry about the fly in the soup."

5. A direct quotation may be placed at the beginning or at the end of a sentence. It may also be divided by the explaining words.

> Examples: "Uncle Paul's car is here. My favorite uncle has finally arrived," said Julie.
>
> Julie said, "Uncle Paul's car is here. My favorite uncle has finally arrived."
>
> "Uncle Paul's car is here," Julie said. "My favorite uncle has finally arrived."

If the divided quotation is all one sentence, do not capitalize the word that begins the second part of the quotation.

Example: "Uncle Paul," Julie said, "has finally arrived."

Brush Up on the Basics

Make sure to put a period, a comma, a question mark, or an exclamation point before the closing quotation mark.
(See Punctuation 16 in the Reference Guide.)

---

6. Begin a new paragraph each time a different character speaks.

> Examples: Mrs. Marcus said, "Today's lesson deals with writing quotations and punctuating them properly."
>
> "Ugh!" exclaimed Rose. "I would rather be sailing."

7. If you do not use the speaker's exact words but you use some other form of their words, do not use quotation marks. This method is called an **indirect quotation**.

> Example: Rose said that she would rather be sailing.

Practice B

On a separate sheet of paper, copy each of the following direct quotations. Punctuate them correctly.

1. Wendy whispered I think this will be an exciting adventure.

2. This ship will leave in one hour the captain announced.

3. Where can I buy a ticket I asked.

4. The ticket booth, a woman answered, is at the end of the hall.

5. All aboard for Boston the captain shouted.

1. Wendy whispered, "I think this will be an exciting adventure."
2. "This ship will leave in one hour," the captain announced.
3. "Where can I buy a ticket?" I asked.
4. "The ticket booth," a woman answered, "is at the end of the hall."
5. "All aboard for Boston," the captain shouted.

Read the following selection. Dialogue has been used to tell a story. Notice how each character reveals his personality through conversation.

> "What is the matter?" Alfred asked Jerry. "You don't really believe in haunted houses, do you?"

"Of course not," Jerry lied. He looked around at the spider webs in the empty room. "Maybe we should get out of this old house. We don't really belong here."

"Don't be silly," Alfred said. "Those guys dared us to spend the night here, and I have never turned down a dare."

"What's that?" Jerry cried. He looked up at the top of the wooden staircase and pointed. "What... what... what...." Jerry could no longer speak. His words froze in his throat.

"Don't be afraid," Alfred said. "It's only someone dressed in a bed sheet playing tricks on us."

How would you describe Alfred?

How would you describe Jerry?

Practice C

Answers will vary. Evaluate students on their ability to punctuate dialogue correctly and to describe characters through dialogue.

On a separate sheet of paper, write a conversation between two people. Let what the characters say show their personalities. Choose one of the following situations.

Write a conversation between

- a clerk in a store and a customer trying to return an item.

- an umpire and an angry baseball fan.

- a police officer and a person getting a speeding ticket.

- two children who have run away from home.

Practice D

The names you choose for your characters can be important. Different kinds of names give the readers different mental pictures of how a character looks and acts. British novelist Charles Dickens was famous for giving his characters names that suggested something about their appearance or personality. Think about the names in the following list of Dickens's characters. Then, write a short description of what you imagine each character's physical appearance or personality to be.

Mr. Gradgrind	Miss Havisham
Lady Dedlock	Mr. Wopsle
Tiny Tim	Harold Skimpole
Mr. Crook	Ebenezer Scrooge
Doctor Strong	Oliver Twist

Now, choose one pair of characters from the above list. On a separate sheet of paper, write a short conversation that these characters might have with one another. For example, what might Mr. Crook have to say to Miss Havisham? What might Harold Skimpole and Tiny Tim talk about? Make your dialogue at least four sentences long.

WRITING WITH STYLE
Creating Characters

Which of the following selections makes you care more about what happens to the main character?

What do you know about Christine in Paragraph 1? What do you know about Christine in Paragraph 2? What is the difference between the paragraphs?

1. When Christine woke up, she found herself at the bottom of a deep canyon. She realized that she had fallen from a cliff. She had been knocked out when her head hit the rocks. She moved carefully, checking to see if any bones were broken. Luckily, she was all right. She looked up the smooth sides of the steep cliff. Then she realized the truth. There was no way out of the canyon. She was trapped.

2. When Christine woke up, she found herself at the bottom of a deep canyon. She realized that she had fallen from a cliff while walking with her dog. She moved carefully, checking to see if any bones were broken. Her blue jeans were torn and her knee was cut, but otherwise she was all right. Then Christine thought about her family. Her husband, Gary, would be worried. She should have returned long ago. What about Jake, her little boy? He would be crying for his mother. Christine looked up the smooth sides of the steep cliff. She could hear her dog, Snowball, barking wildly from somewhere far away. Christine's gentle, blue eyes filled with determination as she realized the truth. There seemed to be no way out of the canyon. Nothing was going to keep her from getting out of there and back to her family.

Selection 2 wins more sympathy for the main character. In Selection 1, the readers know what happens but know nothing about the character or her past. In Selection 2, the readers learn that Christine is a wife and mother and that she has a dog. The writer describes Christine's clothing and eyes so the readers can picture her. These things make the readers care more about Christine.

VOCABULARY BUILDER
Letting Your Imagination Go

Create a new word. Then, use it in a paragraph. Let the context (the way you use the word in sentences) reveal the word's meaning.

Example: created word—quimble

I went to Miller's Pet Shop to buy a quimble. I had been saving my money for months because a quimble is very expensive. The clerk at Miller's said that he kept the quimbles in the back of the shop because most people were not interested in them. The back of the shop was dark and cool. Quimbles like it that way. I heard the quimbles making a tiny chirping sound. The first quimble I saw was the one I wanted. It was soft and brown and furry. I paid my money, and the clerk put my new quimble in a little cage. I hurried out of the store, anxious to take my new quimble home.

Create your own new word, and use it in an original paragraph. Write your paragraph on a separate sheet of paper.

Answers will vary. You may wish to have students exchange papers to see if they can figure out the meaning of their made-up words.

Chapter

22 ⟩ Review

Summary Have students use the summary to outline the main idea and details of the chapter.

Summary

Think about the interesting traits that real people have to create fictional characters.

Include all the senses—not just sight—when you describe people.

A good writer creates characters that readers care about.

Try to see things from that character's point of view.

A character's dialogue can show a lot about his or her personality.

Be sure to punctuate your dialogue correctly.

More Vocabulary Review is provided in the Classroom Resource Binder.

Vocabulary Review

Complete each sentence with a term from the box. Write your answers on a separate sheet of paper.

hero
trait
point of view
unique
indirect quotation
imaginary
habit
dialogue
villain

1. Courage is the character's strongest _____.

2. A _____ is something we do without thinking.

3. The author wrote about story events that were made up, or _____.

4. The _____ in the novel sounds just like real people talking.

5. The main character, who saved the children, was the novel's _____.

6. The _____ of the story is an evil person.

7. An _____ uses other words to show what a character says.

8. The character is considered _____ because there is no one like her.

9. When you know who is telling a story, you know the _____.

1. trait
2. habit
3. imaginary
4. dialogue
5. hero
6. villain
7. indirect quotation
8. unique
9. point of view

350   Unit 7 • Imaginative Writing

Chapter Quiz

Complete the following items. Write your answers on a separate sheet of paper.

1. Why is it important to use all five senses when you create a character?

2. What are two ways that writers use the people they know to create characters?

3. How do writers use traits of real people to create characters?

4. How might a writer use dialogue to build a character's personality?

5. Punctuate the following quotation: *The bandstand, John explained, is next to the lake.*

Critical Thinking

How can writers use point of view to create sympathy for a story character? Write your answer on a separate sheet of paper.

Critical Thinking Answers will vary. Possible answer: Telling a story from a particular character's point of view usually helps create more sympathy for him or her.

▶ **Test Tip**
Finish answering all of the questions. Then, go back and check your work.

Chapter Quiz

1. Using the five senses can help give readers a tangible picture of a character.

2. A writer might give a character the special traits or habits of people he or she knows. A writer can also combine traits from real people to create an imaginary character

3. To create a "bad guy," a writer emphasizes a real person's bad actions and negative traits. To create a "good guy," a writer emphasizes a real person's good actions and positive traits.

4. The things characters say and the ways in which they say them can show their personality.

5. "The bandstand," John explained, "is next to the lake."

Writing Activity

Find a picture of someone in a magazine. Look carefully at the person. Give this person a name, and make him or her a character. Think about what kind of life this character might lead. On a separate sheet of paper, describe an incident in which the character might be involved. The incident you describe needs to give clues to the character's personality.

Writing Activity Answers will vary. Evaluate students' ability to analyze a person's personality and actions based on their physical appearance.

Real-life experiences give writers many ideas for stories.

O. Henry (1862–1910) is one of America's most popular short-story writers. His real-life stories are known for their surprise endings. A friend once asked O. Henry where he got his story ideas. "There are stories in everything," the author replied. Three of O. Henry's most popular stories are "The Gift of the Magi," "After Twenty Years," and "The Last Leaf."

Extra Reading See the Pacemaker® Classics series for O. Henry's *O. Henry.*

To help students tap their prior knowledge of the chapter topic, see the **Chapter Project** in the Classroom Resource Binder.

Learning Objectives

- Identify character as a story element.
- Identify setting as a story element.
- Identify plot as a story element.
- Identify mood as a story element.
- Show an understanding of resolution of conflict.

Chapter 23 / Writing a Story

Words to Know

distinct	different
mood	a state of mind or a feeling
background	the events that came before

23-1 / What Is a Story?

Storytellers can transport others into a different world. For a little while, they can turn dreams into reality.

The cave people drew pictures on the walls of their caves. Their pictures told stories of struggles with wild animals. They told stories of hard times when food was scarce and the weather was bad. People continued telling stories throughout the years. In all lands, they told tales of troubles, of triumphs, and of people with courage. We are still telling stories today.

A teacher might say, "Today's assignment is to write a story. Let your imagination go. This will be fun."

Writing a story can, indeed, be fun if you understand what a story is. A story tells what happened.

The tale of what happened can be true, or it can be made up. It can be as short as a paragraph or as long as hundreds of pages.

A story also has a conflict. You may call a conflict a problem, or a struggle. The conflict is at the heart of the story. Everything else revolves around it.

The conflict can be between two people, as in the following example.

> Tim comes to live at his cousin John's house. John thinks that Tim is a boring pest. John teases Tim all the time. The two boys fight and argue. Tim, who is really a very lonely boy, must not only live in John's house but must share his room.

The conflict can be between a person and some outside force, as in the following example.

> Connie takes the little girl whom she is baby-sitting on a rowboat ride on the lake. When a storm comes up, she has to save not only her own life, but the child's life, too.

The conflict can be within one character's mind. It can involve a decision that he or she must make, as in the following example.

> Diane knew that the other girls in school were not friends with Becky. She knew that they would laugh at her if she invited Becky to her party. She also knew that Becky needed a friend. A party invitation would mean more to Becky than anything in the world. Diane could make Becky happy, but it could mean losing other friends. What would Diane do?

Practice A

To write a story of your own, you need to be able to recognize conflict. Read about each of the following situations. Decide if each contains a conflict. On a separate sheet of paper, number from 1 to 5. Then, write *conflict* or *no conflict* by each number.

1. Pete has skipped school and is spending the day in the park. While he is at the park, he sees a robbery. He is the only one who sees the attack on the old man, and he can clearly identify the robber. However, if Pete tells police what he saw, his parents will find out that he skipped school. He will be punished.

2. Pete has skipped school and is spending the day in the park. It is a beautiful day. The sun is shining, and the park is not crowded as it is on the weekends. Pete buys some popcorn and feeds the ducks in the duck pond. He has a great day.

3. Sarah and Kim have always been good friends. They both try out for the same swim team. They both make the team. They both want to swim in the butterfly event, but only one of them can swim in that event.

4. Sarah and Kim have always been good friends. They both try out for the same swim team. They both make the team. The team is great, and they have a winning season.

5. Lisa discovers that her father's factory is dumping dangerous waste material in the town river. She wants to be loyal to her family, but she knows that the river could be destroyed.

1. conflict
2. no conflict
3. conflict
4. no conflict
5. conflict

Practice B

Think of a situation that contains conflict. It can be a real experience that you have had or have heard about. Perhaps you were once lost, faced danger, or competed with someone. The situation can also be imaginary. On a separate sheet of paper, write a brief description, like those in Practice A on page 355, of the situation.

23-2 ▶ The People in the Story

A story must have characters, a setting, and a plot. The characters are the people in the story. In a good story, the characters seem real, and the readers care what happens to the characters. Remember the discussion of character in the last chapter. Review it if you need to.

When you write a short story, you should limit the number of characters. If you have too many characters, your readers may not be able to remember all of them. Have you ever read a story in which you were confused by too many characters?

It is better to concentrate on getting your readers to know two or three characters well than to introduce a lot of people. Remember your goal. You want your readers to care about your characters.

The Writing Process

How can brainstorming help you to create exciting characters? (See The Writing Process, page WP5.)

Give your characters names that are very different from each other. Give them different problems, different hair colors, and different personalities. Make them wear different types of clothing. Make sure the characters are **distinct**, or different, from each other.

Practice

On a separate sheet of paper, copy and complete the following lists. Create two characters that are distinct from each other. You might base your characters on two real people you know who are quite different from each other.

Answers will vary. Check to make sure that students have created two distinct characters.

Character 1	Character 2
name	name
age	age
hair color	hair color
height	height
clothing style	clothing style
personality	personality
interests	interests

Portfolio Project

On a separate sheet of paper, rewrite the following two paragraphs. Change the characters' names so that they are not so similar. Give each character some distinct characteristics. You might consider these qualities as you rewrite: hair color, personalities, and interests. You might try making the reader like one of the characters and dislike the other one. You might decide their conflict is not very important. Create a different conflict for them if you like.

Annie and Amy are on their own at last. It is their first year of college, and they are roommates. They have been friends since grade school. They have been at the university for only one week, and already both have fallen in love. Annie describes her new boyfriend as tall, handsome, and athletic. Amy says her boyfriend is all those things, too. She says that he is also smart, sweet, and gentle.

Then, Annie sees Amy and a young man walking hand in hand in front of the library. Annie is shocked and angry. Amy is holding hands with Annie's boyfriend! They are both in love with the same man.

Answers will vary. Evaluate students on their ability to create two distinct characters and a more interesting conflict.

The Setting Can Create a Mood

The setting is where and when the story takes place. The writer must make the setting clear early in the story. The setting can create a **mood**, or feeling, for a story.

What kind of a mood is created by the following description of a setting?

> Dark clouds moved in over the lake. The outline of the shore seemed far away. Although the sky was dark, the late afternoon was very calm. There was not a breath of wind. It was strange for the air to be so still. The water was as dark as the sky. Not a ripple disturbed its black surface. Then, I saw a strange shape pass by my little rowboat. It was a long, white shape that seemed to be just a few feet under the water. It passed again, going against the current now. This large object was no fish!

How does the description create an air of mystery and danger? What words make you feel this way? Using the right details is important.

Think About It

How can details help you to create a mood?

Practice A

On a separate sheet of paper, rewrite the following paragraph so that it has a mood of danger, evil, and mystery.

> It was night. I walked up the steps of the house. I opened the door and stepped inside. The clock on the mantel was just striking. I looked around the room. At first, I thought the room was empty. Then, I saw a woman standing in the corner with her back to me. She turned around.

Answers will vary. Sample response: It was a dark, stormy night. I crept up the steps of the abandoned house. I slowly pushed open the rickety door and cautiously stepped inside. The antique clock on the cold, dusty mantel was just striking midnight. I spun around the room. At first, I thought the room was empty. Then I saw a ghostly old woman standing in the corner with her back to me. She slowly turned around.

You are responsible for letting your readers know the setting early in your story. You are also responsible for giving your readers a little **background** material. Background includes the events that come before another event. Let your readers know the situation as the story opens. Tell a bit about what has already happened in the characters' lives.

Notice how the following paragraph gives the readers background details.

> Jenny has decided to enter a pie-baking contest. Now, this may not seem very unusual or very exciting, but for Jenny, it is an amazing event. She grew up in an apartment in Chicago. Her family often dined in restaurants. Then, last September, Jenny got married and moved to a farm in Ohio. Jenny had never cooked a meal or shopped in a grocery store. However, once she got into her own kitchen, she found that she liked it there. When the Ohio State Fair opened this summer, Jenny decided that she would not only enter the pie-baking contest but that she would win it!

The conflict is set up: Will Jenny bake a prize-winning pie or not?

Enough background is provided so that the readers will know why pie-baking is so unusual for Jenny. The readers also have been introduced to the main character and already know quite a bit about her.

Notice that all of the details have something to do with the story. We are not told, for example, that Jenny was an orchestra member in high school. We are not told that her parents are divorced or that her new husband is a champion chess player. These things would not affect this story, so they are not mentioned.

Practice B

1, 2, 4, 6, 8, 9

Read the following story idea.

Conflict: The Websters' house is on fire. Eight-year-old Will Webster is inside. Can anyone save him?

On a separate sheet of paper, write the numbers of the details that are important to the story. Explain your choices. Do not write the numbers of details that seem unnecessary.

1. The Websters live in the country. The only fire station is 50 miles away.

2. Will Webster has a broken leg.

3. Mr. Webster is a clerk in a clothing store.

4. The Websters' house is old and is made of wood.

5. The Websters grow vegetables in a garden behind their house.

6. Will Webster has been known to play with matches.

7. Will Webster goes to Junction City Grade School.

8. A next-door neighbor, Stan Swift, is home when the fire breaks out.

9. Stan Swift is an excellent athlete. He is strong and brave and likes Will very much.

10. Stan's mother is a teacher.

23-4 ▶ The Plot—Resolving the Conflict

The plot is the series of events that leads to the resolution of the conflict. The plot includes the events that happen to make the problem better or worse and that cause the problem to be resolved. These events make up the body of the story.

You should be able to list the events in a plot, as in the following example.

> Linda Gray is frightened when she cannot find her two-year-old daughter, Tammy.
>
> She looks all around the backyard where she last saw Tammy playing. She calls the neighbors, but no one has seen Tammy.
>
> She sees an unfamiliar van pull away from the curb and speed off down the street.
>
> Sure that her daughter has been kidnapped, Linda calls the police.
>
> The police arrive and question Linda. They ask her if she has searched the house. Linda realizes that she has not.
>
> The police search the house and find Tammy asleep on her bedroom floor.

Brush Up on the Basics

Adjectives can help to describe characters and events. Make sure to use a comma to separate adjectives in a series. (See Punctuation 7 in the Reference Guide.)

Why do you think the detail about the van was included in the story? It really has nothing to do with final outcome. The detail about the unfamiliar van adds suspense. It plants the idea that Tammy may have been kidnapped.

Before you write a story, do the following things.

1. Write a sentence describing the conflict.

2. List your characters.

3. Write a brief outline of the events.

4. Write a sentence telling how the conflict will be resolved.

If you follow the four steps listed above, you should write a good story. You will know where you are heading the moment you begin writing. Your story will not go on and on. You will not find yourself well into the story and suddenly ask yourself: *How am I going to end this?*

English and Technology

You can use the Internet to find books. Then, you can read them on your computer screen.

If the ending goes on and on, it shows that the writer did not plan ahead. The writer had no idea how the story was going to end when he or she began writing. With no way to solve the character's problem, the writer took an easy and uninteresting way out. Your ending should be as strong as your beginning. Plan ahead, and it will be.

Choose one of the following story endings. On a separate sheet of paper, write a beginning, with the setting and background, and a middle, with the events of the plot, so that you have a complete story.

- Then, I saw the window, and I knew I could escape. When I was free, I hurried down the road without looking back. I left the big, dark house behind me. I knew I would never forget that place. I knew, too, that I would never talk to strangers again.

- I watched as the father and his child hugged each other. I had been through a lot to make this moment happen, but it had been worth it. They were together again.

- When I opened my eyes, the people around my bed were crying. "Welcome home," they said.

- In spite of everything, we won that game. No one had been able to stop us. We were the champs.

Answers will vary. Students' stories should contain all the elements of a short story.

Practice

On a separate sheet of paper, number from 1 to 4. Use complete sentences to answer the following questions.

1. A story is built around a conflict. What is the meaning of *conflict?*

2. A story must have characters. What are *characters?*

3. A story needs a setting. What is a *setting?*

4. Every story has a plot. What makes up the *plot?*

Answers will vary but should be similar to the following.

1. The conflict is the problem or struggle going on in the story.
2. Characters are the people in the story.
3. The setting tells where and when the story takes place.
4. The plot includes the events of the story and the conflict.

WRITING WITH STYLE
Beginning a Story

Which of the following beginnings, 1 or 2, makes you want to read the story? Why?

1. Janie Nichols met the old man in the park one Saturday. He seemed lonely and sad. Janie decided that he needed a friend. Janie, in fact, also needed a friend. She had just moved to the city and knew very few people. She had not found a job yet, and she lived alone in a little apartment. The old man wanted to talk, and Janie wanted to listen.

   He told Janie stories. He told her about all the strange places he had visited when he was young. One day, he gave Janie a gift.

   "This box," he said, "contains a precious treasure. Do not open it until you are alone." He smiled a crooked smile from behind his thick, gray beard.

   In her apartment that evening, Janie began to unwrap the box. She had just pulled off the dirty old string when the box moved. The movement made Janie jump. She stared at the box, not sure what to do next.

2. Janie Nichols met the old man in the park one Saturday. He seemed very nice. The man and Janie became good friends. They would sit and talk for hours every time they met. Some days, they would feed the pigeons. The park was filled with pigeons. There were gray ones and white ones, and there were some with brightly colored feathers.

   One day, the old man said, "I have a present for you, Janie." He gave her a box. She was very grateful for the gift. She did not get many presents. When she opened it, she found it was a blue sweater. It was beautiful and soft and had come from the finest department store in town.

Beginning 1 makes the reader more interested in reading the whole story. It sets up a conflict (Should Janie open the box?) and suggests something mysterious to come (What could be in the box?). There is no conflict suggested in Selection 2.

VOCABULARY BUILDER
Using the Word "Said"

Sometimes, you will use dialogue in a story. Your story will be more exciting if you do not always use the word *said* in conversations. Vary your writing. Try to use more descriptive verbs to replace *said.*

This lesson presents some words you might use to replace *said.* On a separate sheet of paper, complete each sentence by giving the speaker something to say. Use the meaning of the verb in italic type to decide just what the speaker would say. If you do not know what the verb means, look it up in the dictionary before you complete the sentence.

Example: "Save me! I'm drowning!" *exclaimed* Jill.

1. "_____!" exclaimed Joan.

2. "_____!" bawled Dora.

3. "_____!" shouted the boss.

4. "_____," Doug mumbled.

5. "_____?" Luke questioned.

Answers will vary. Possible responses:

1. "Fire! Everyone get out!" exclaimed Joan.

2. "I don't want that doll!" bawled Dora.

3. "Get that report done now!" shouted the boss.

4. "He'll never learn," Doug mumbled.

5. "Do we have to go now?" Luke questioned.

Summary Have students use the summary to outline the main idea and details of the chapter.

Summary

A story tells what happened. It must have characters, a setting, and a plot.

Every story has a conflict, or problem, that the characters face. The conflict can be between two people. It can be between a person and an outside force. A conflict can also be within one character's mind.

Make sure that the characters of a story are distinct from one another.

You can use the setting of a story to create a mood.

Before you begin to write a story, write a sentence describing the main conflict. Then, list the story's characters, write an outline of the events, and write a sentence that tells how the conflict will be resolved.

| distinct |
| mood |
| background |

1. false, background
2. true
3. false, mood

More Vocabulary Review is provided in the Classroom Resource Binder.

Vocabulary Review

Write *true* or *false* after each sentence. If the sentence is false, change the underlined word to make it true. Choose a term from the box. Write your answers on a separate sheet of paper.

1. The <u>mood</u> in a story fills in the readers about what has already happened in the characters' lives.

2. The characters in a story must be <u>distinct</u> from one another. Otherwise, readers might confuse them.

3. The setting of the story, an old, empty house, created a creepy <u>background</u> in the readers' minds.

Chapter Quiz

1. The conflict is the heart of a story around which everything revolves.

It is the conflict that makes a story exciting to read.

2. A conflict can occur between two characters, between a character

and an outside force, or within a character's own mind.

Chapter Quiz

Complete the following items. Write your answers on a separate sheet of paper.

1. Why is it important for a story to have a conflict?

2. What are the three main types of conflicts that a story can have?

3. Why are details important when you are creating a character?

4. How can a writer create the mood for a story?

5. Why does a writer give background information at the beginning of a story?

▶ **Test Tip**
Make sure to use proper capitalization and punctuation when you write your answers.

3. Details are important when creating a character because they help paint a picture of the character.

4. A writer can create the mood for a story through details, setting, and the words he or she uses.

5. Background information lets the reader know the situation as the story opens.

Critical Thinking

Why would a writer need to know how the conflict in a story will be resolved? Write your answer on a separate sheet of paper.

Critical Thinking Answers will vary. Possible answer: Knowing how the conflict will be resolved keeps a writer focused on the story and its ending.

Writing Activity

On a separate sheet of paper, write a two-paragraph story using these four steps. (1) Write a sentence describing the conflict. (2) List your characters. (3) Write a brief outline of the story's events. (4) Write a sentence that tells how the conflict will be resolved.

Writing Activity Answers will vary. You may wish to discuss students' four-step plan before they begin the actual writing of their story.

The art of the poet is to make ordinary words send extraordinary messages.

Countee Cullen
(1903–1946) became well known during the Harlem Renaissance of the 1920s. His poems explore how racial prejudice affects people. His poems also look at an African American's search for his African heritage. Cullen used ordinary, everyday words to send important messages to his readers.

To help students tap their prior knowledge of the chapter topic, see the **Chapter Project** in the Classroom Resource Binder.

Learning Objectives

- Identify devices of alliteration and onomatopoeia.
- Write a cinquain.
- Write a haiku.
- Write concrete words and poems.

Chapter **24** Writing Poetry

Words to Know

verse	a short poem or a section of a poem
alliteration	the repetition of the same first sound in a group of words or a line of poetry
onomatopoeia	a word whose sound suggests its meaning
rhyme	the repetition of similar end sounds
rhythm	any regular, repeating pattern
cinquain	a five-line poem that follows a particular pattern
haiku	a Japanese-style of verse that is usually about nature; the verse is formed by three lines of five, seven, and five syllables

24-1 Listening to Words

Writing poetry lets you relax, play with words, and dream a little. So far in this book, you have learned to follow a lot of writing rules. You have written some fairly long papers. However, there are very few rules for writing poetry. Poems are often short. Sometimes, they are only a few words. Sometimes, they are more than one **verse** long. A verse is a short poem or a section of a poem.

Writing poetry lets people take a close look at their world and at their feelings. It lets people express those feelings in just a few carefully chosen words.

Listen to the words of poems. Each word plays a part in creating a mood and expressing an idea. Each word in a poem has more than one job. The word expresses an idea through its meaning. It also creates a kind of music. The very sounds of the words often add to a poem's effect on us.

One way poets can use sound in their writing is to use a figure of speech called **alliteration**. Alliteration means that the same first letter or letters are repeated in several words. This method can create an interesting effect. The repeated letter not only makes a sound, but it can also add meaning.

Look at the following example of alliteration.

> The strong, smooth snake slithered across the sun-baked sand.

Did you notice how all the *s* sounds created a hissing, snaky feeling?

The following are two more examples.

> Forceful winds fanned the fierce, flashing flames.

> Donna definitely disliked doughnuts.

Practice A

On a separate sheet of paper, write a sentence of description for two subjects on page 371. Use alliteration in your description. Begin two, three, or four words with the same letter.

> Example: summer—Sweet summer sounds filled the air like singing.

> Example: autumn leaves—The crisp, crunchy autumn leaves crackled underfoot.

1. a train
2. summer
3. rain
4. a bee
5. a fire engine
6. snow
7. autumn leaves
8. flowers
9. bugs
10. any other subject

Some words actually copy sounds. For example, the word *buzz* imitates the sound a bee makes. This type of word is another figure of speech. It is called **onomatopoeia** (on-a-ma-ta-PEE-a). Think about these sound words as you do the following practice.

Practice B

On a separate sheet of paper, write a sound word for each of the following things.

Example: pig = oink

1. a faucet
2. an alarm clock
3. a train
4. a horn
5. rain
6. a cow
7. a donkey
8. a rooster
9. bacon frying
10. a person who has been hit in the stomach
11. a laugh
12. a strong wind
13. a home run

Answers will vary. Possible responses:
1. A train trekked across the tough terrain.
2. Summer on the seaside coast smells sweet.
3. The rain rattled and roared, scaring the restless children.
4. A bee buzzed between the brambles.
5. The fire engine flew in a frenzy to free the family from the fire.
6. Snow seized the small town.
7. The autumn leaves create a cheerful cornucopia of colors.
8. Brightly colored flowers bring a bounty of beauty.
9. Disgusting bugs diligently dug into the dark dirt.

Answers will vary. Possible responses:
1. drip
2. beep
3. clackety clack
4. honk
5. plip plop
6. moo
7. hee-haw
8. cock-a-doodle-doo
9. sizzle
10. ugh
11. ha, ha
12. whoosh
13. crack

Do you remember the goal of writing that has been repeated so often in this book? You want to let your readers experience what you are experiencing. Poems can do that using very few words. Before you write any poems for the following practices, take time to picture what you will write about. Go slowly. See it. Hear it. Smell it. Taste it. Feel it. Think about how your topic makes you feel.

Practice A

Answers will vary. Encourage students to play with language and to look at their subject from a variety of perspectives.

Think of this practice as making a picture poem. You will be describing something. Your poem does not have to **rhyme**. A rhyme is the repetition of similar sounds. It does not have to have any special **rhythm**. Rhythm is a regular, repeated pattern. There is only one rule. Each line should paint a picture.

Highway

The highway stretches out ahead of me,
Hard, black asphalt as far as I can see.
A yellow line runs down the middle.
That line is faded now but once was bright.
The highway goes on and on, flat and straight,
   right toward the sun.
I cannot see the end.

Can you picture the highway? Notice that each line is like a brush stroke on canvas, adding to the picture of the highway.

On a separate sheet of paper, write your picture poem. You may choose your topic from the following list. You may also create a topic of your own.

clouds	a waterfall	a car
headlights	a ski slope	an insect
a swimming pool	snow	night
the last day of school	a hurricane	a sunrise
a desert	a police officer	a rock star

Before you write, take time to picture your subject. Use all of your senses. Think about how your subject makes you feel. Suppose, for example, you are going to write about a fruit stand. You picture it. It is bright and full of fruit. You see many different kinds of fruits on the shelves. You smell the sweet odor of the oranges. You feel the slippery coating of the apples. Finally, you think about how sad you feel because you cannot eat it all.

The next practices will give you a chance to write some different types of poems.

Think About It

How can senses help you write poetry?

Practice B

By taking just five steps found on the next page, you can write a poem. These five-line poems are called **cinquains** (SIN-kānz).

(Practice B continues on next page.) ⏩

(Practice B continued.)

Read the following five steps carefully Take a look at some of the examples, and then begin.

STEP 1: Write a noun, which is a person, a place, a thing, or an idea.

Icicles

STEP 2: On the next line, write two adjectives that describe the noun in Line 1. Separate the two adjectives with a comma.

Long, silver

STEP 3: On the third line, write three verbs. These verbs should be things that the noun on the first line does. Separate the three verbs with commas.

Glitter, sparkle, drip

STEP 4: On the fourth line, tell how you feel about your noun, or compare it to something else by writing a simile.

They are silver daggers.

STEP 5: On the fifth line, repeat the word that you wrote on the first line, or write a synonym for that word.

Icicles

Read a few more examples of cinquains before you write your own. Notice that the first word on each line begins with a capital letter.

Actress,
Beautiful, glamorous
Smiling, bowing, gesturing
Who is she, really?
Star.

Stream
Shallow, icy
Bubbling, gurgling, flowing
A friend that cools my toes
Tiny river.

On a separate sheet of paper, write a cinquain. Just follow the five steps.

You may write about one of the following topics, or choose a topic of your own.

Answers will vary. The secret to writing these poems is following the steps. Be sure students understand what to write for each line.

trees	fire engines	love
babies	eagles	television
teachers	moon	books
baseball	ocean	dogs

Practice C

The Japanese invented a form of verse called **haiku** (HI-koo). Haiku is a verse formed by three lines of five, seven, and five syllables. Students often enjoy writing haiku because they are short and follow a simple pattern. Think of haiku as an expression of one brief moment in time.

The haiku pattern is based on the number of syllables in a line. The entire poem has only seventeen syllables. The first line has five syllables. The second line has seven syllables. The third line has five syllables.

Read the following examples of haiku before you write your own.

Fog blankets the bay
Fishing boats are like white
   ghosts
Ropes moan against docks.

Race cars on the track
Tires shrieking, around and round
Going nowhere fast.

The flag flaps wildly
Declaring a nation's pride
Bright, brave colors wave.

A fiery wind blows
Across the empty desert
Nothing can live here.

(Practice C continues on next page.) ➠

(Practice C continued.)

Answers will vary. Writing
haiku is very challenging.
You may wish to have students
work in pairs or only have your
more advanced students
complete this activity.

On a separate sheet of paper, write your own haiku.
Remember that the point is to capture a moment and
share it with your readers. Also, remember the number
of syllables in each line. Write about one of the topics
listed below, or choose your own topic.

flower	jazz	sunset
turtle	frozen pond	junkyard
sun	spider web	cemetery
caterpillar	candy	rooftop
quilt	football	slums

Express Yourself
So far in this chapter, you have used your picturing
and describing skills to write some poems. You have
been looking at things in the world. Now, look inside
your own mind.

Brush Up on the Basics

You can use punctuation
to make your poetry clear.
(See Punctuation 1 in the
Reference Guide.)

1. and 2. Answers will vary.
Encourage students
to be honest about
themselves, so they will write
more powerful, heartfelt
poems.

Practice D

1. On a separate sheet of paper, complete each
    of the following sentences in a different way.

    a. I wish . . .

    b. I wish . . .

    c. I wish . . .

    d. I am happy when . . .

    e. I am happy when . . .

    f. I am happy when . . .

    g. I am sad when . . .

    h. I am sad when . . .

    i. I am sad when . . .

2. Now, choose the one sentence from Part 1 that you like best. On a separate sheet of paper, expand that sentence into a poem. Build on the idea expressed in the sentence. The poem should reveal the way you feel. Look at some of the following examples before you write your own poem.

I wish . . .
That people wouldn't call me
    a shrimp
And laugh at me because I'm
    small.
Sometimes, it makes me feel as
    if I don't exist at all.

I wish . . .
I had a million bucks,
And I could buy all my friends
The most amazing presents.
I'd watch them smile bigger
And bigger until their faces
Almost burst.

I am happy when . . .
It is late at night, and the
    house is quiet.
Then darkness wraps around
    me like a blanket.
My brothers and sisters are
    safe in bed.
We are together.
No one can get in or out.

I am sad when . . .
Halloween is past,
And I pack my mask away.
I have to be myself again.
No more daring, dashing
    pirate—
Time to get back to real life.

Think of the word *concrete*. Your first thought might be about the hard substance that is used to make sidewalks. *Concrete* has another meaning. It means real or having a physical existence. Something concrete is something you can actually see. Objects you can touch are concrete. Ideas are not.

You can have some fun with words by thinking in a concrete manner.

Look at the following examples of concrete words.

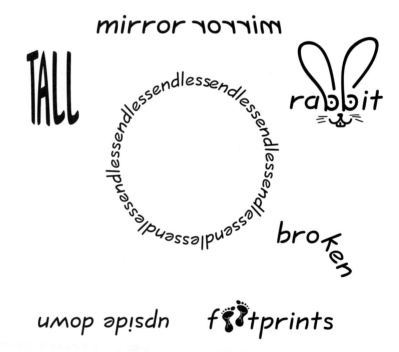

The Writing Process
What is the purpose of publishing your poetry? (See The Writing Process, page WP40.)

Practice

On a separate sheet of paper, write some concrete words of your own. You can use any words you want. Look at the following suggestions.

Answers will vary. You may wish to post students' poetry around the classroom.

flower	rain	huge
flag	waterfall	repeat
parallel	war	dizzy
downhill	sad	absent
mountain	snake	crowded

You can write concrete poems, too. Remember that the physical shape will show meaning. Read the following example of a concrete poem.

From the top of
   the park slide, I
            could
                see
                    the
                        whole
                            world
                                then
                                    Z
                                     o
                                      o
                                       M I was back on earth again.

Portfolio Project

Write a concrete poem on a separate sheet of paper. Look at the following suggested topics.

a cat	love	a frog
a mountain	the moon	snowflakes

Answers will vary.

WRITING WITH STYLE
Writing Poetry

What makes a collection of words a poem? Look at the following two descriptions. Which one would you define as the poem? What qualities does it have that make it a poem?

1. The Moon

> The moon is a natural satellite of Earth. It is sometimes seen in a full, rounded shape. At other times, it can be seen as a crescent shape. Some people say that the moon has strange powers. Some people even say that people can become insane from looking at the moon. Such people are said to be "moonstruck."

2. The Moon

> Great, white orb of the night
> You are a mystery.
> Some evenings just a pale sliver of light,
> Your surface hidden by the dark.
> Sometimes, full and round and glorious
> You invite all to come stand and stare
> At your brilliance.

Selection 2 is a poem. It is written in verse form. It is very descriptive, with each line presenting an image. Selection 1 is written in prose style and is more informative than descriptive.

VOCABULARY BUILDER
Using Clichés

Clichés are overused expressions. People often use them so that they do not have to say things in their own words. Most people use clichés once in a while when speaking. However, it is wise to avoid using clichés in your writing. It is better to be original than to rely on overused expressions. Use your own voice. Express yourself.

You will often hear clichés, and it is interesting to think about what they mean. Clichés often do not actually mean what they seem to say. For example, "turn over a new leaf" is a cliché. It means, "make a new start." A person who uses this cliché is not talking about trees.

1. Read the following sentences. The words in italic type are clichés. On a separate sheet of paper, tell what each cliché means in your own words. Use context clues to help you figure out meanings.

   a. Hank worked so hard at the factory that he would sleep *like a log* every night.

   b. Susan always uses the same excuse. She sounds like *a broken record.*

   c. I bet a dollar that the Golden Bears would win the game, even though it was *a long shot.*

   d. Steven always gets angry. He has a real *chip on his shoulder*.

   e. I have heard that joke before. It is *as old as the hills*.

   f. Do not say the wrong thing to Cindy. She has a *short fuse*.

2. Think of three more clichés. List them on a separate sheet of paper, and explain what they mean.

1. Answers will vary but should be similar to the following:

   a. Sleep *like a log* means to sleep very soundly.

   b. Sounds like *a broken record* means to repeat something over and over again.

   c. A *long shot* is an unlikely possibility.

   d. A *chip on his shoulder* means he is always grouchy.

   e. *As old as the hills* is used to describe something that is very old.

   f. Someone with a *short fuse* has a very quick temper.

2. Answers will vary.

Summary Have students use the summary to outline the main idea and details of the chapter.

Summary

Choose each word in a poem carefully to create an image or express an idea.

Poets sometimes use alliteration and onomatopoeia to emphasize meaning through sound.

A poem may or may not rhyme or have a special rhythm.

Cinquains and haiku are short poems that follow definite patterns.

You can show meaning with an actual picture by writing concrete words and poems.

More Vocabulary Review is provided in the Classroom Resource Binder.

Vocabulary Review

Match each term in the box with its meaning. Write your answers on a separate sheet of paper.

onomatopoeia
verse
haiku
alliteration
cinquain
rhythm
rhyme

1. **1.** a short poem or section of a poem
2. **2.** the repetition of similar end sounds
3. **3.** any regular, repeated pattern
4. **4.** a five-line poem that follows a particular pattern
5. **5.** a Japanese verse formed by three lines
6. **6.** the repetition of the same first sound in a group of words or line of poetry
7. **7.** a word whose sound reminds you of its meaning

1. verse
2. rhyme
3. rhythm
4. cinquain
5. haiku
6. alliteration
7. onomatopoeia

Chapter Quiz

1. Writing poetry is different because it uses a fewer number of words. The poet tries to create images using as few words as possible. The lines or images are not written in complete sentences. Also, there are not many rules for writing poetry. A poet is free to relax and play with words.

Chapter Quiz

Complete the following items. Write your answers on a separate sheet of paper.

1. How is writing a poem different from the other types of writing you have learned in this book?

2. What is the purpose of using alliteration in a poem?

3. Describe how to write a cinquain. Tell what appears on each of its five lines.

4. Describe the form of a haiku.

5. Why is the form of a concrete poem important?

Critical Thinking

How does a poet use language to create an image? Write your answer on a separate sheet of paper.

Critical Thinking Answers will vary. Possible answer: A poet uses strong, specific words to create an image and feeling with each line. This can be done through the choice of words and how they are used, for example, in forms such as alliteration and onomatopoeia.

▶ **Test Tip**
If you need help answering a question, try to picture what you learned in class.

2. Alliteration creates a kind of music by repeating the same first sound in a group of words or a line of poetry.

3. Line 1 of a cinquain is a noun. Line 2 lists two adjectives that describe the noun. Line 3 lists three verbs that tell what the noun does. Line 4 tells more about the noun. Line 5 repeats the noun in Line 1 or gives a synonym for it.

4. A haiku has three lines of five, seven, and five syllables.

5. A concrete poem's form looks like the subject of the poem. It serves as an illustration.

Writing Activity

On a separate sheet of paper, write the letters of your first and last names going down. Each letter will be on its own line. Think of words that describe who you are or what you like. Each word must begin with a different letter of your name. Write the word next to the letter.

Writing Activity Answers will vary. These poems are generally funny but should also be viewed as a means for celebrating who students are.

Unit 7 Review

Read each of the following items. On a separate sheet of paper, write the letter that best answers each one.

1. The special qualities that make a character distinct from others are called
   A. sympathy.
   B. habits.
   C. traits.
   D. moods.

2. Which of the following quotations is written correctly?
   A. It's me out here, called John, "so open the door."
   B. "It's me," out here, said John, "so open the door."
   C. "It's me out here, said John, so open the door."
   D. "It's me out here," said John, "so open the door."

3. The mood of a story is often created by the
   A. characters.
   B. plot.
   C. setting.
   D. all of the above

4. The conflict in a story can be
   A. between two people.
   B. between a person and an outside force.
   C. within one character's mind.
   D. all of the above

5. This sentence *The cat crept carefully across the carpet* is an example of
   A. onomatopoeia.
   B. alliteration.
   C. rhyme.
   D. concrete words.

6. Both a haiku and a cinquain
   A. have three lines and 17 syllables.
   B. must contain onomatopoeia.
   C. have end-of-line rhyme.
   D. are short verse forms.

Critical Thinking Answers will vary. Details are important in all types of writing because they help readers understand what the writer is trying to communicate.

Writing Activity Answers will vary. You may wish to post students' work around the classroom or compile them in a booklet.

Critical Thinking

Why are details important in all types of writing? Write your answer on a separate sheet of paper.

WRITING ACTIVITY Write a short poem about your world today. It could be a haiku, a cinquain, or another verse form. Remember to use words that both express ideas and create a kind of music. Write your poem on a separate sheet of paper.

Appendix

Glossary

abbreviation   a shortened form of a word

acceptance   answering "yes" to an invitation

adjective   a word that describes a noun or pronoun

adverb   a word that describes a verb, an adjective, or another adverb

alliteration   the repetition of the same first sound in a group of words or a line of poetry

anecdote   a short, interesting story about an event or a person

antecedent   the noun a pronoun replaces

application   a form with questions that a person must answer when applying for a job

audience   the people who read a piece of writing

background   the events that came before

bibliography   a list of books or sources for a particular topic

body   the main part of a paragraph that gives the supporting details

brainstorming   working with others to list ideas for writing

card catalog   a file in a library that contains information for every book

character   a person in a story or play

characteristics   features that make something or someone special and individual

checklist   a list of things to look for and check off when done

chronological order   events arranged in the order in which they happened

cinquain   a five-line poem that follows a particular pattern

classified ad   a short newspaper advertisement arranged in a group, or class, with similar ads

combine   to join together

command   a sentence that gives an order

communication   sending and receiving messages

comparison   the act of noting the likenesses and differences of things

complex sentence   a sentence with a subordinate clause and an independent clause

composition   an essay

compound predicate   two or more predicates with the same subject

compound sentence   two simple sentences joined by a comma and a coordinating conjunction, such as *and, but,* and *or*

compound subject   two or more subjects with the same predicate

concluding sentence   a sentence that ends a paragraph

conclusion   the end of a paragraph

conflict   a problem or struggle that is at the center of the story

conjunction a word used to join or link words, phrases, ideas, and sentences; common conjunctions are *and, but,* and *or*

connotation ideas or feelings associated with a word in addition to its actual meaning

content the ideas in a piece of writing

contribute to give something to others

cross-reference a reference to another part of a book or to another source of information on the same subject

define to give the meaning of a word

description a picture in words; the details that create a picture of something

descriptive giving a picture in words; telling about something in great detail

details all the small parts of something that make up the whole

Dewey Decimal system a system used in libraries to put books in order; the specific number assigned to each book, pamphlet, and so on that classifies the item according to subject

dialogue a conversation between characters

differences points that are not alike; ways that things are different

distinct different

drafting the writing stage of the writing process

edit to prepare a piece of writing for the final copy by correcting any mistakes in facts, grammar, usage, and mechanics

editing correcting mistakes in a piece of writing

element a basic part or feature of the whole

essay a short piece of writing about a particular subject

exaggeration something stretched beyond the truth; something made larger or greater than it really is

example one of a group that shows what the rest are like or explains the general rule; a sample

explanatory paragraph a paragraph that explains, clarifies, and gives details

fact something that is known to be true

fiction imaginative writing; something made up or invented

figure a number

figure of speech an expression in which words suggest an image that is different from the literal meaning of words

format the plan, style, or layout of a piece of writing

fragment a group of words that is not a complete sentence but is punctuated as if it were

gender tells if a noun or a pronoun is masculine or feminine

grammar a set of rules for writing and speaking a language

habit a thing that a person does regularly without thinking about it

haiku a Japanese-style verse that is usually about nature; the verse is formed by three lines of five, seven, and five syllables

hero the main character in a story; he or she is usually good

identify to show to be a particular person, place, or thing

imaginary not real; existing only in one's mind

implies suggests in an indirect way

incident an event

indented set in from the margin of a page

independent clause a clause that can stand alone as a complete sentence

indirect quotation repeating what a character says but not in the exact words

informative paragraph a paragraph that gives information and shares knowledge

inquire to ask about something

interview a meeting between a job seeker and an employer during which questions are asked and answered

irregular verbs verbs that do not use –d or –ed to form their past tense

literally actually, really, exactly as things are

logical something that makes sense or is reasonable

main idea the point a writer wants to make about a topic

mechanics the spelling and punctuation of a piece of writing

metaphor a figure of speech in which one thing is compared to another by suggesting a likeness between the two

mood a state of mind or a feeling

narrative paragraph a paragraph that tells of events and experiences

nonfiction writing that tells about real people and events

noun a word that names a person, a place, a thing, or an idea

novel a long work of fiction

object of the preposition a noun or pronoun that follows a preposition in the prepositional phrase

onomatopoeia a word whose sound suggests its meaning

opinion a belief, an attitude, or a viewpoint

oral presentation a talk given to a group

order of importance organizing sentences from most important to least important

organize to put the parts of something in order

outline a plan that shows how a main idea and its details connect to each other

outlining creating a plan for a piece of writing

paragraph a group of sentences placed together because they all relate to the same idea

periodical a publication, such as a newspaper or a magazine, that is published at regular intervals

persuade to get someone to do something or believe something; to convince

plot   the main story of a novel or play

plural   expressing more than one

point of view   who is telling a story

predicate   the part of the sentence that tells something about the subject

preposition   a word that shows the relationship of a noun or pronoun to some other word in a sentence

prepositional phrase   a preposition and its object taken together

prewriting   the planning stage of the writing process

pronoun   a word used in place of a noun

proofread   to mark errors in a piece of writing

proofreading marks   marks used to show editing changes

publishing   sharing your writing with others

punctuation marks   marks used to make the meaning of writing clear

purpose   the reason for writing something

qualify   (1) to limit or make less strong; (2) to be suited; to have the necessary training

quote   to repeat or copy exactly the writing or speech of another

reference   a person who can give information about someone else

reference book   a source of information

regrets   the polite refusal of an invitation

report   an account of a particular subject

research   the gathering of facts and other information

resolution of the conflict   a solution; an end to the conflict

restate   to say or write something again in different words

restating   saying something again or in a different way

résumé   an account of a person's education, experience, and qualifications

revise   to make changes in a piece of writing

rhyme   the repetition of similar end sounds

rhythm   any regular, repeating pattern

rough draft   the first, unpolished copy of a piece of writing

run-on sentence   two or more sentences that have not been properly joined

senses   sight, hearing, smell, taste, and touch

sentence   a group of words that expresses a complete thought; a sentence has a subject and a predicate. It begins with a capital letter and ends with a punctuation mark

sentence structure   the way in which a sentence is written

setting   the time and place of an event, story, or play

similarities   points of likeness; ways that things are alike

simile   a figure of speech in which two things are compared by using the words like or as

simple predicate   the verb or verb phrase in the sentence

simple sentence   a group of words that expresses a complete thought and has one subject-predicate combination

simple subject   the most important noun or pronoun in the sentence; what the sentence is about

singular   expressing only one

source   any book, place, person, or material from which you gather information

subject   the part of the sentence that tells who or what the sentence is about

subordinate clause   a clause that adds to the meaning of another clause but makes no sense by itself

subordinate conjunction   a conjunction that introduces a subordinate clause

summary   a short statement that brings together the important points and details

support   to add strength to

sympathy   the act of sharing another's feelings; feeling sorry for another's suffering

synonym   a word with the same or nearly the same meaning as another word

thesaurus   a book that lists words that are similar in meaning

thesis statement   a sentence that presents the idea that the essay will support

topic   the subject of a piece of writing

topic sentence   a sentence that states the main idea of a paragraph

trait   a special quality

transition   the act of moving from one thing to another

transitional word   a word that helps a reader move from one idea to another; it shows how one idea relates to and connects with another idea

typeface   a style of type

unique   being the only one of its kind

variety   many different forms or kinds of things

verb   a word that expresses action or being

verse   a short poem or a section of a poem

villain   an evil or wicked character in a story

vivid   clear, distinct, colorful

word processing   a computer software, or program, used to type and change text

writing assignment   a writing task

writing process   a five-step process for writing that includes prewriting, drafting, revising, editing, and publishing

ZIP code   a postal code designed to speed up mail service by assigning special numbers to each area of the country

REFERENCE GUIDE

SENTENCES

GRAMMAR 1 **Definition of a sentence**

A sentence is a group of words that expresses a complete thought. Every sentence must have a subject and a predicate. (See Grammar 3–6.) Every sentence begins with a capital letter and ends with a punctuation mark.

> That leopard has already killed 400 people.

> Is it still hungry?

> Be careful!

Sometimes a sentence may have only one word. (See Grammar 5.)

> Listen.

> Hurry!

GRAMMAR 2 **Kinds of sentences**

There are four different kinds of sentences.

A *declarative sentence* makes a statement. A declarative sentence ends with a period.

> A volcano in the Canary Islands is for sale.

An *interrogative sentence* asks a question. An interrogative sentence ends with a question mark.

> Who would want to buy a volcano?

An *imperative sentence* gives a command. An imperative sentence ends with a period or an exclamation point.

Show me the list of buyers.

An *exclamatory sentence* expresses excitement. An exclamatory sentence ends with an exclamation point.

They must be crazy!

GRAMMAR 3 ## Subjects and predicates in declarative sentences

Every sentence has two main parts, the subject and the predicate. The subject names what the sentence is about. The predicate describes an action by or a state of being of the subject.

In most declarative sentences, the subject is the first part. The predicate is the second part.

A famous sea captain — was often sick.
subject — predicate

He — suffered from seasickness.
subject — predicate

In some declarative sentences, the predicate is the first part. The subject is the second part.

Back and forth rolled — the captain's ship.
predicate — subject

GRAMMAR 4 ## Subjects and predicates in interrogative sentences

Every interrogative sentence has a subject and a predicate. In some interrogative sentences, the subject is the first part. The predicate is the second part.

Who — solved the mystery?
subject — predicate

Which clue — was most important?
subject — predicate

In most interrogative sentences, part of the predicate comes before the subject. To find the subject and predicate, rearrange the words of the interrogative sentence. Use those words to make a declarative sentence. The declarative sentence will not always sound natural, but it will help you. The subject and predicate of the two sentences are the same.

Did	the butler	lie about it?
predicate	subject	predicate

The butler	did lie about it.
subject	predicate

GRAMMAR 5 ## Subjects and predicates in imperative sentences

Only the predicate of an imperative sentence is spoken or written. The subject of the sentence is understood. That subject is always *you*.

(You)   Try an underhand serve.

(You)   Please show me how to do it.

GRAMMAR 6 ## Subjects and predicates in exclamatory sentences

Every exclamatory sentence has a subject and a predicate. In most exclamatory sentences, the subject is the first part. The predicate is the second part.

Kotzebue Sound, Alaska,	is frozen over nearly all of the time!
subject	predicate

In some exclamatory sentences, part of the predicate comes before the subject.

What terrible weather	that city	has!
predicate	subject	predicate

(That city	has terrible weather!)
subject	predicate

Compound subjects in sentences

A sentence with a compound subject has two or more subjects with the same predicate.

> Jesse James and his brother Frank were famous outlaws in the Old West.

> Cole Younger, James Younger, and Robert Younger were all members of the James gang.

Compound predicates in sentences

A sentence with a compound predicate has two or more predicates with the same subject.

> The postal workers took in the tailless cat and named it Kojak.

> Kojak lives in the post office, catches mice, and plays with yarn.

Compound sentences

A compound sentence is made up of two shorter sentences joined by a coordinating conjunction. (See Grammar 45.) A compound sentence has a subject and a predicate followed by another subject and another predicate.

> G. David Howard set a record in 1978, and it remains unbroken.

> Howard told jokes for more than 13 hours, but not all of them were funny.

NOUNS

GRAMMAR 10   **Definition of a noun**

A noun is a word that names a person, a place, an idea, or a thing.

> That brave man crossed the ocean in a rowboat.

GRAMMAR 11   **Singular and plural forms of nouns**

Almost every noun has two forms. The singular form names one person, place, idea, or thing.

> Only one worker in that factory can name the secret ingredient.

The plural form names more than one person, place, idea, or thing.

> Several workers in those two factories can name the secret ingredients.

GRAMMAR 12   **Spelling plural forms of nouns**

For most nouns, add -s to the singular form to make the plural form.

> joke—jokes   character—characters
>
> cartoon—cartoons

If the singular form ends in -s, -ss, -sh, -ch, or -x, add -es.

> bus—buses   witch—witches
>
> kiss—kisses   wish—wishes
>
> fox—foxes

If the singular form ends in a consonant and *-y*, change the *-y* to *-i-* and add *-es*.

spy—spies   discovery—discoveries

mystery—mysteries

If the singular form ends in *-f,* the *-f* is usually changed to *-v-,* and *-es* is added. If the singular form ends in *-fe, -f* is usually changed to *-v-* and *-s* is added. There are some important exceptions to these rules. Look in a dictionary if you are not sure of the correct plural form.

half—halves   wife—wives

loaf—loaves   knife—knives

Some exceptions include the following.

roof—roofs   chief—chiefs   safe—safes

If the singular form ends in *-o,* add *-s* to some words and *-es* to others. Look in a dictionary if you are not sure of the correct plural form.

studio—studios   tomato—tomatoes

piano—pianos   zero—zeros

Some nouns change in other ways to make the plural form.

child—children   mouse—mice

woman—women   goose—geese

A few nouns have the same singular form and plural form.

sheep—sheep   deer—deer

moose—moose

Proper nouns and common nouns

A proper noun is the special name of a particular person, place, idea, or thing. Each word in a proper noun begins with a capital letter.

> Max stopped in Junctionville and went to the Smith House Museum.

A common noun is the name of any person, place, idea, or thing.

> The man stopped in a small town and went to the museum.

Possessive nouns

The possessive form of a noun shows ownership. Usually, the possessive form of a noun is made by adding an apostrophe and -*s*. (See Punctuation 20.)

> A piranha's teeth are as sharp as razors.

The possessive form of a plural noun that ends in -*s* is made by adding only an apostrophe. (See Punctuation 20.)

> Nobody believed the explorers' story.

Nouns of address

A noun of address names the person being spoken to. One or two commas separate a noun of address from the rest of a sentence. (See Punctuation 9.)

> Where are you going, Ricky?

> I told you, Lucy, that I have a rehearsal tonight.

Appositive nouns

An appositive noun renames or identifies the noun that comes before it in a sentence. An appositive noun is usually part of a group of words. The whole group of words is called an appositive. One or two commas separate an appositive from the rest of a sentence. (See Punctuation 10.)

> A Ford was the preferred car of John Dillinger, *the famous gangster.*

> Even his sister, *the president* of her own company, would not hire him.

VERBS

Definition of a verb

A verb is a word that expresses action or being.

> The volcano *erupted* suddenly.

> It *was* a terrific surprise.

Almost all verbs have different forms to show differences in time.

> Puffs of smoke *rise* from the volcano sometimes.

> A huge cloud of heavy gray smoke *rose* from it last week.

Action verbs

Most verbs are action verbs. An action verb expresses physical or mental action.

> The committee members banned comic books.

> They disliked the characters' behavior.

Linking verbs

Some verbs are linking verbs. A linking verb tells what a sentence's subject is or is like. The most common linking verb is *be*. (See Grammar 23.)

> A black and white dog became a mail carrier in California.

> The dog's name was Dorsey.

Verb phrases

A verb phrase is made up of two or more verbs that function together in a sentence. The final verb in a verb phrase is the main verb.

> The 13,000–pound bell had disappeared.

> Somebody must have stolen it.

The verbs before the main verb in a verb phrase are helping verbs. The most common helping verbs are forms of *be* (*is, are, am, was, were*), forms of *have* (*has, have, had*), and forms of *do* (*does, do, did*). (See Grammar 23.)

> That radio station is sponsoring a concert.

> The station has already received 45,217 postcards.

Agreement of verbs with nouns

Verbs that express continuing action or existence and verbs that express current action or existence are in the present tense. Almost all present-tense verbs have two different forms. These two different forms go with different sentence subjects. The main verb or the first helping verb in a sentence must agree with the most important word in the subject of that sentence.

One present-tense form of a verb agrees with singular nouns. This verb form ends with -*s*.

> A tick sucks blood from larger animals.

The other present-tense form of a verb agrees with plural nouns.

> Ticks suck blood from larger animals.

Agreement of verbs with compound subjects

The present-tense verb form that agrees with plural nouns also agrees with compound subjects. (See Grammar 7.)

> Beth Obermeyer and her daughter Kristen hold a record for long-distance tap dancing.

GRAMMAR 23 ## Forms of the verb *be*

The verb *to be* has more forms than other verbs. It has three present-tense forms: *is*, *are*, and *am*. *Is* agrees with singular nouns. *Are* agrees with plural nouns. *Am* agrees with the pronoun *I*.

> Mary Lou Retton is a famous gymnast.

> Many people are her fans.

> I am a pretty good gymnast, too.

Most verbs have one past-tense form that tells about action or existence in the past. The verb *to be* has two past-tense forms: *was* and *were*. *Was* agrees with singular noun subjects. *Were* agrees with plural noun subjects.

> The argument was noisy.

> Several neighbors were very angry about it.

GRAMMAR 24 ## Irregular verbs

Usually the past-tense form of a verb ends in *-d* or *-ed*.

> William Baxter invented an important part of the Morse code.

Some verbs change in other ways to form the past tense. These are called irregular verbs. Look in a dictionary if you are not sure of the correct past-tense form of a verb.

> Samuel Morse took all the credit.

PRONOUNS

GRAMMAR 25 **Personal pronouns**

A personal pronoun is a word that takes the place of one or more nouns.

> Patrick tried to enlist in the army during World War II, but he was found unfit to serve.

GRAMMAR 26 **Subject forms and object forms of personal pronouns**

Each personal pronoun has a subject form and an object form. These different forms are used in different ways in sentences. The pronouns *it* and *you* are the same in the subject and object forms. The subject forms of personal pronouns are *I, you, he, she, it, we,* and *they.* The object forms of personal pronouns are *me, you, him, her, it, us,* and *them.*

> He saw through a wall and read the wrong eye chart.
>
> The army did not accept him.

GRAMMAR 27 **Antecedents of pronouns**

A personal pronoun refers to the noun it replaces. That noun is the antecedent of the pronoun.

> Roy Rogers became famous in movies. He was usually accompanied by his horse, Trigger, and his dog, Bullet.

If a pronoun takes the place of two or more nouns, those nouns together are the antecedent of the pronoun.

Roy Rogers and Dale Evans often worked together.

They made dozens of movies.

Subject-verb agreement with personal pronouns

The present-tense verb form that agrees with singular nouns also agrees with the pronoun subjects *he, she,* and *it.*

She tests new planes.

The present-tense verb form that agrees with plural nouns also agrees with the pronoun subjects *I, you, we,* and *they.*

They test new planes.

Indefinite pronouns

A word that refers to a general group but does not have a specific antecedent is an indefinite pronoun.

Nobody can be right about everything.

One common indefinite pronoun, *no one,* is written as two words.

Subject-verb agreement with indefinite pronouns

The present-tense verb form that agrees with singular nouns also agrees with most indefinite pronouns.

> Almost everyone remembers the Alamo.

> No one knows exactly what happened there.

> Of all the accounts written about the battle, several claim to be factual.

Possessive pronouns

A personal pronoun that shows ownership is a possessive pronoun.

These possessive pronouns are used before nouns in sentences: *my, your, his, her, its, our,* and *their.*

> Why are my gym shoes in your locker?

These possessive pronouns stand alone in sentences: *mine, yours, his, hers, its, ours,* and *theirs.*

> Are these gym shoes mine, or are they yours?

Unlike possessive nouns, possessive pronouns are not written with apostrophes.

Reflexive pronouns

A pronoun that refers back to a noun or pronoun in the same sentence is a reflexive pronoun. These words are reflexive pronouns: *myself, yourself, himself, herself, itself, ourselves, yourselves,* and *themselves.*

> The witness had been talking to himself.

> You should have bought yourself a ticket.

Demonstrative pronouns

A word that points out one or more people or things is a demonstrative pronoun. These words can be demonstrative pronouns: *this, that, these,* and *those.*

> These are the funniest cartoons.

> Nobody laughed at those.

If the word *this, that, these,* or *those* is followed by a noun, the word is not a demonstrative pronoun. (See Grammar 34.)

ADJECTIVES

Definition of an adjective

A word that adds to the meaning of a noun or pronoun is an adjective. Adjectives usually tell *what kind, which one,* or *how many.*

> Those exhausted men have been playing tennis for nine hours.

Adjectives that tell *what kind* can sometimes stand alone.

> They were exhausted.

Adjectives that tell *which one* or *how many* always come before nouns.

> Both players have used several rackets.

GRAMMAR 35 **The adjectives *a* and *an***

The adjectives *a* and *an* are usually called *indefinite articles*. The adjective *the* is usually called a *definite article*. *A* is used before words that begin with consonants or with the sound "yew."

> A penguin cannot fly.
>
> Cooking is a useful activity.

An is used before words that begin with vowels or with an unsounded *h*.

> An ostrich cannot fly.
>
> Brutus is an honorable man.

GRAMMAR 36 **Predicate adjectives**

An adjective that comes after a linking verb and adds to the meaning of the subject noun or pronoun is a predicate adjective.

> Maria Spelterina must have been brave.
>
> Her tightrope walks across Niagara Falls were dangerous.

Proper adjectives

An adjective that is formed from a proper noun is a proper adjective. Each word in a proper adjective begins with a capital letter.

> The American dollar is worth less than the British pound.

> The new Spielberg film is great!

Comparative and superlative forms of adjectives

Adjectives can be used to compare two or more people or things. When only two people or things are compared, use the comparative form of an adjective. To make the comparative form, add -*er* to adjectives with one syllable. Use *more* or *less* before some adjectives with two syllables. Look in a dictionary if you are not sure of the correct comparative form of an adjective.

> Tom is taller than my friend, Mike.

> Tom is more amusing than my friend, Mike.

When more than two people or things are compared, use the superlative form. Add -*est* to adjectives with one or more syllables. Use *most* or *least* before some adjectives with two syllables and all adjectives with more than two syllables. Look in a dictionary if you are not sure of the superlative form of an adjective.

> Tom is the funniest friend I have.

> Tom is the most amusing friend I have.

The comparative and superlative forms of the adjective *good* are *better* and *best*.

> Tom is a better friend than Mike.

> Tom is the best friend I have ever had.

The comparative and superlative forms of the adjective *bad* are *worse*, and *worst*.

> *The Morning Sun* was a worse movie than *The Evening Star*.

> *The Morning Sun* was probably the worst movie ever made.

ADVERBS

GRAMMAR 39 **Definition of an adverb**

A word that adds to the meaning of a verb, an adjective, or another adverb is an adverb. Adverbs usually tell *where, when, how,* or *how often.*

> The rodeo rider bravely mounted the mustang again.

Comparative and superlative forms of adverbs

Adverbs can be used to compare the actions of two or more people or things. When only two people or things are compared, use the comparative form of an adverb. To make the comparative form, the word *more* or *less* is usually used before the adverb. Add *-er* to a few short adverbs.

> Polly speaks more clearly than that other parrot.

> Polly can fly higher than that other parrot.

When the actions of more than two people or things are compared, use the superlative form. To make the superlative form, the word *most* or *least* is usually used before the adverb. Add *-est* to a few short adverbs.

> Of all those parrots, Polly speaks most clearly.

> Of all those parrots, Polly can fly highest.

The comparative and superlative forms of the adverb *well* are *better* and *best*.

> That parrot behaved better than your pet cat.

> Of all the unusual pets in the show, the parrot behaved best.

The comparative and superlative forms of the adverb *badly* are *worse* and *worst*.

> Your pet monkey behaved worse than that parrot.

> Of all the unusual pets in the show, your cat behaved worst.

GRAMMAR 41   **Using adjectives and adverbs**

Use an adjective to describe a noun or a pronoun.

The proud actor accepted the prize.

Use an adverb to describe a verb, an adjective, or another adverb. Many (but not all) adverbs end in *-ly*.

The actor accepted the prize proudly.

GRAMMAR 42   **The adverb *not***

The adverb *not* changes the meaning of a verb, an adjective, or another adverb in a sentence.

The soldiers in the fort would not surrender.

Help did not arrive in time.

GRAMMAR 43   **Avoiding double negatives**

The adverb *not* is a negative word. Other common negative words are *no, never, no one, nobody, nothing, nowhere, hardly, barely,* and *scarcely*. Use only one negative word to make a sentence mean *no* or *not*.

No one ever understands how I feel.

My friends never understand how I feel.

Hardly anyone understands how I feel.

GRAMMAR 44 **Adverbs used as intensifiers**

Certain adverbs add to the meaning of adjectives or other adverbs. These special adverbs are sometimes called intensifiers.

> One terribly nosy neighbor heard the whole conversation.

> Very nervously, she told the police all about it.

CONJUNCTIONS

GRAMMAR 45 **Coordinating conjunctions**

A word used to join two equal parts of a sentence is a coordinating conjunction. The most common coordinating conjunctions are *and*, *but*, and *or*. (See Grammar 9.)

> Many people have driven across the country, but these two men did it the hard way.

> Charles Creighton and James Hargis drove across the country and back again.

> They never stopped the engine or took the car out of reverse gear.

Subordinate conjunctions and complex sentences

A word used to begin an adverb clause is a subordinate conjunction. The most common subordinate conjunctions are listed below.

after	before	though	when
although	if	unless	whenever
because	since	until	while

An adverb clause is a group of words that has a subject and a predicate but cannot stand alone as a sentence. An adverb clause functions like an adverb. It tells *when*, *where*, *how*, or *why*. An adverb clause usually comes at the end or at the beginning of a sentence. (See Punctuation 8.) A sentence formed from an adverb clause (which cannot stand alone) and a main clause (which can stand alone) is called a *complex sentence*.

Otto E. Funk played his violin while he walked from New York City to San Francisco.

When he finished his musical journey, both his feet and hands were tired.

Whenever it is threatened, an opossum plays dead.

It can be poked, picked up, and even rolled over while it remains completely rigid.

INTERJECTIONS

Definition of an interjection

A word that simply expresses emotion is an interjection.
A comma or an exclamation point separates an
interjection from the rest of a sentence. (See
Punctuation 11.)

Oh, now it makes sense.

Wow! That's terrific news!

PREPOSITIONS

Definition of a preposition

A word that shows the relationship of a noun
or pronoun to some other word in a sentence is
a preposition. The most common prepositions are
listed below.

about	before	during	over
above	behind	for	since
across	below	from	through
after	beneath	in	to
against	beside	into	under
along	between	like	until
among	beyond	of	up
around	by	off	upon
at	down	on	with

Prepositional phrases

A preposition must be followed by a noun or a pronoun. The preposition and the noun or pronoun that follows it form a prepositional phrase.

> A new record for sit-ups was set by Dr. David G. Jones.

> His family and friends were very proud of him.

Often, other words come between the preposition and the noun or pronoun. These words are also part of the prepositional phrase.

> He set a new record for consecutive straight-legged sit-ups.

Objects of prepositions

A preposition must be followed by a noun or a pronoun. That noun or pronoun is the object of the preposition.

> One of the main characters of *Fall Leaves* did not appear until the second season.

Personal pronouns in prepositional phrases

A personal pronoun that is the object of a preposition should be in the object form. These are object-form pronouns: *me, you, him, her, it, us,* and *them.*

> The other presents for her are still on the table.

> The most interesting present is from me.

Prepositional phrases used as adjectives

Some prepositional phrases are used as adjectives. They add to the meaning of a noun or pronoun in a sentence.

> The Caribbean island of Martinique is a department of the French government.

Prepositional phrases used as adverbs

Some prepositional phrases are used as adverbs. They add to the meaning of a verb, an adjective, or another adverb in a sentence.

> In 1763, Napoleon Bonaparte's wife, Josephine, was born on Martinique.

SENTENCE PARTS

Simple subjects

The most important noun or pronoun in the subject of a sentence is the simple subject of that sentence. The object of a preposition cannot be the simple subject of a sentence.

> A 27-year-old man from Oklahoma swam the entire length of the Mississippi River.

> He spent a total of 742 hours in the river.

Simple predicates

A verb, an adjective, or an adverb of a sentence is the simple predicate of that sentence.

> Actor W. C. Fields may have had 700 separate savings accounts.

> Fields used a different name for each account.

Direct objects

A word that tells *who* or *what* receives the action of a verb is the direct object of the verb. A direct object must be a noun or a pronoun. A personal pronoun that is a direct object should be in the object form. These are object-form pronouns: *me, you, him, her, it, us,* and *them.*

> The first aspirin tablets contained heroin.

> A German company sold them for 12 years.

Indirect objects

A word that tells *to whom* or *to what* or *for whom* or *for what* something is done is the indirect object of the verb. An indirect object comes before a direct object and is not part of a prepositional phrase. An indirect object must be a noun or a pronoun.

A personal pronoun that is an indirect object should be in the object form. These are object-form pronouns: *me, you, him, her, it, us,* and *them.*

> Professor Sommers gave his students the same lecture every year.

> He told them a familiar story.

Predicate nominatives

A word that follows a linking verb and renames a sentence's subject is the predicate nominative of the sentence. A predicate nominative must be a noun or a pronoun. A personal pronoun that is a predicate nominative should be in the subject form. These are subject-form pronouns: *I, you, he, she, it, we,* and *they*.

> The best candidate was Andrea.

> In my opinion, the winner should have been she.

CAPITALIZATION RULES

First word in a sentence

Begin the first word of every sentence with a capital letter.

> Who won the eating contest?

> That man ate 17 bananas in two minutes.

Personal pronoun *I*

Write the pronoun *I* with a capital letter.

> At the last possible minute, I changed my mind.

Names and initials of people

Almost always, begin each part of a person's name with a capital letter.

Hernando Jones   Rosie Delancy   Sue Ellen Macmillan

Some parts of names have more than one capital letter. Other parts are not capitalized. Check the correct way to write each person's name. Look in a reference book, or ask the person.

JoAnne Baxter   Tony O'Hara   Jeannie McIntyre

Use a capital letter to write an initial that is part of a person's name.

B. J. Gallardo   J. Kelly Hunt   John F. Kennedy

Titles of people

Begin the title before a person's name with a capital letter.

Mr. Sam Yee   Captain Cook

Dr. Watson   Governor Maxine Stewart

Do not use a capital letter if this kind of word is not used before a person's name.

Did you call the doctor?

Who will be our state's next governor?

CAPITALIZATION 5   **Names of relatives**

A word like *grandma* or *uncle* may be used as a person's name or as part of a person's name. Begin this kind of word with a capital letter.

> Only Dad and Aunt Ellie understand it.

Usually, if a possessive pronoun comes before a word like *grandma* or *uncle,* do not begin that word with a capital letter.

> Only my dad and my aunt understand it.

CAPITALIZATION 6   **Names of days**

Begin the name of a day with a capital letter.

> Most people do not have to work on Saturday or on Sunday.

CAPITALIZATION 7   **Names of months**

Begin the name of a month with a capital letter.

> At the equator, the hottest months are March and September.

CAPITALIZATION 8   **Names of holidays**

Begin each important word in the name of a holiday with a capital letter. Words like *the* and *of* do not begin with capital letters.

> They usually have a picnic on the Fourth of July and a fancy dinner party on Thanksgiving.

CAPITALIZATION 9 **Names of streets and highways**

Begin each word in the name of a street or highway with a capital letter.

Why is Lombard Street known as the most crooked road in the world?

CAPITALIZATION 10 **Names of cities and towns**

Begin each word in the name of a city or town with a capital letter.

In 1997, the Mountaineers moved from Sparta to Newton.

CAPITALIZATION 11 **Names of states, countries, and continents**

Begin each word in the name of a state, country, or continent with a capital letter.

The story was set in Nevada, but the film was shot in Mexico.

Many mountain peaks in Antarctica are very high.

CAPITALIZATION 12 **Names of mountains and bodies of water**

Begin each word in the name of a mountain, river, lake, or ocean with a capital letter.

Amelia Earhart's plane was lost somewhere over the Pacific Ocean.

Abbreviations

If a word would begin with a capital letter, begin its abbreviation with a capital letter.

On a scrap of paper, the patient had written, "Wed.—Dr. Lau."

Titles of works

Use a capital letter to begin the first word, the last word, and every main word in the title of a work. The words *the*, *a*, and *an* do not begin with capital letters except at the beginning of a title. Coordinating conjunctions and prepositions also do not begin with capital letters. (See Grammar 45 and Grammar 48.)

Joe and Jen were the main characters in the television series *Friends for Life*.

Other proper nouns

Begin each major word in a proper noun with a capital letter. A proper noun is the special name of a particular person, a place, an idea, or a thing. (See Grammar 13.) Usually, the words *the*, *a*, and *an*, coordinating conjunctions, and prepositions do not begin with capital letters. (See Grammar 45 and Grammar 48.)

Jerry rushed to Mario's Restaurant and ate Spaghetti Romano.

Proper adjectives

Begin a proper adjective with a capital letter. A proper adjective is an adjective that is formed from a proper noun. If the proper adjective is made with two or more nouns, capitalize each of them. (See Grammar 37.)

That American author writes about English detectives.

She loves Alfred Hitchcock movies.

Direct quotations

Begin the first word in a direct quotation with a capital letter. (See Punctuation 14–16.)

Dr. Pavlik said, "There are simply no teeth in the denture law."

If the words that tell who is speaking appear in the middle of a quoted sentence, do not begin the second part of the quotation with a capital letter.

"There are simply no teeth," said Dr. Pavlik, "in the denture law."

Greetings and closings in letters

Begin the first or only word in the greeting of a letter with a capital letter.

Dear Mr. Lincoln: Dear Uncle Abe,   Madam:

Begin the first or only word in the closing of a letter with a capital letter.

Sincerely yours,   Very truly yours,   Love,

Outlines

In an outline, begin the first word of each heading with a capital letter.

    II. Houses by mail order

        A. First sold by Johnson Builders in 1903

            1. Build-it-yourself kits

            2. Included all materials and instructions

        B. Other companies now in business

In an outline, use capital Roman numerals to label main ideas. Use capital letters to label supporting ideas. For ideas under supporting ideas, use Arabic numerals. For details, use small letters. Use a period after each Roman numeral, capital letter, Arabic numeral, or small letter.

    I. Miner George Warren

        A. Risked his share of Copper Queen mine in bet

            1. Bet on race against George Atkins

                a. Warren on foot

                b. Atkins on horseback

            2. Lost property worth $20 million

PUNCTUATION RULES

Periods, question marks, and exclamation points at the ends of sentences

Use a period, a question mark, or an exclamation point at the end of every sentence. Do not use more than one of these marks at the end of a sentence. For example, do not use both a question mark and an exclamation point, or do not use two exclamation points.

Use a period at the end of a declarative sentence, or a sentence that makes a statement.

> A hockey player must be able to skate backward at top speed.

Also use a period at the end of an imperative sentence, or a sentence that gives a command.

> Keep your eye on the puck.

Use a question mark at the end of an interrogative sentence, or a sentence that asks a question.

> Who is the goalie for their team?

Use an exclamation point at the end of an exclamatory sentence, or a sentence that expresses excitement.

> That was a terrific block!

Periods with abbreviations

Use a period at the end of each part of an abbreviation.

Most titles used before people's names are abbreviations. These abbreviations may be used in formal writing. (*Miss* is not an abbreviation and does not end with a period.)

Dr. Blackwell   Mr. Bill Tilden

Ms. Maureen Connolly

Most other abbreviations may be used in addresses, notes, and informal writing. They should not be used in formal writing.

Lake View Blvd.   Mon. and Thurs.

Fifth Ave.   Dec. 24

Do not use periods in the abbreviations of names of government agencies, labor unions, and certain other organizations.

Tomorrow night, station MLT will broadcast a special program about the FBI.

Do not use periods after two-letter state abbreviations in addresses. This kind of abbreviation has two capital letters and no period. Use these abbreviations in addresses.

Their new address is 1887 West Third Street, Los Angeles, CA 90048.

Periods after initials

Use a period after an initial that is part of a person's name.

Chester A. Arthur   C. C. Pyle

Susan B. Anthony

Commas in dates

Use a comma between the number of the day and the number of the year in a date.

Hank Aaron hit his record-breaking home run on April 8, 1974.

If the date does not come at the end of a sentence, use another comma after the number of the year.

April 8, 1974, was an exciting day for Hank Aaron's fans.

Do not use a comma in a date that has only the name of the month and number of a year.

Aaron hit his final home run in July 1976.

Do not use a comma in a date that has only the name of a month and the number of a day.

April 8 is the anniversary of Aaron's record-breaking home run.

Commas in place names

Use a comma between the name of a city or town and the name of a state or country.

> The world's largest chocolate factory is in Hershey, Pennsylvania.

If the two names do not come at the end of a sentence, use another comma after the name of the state or country.

> Hershey, Pennsylvania, is the home of the world's largest chocolate factory.

Commas in compound sentences

Use a comma before the conjunction *and*, *but*, or *or* in a compound sentence. (See Grammar 9 and Grammar 45.)

> Eighteen people tried, but no one succeeded.

Commas in series

Three or more words or groups of words used the same way in a sentence form a series. Use commas to separate the words or groups of words in a series.

> Jamie, Mitch, Kim, Lou, and Pablo entered the contest.

> Each contestant swam one mile, bicycled two miles, and ran five miles.

Commas after introductory phrases and clauses

Use a comma after a phrase that introduces, or gives additional information about, the main thought of a sentence and is placed before the subject of the sentence. A phrase is a group of words that cannot stand alone as a complete thought. It usually acts as an adjective or an adverb. One kind of phrase is a prepositional phrase. (See Grammar 49.)

> In the old dresser, **Penny found the diamonds.**

If the entire predicate comes before the subject of the sentence, do not use a comma. (See Grammar 3.)

> In the old dresser lay **the diamonds.**

Use a comma after an adverb clause that is placed at the beginning of a sentence. (See Grammar 46.)

> When he was first named hockey's most valuable player, **Wayne Gretzky was only 18 years old.**

Commas with nouns of address

Use a comma after a noun of address that is placed at the beginning of a sentence. (See Grammar 15.)

> Fernando, **that was a terrific pitch!**

Use a comma before a noun of address that is placed at the end of a sentence.

> **That was a terrific pitch,** Fernando!

If the noun of address is placed in the middle of a sentence, use one comma before the noun and another comma after it.

> **That,** Fernando, **was a terrific pitch!**

Commas with appositives

Use a comma before an appositive at the end of a sentence. (See Grammar 16.)

> This costume was worn by Shelley, our class president.

If an appositive appears in the middle of a sentence, use one comma before the appositive and another comma after it.

> Shelley, our class president, wore this costume.

Commas or exclamation points with interjections

Usually, use a comma after an interjection. (See Grammar 47.)

> Well, we should probably think about it.

Use an exclamation point after an interjection that expresses excitement.

> Wow! That is a terrific idea!

Commas after greetings in friendly letters

Use a comma after the greeting in a friendly letter.

> Dear Karla,   Dear Uncle Theodore,

Commas after closings in friendly letters and business letters.

Use a comma after the closing in a letter.

Love,   Yours sincerely,

Quotation marks with direct quotations

A direct quotation tells the exact words a person said. Use quotation marks at the beginning and the end of each part of a direct quotation.

"Look!" cried Tina. "That cat is smiling!"

"Of course," Tom joked, "it's a Cheshire cat."

Commas with direct quotations

Usually, use a comma to separate the words of a direct quotation from the words that tell who is speaking. (See Punctuation 16.)

Jay asked, "Who won the game last night?"

"The Tigers won it," said Linda, "in 14 innings."

End punctuation with direct quotations

At the end of a direct quotation, use a period, a comma, a question mark, or an exclamation point before the closing quotation marks.

If the direct quotation makes a statement or gives a command *at the end of a sentence*, use a period.

> Linda said, "The Tigers won last night's game."

> Jay said, "Tell us about the game."

If the direct quotation makes a statement or gives a command *before the end of a sentence*, use a comma.

> "The Tigers won last night's game," said Linda.

> "Tell us about the game," Jay said.

If the direct quotation *asks a question*, use a question mark.

> "Was it an exciting game?" asked Jay.

If the direct quotation *expresses excitement*, use an exclamation point.

> Linda yelled, "It was great!"

Quotation marks with titles of works

Use quotation marks around the title of a story, poem, song, essay, or chapter.

"Have a Happy Day" is a fun song to sing.

If a period or a comma comes after the title, put the period or comma inside the closing quotation mark.

A fun song to sing is "Have a Happy Day."

Underlines with titles of works

Underline the title of a book, play, magazine, movie, television series, or newspaper when you write a paper by hand.

One of the best movies about baseball was The Champion.

Put the title of a book, play, magazine, movie, television series, or newspaper in italic type when you use a word-processing program.

One of the best movies about baseball was *The Champion*.

Apostrophes in contractions

Use an apostrophe in place of the missing letter or letters in a contraction.

is not—isn't   Mel is—Mel's   I will—I'll

Apostrophes in possessive nouns

Use an apostrophe and -*s* to write the possessive form of a singular noun. (See Grammar 14.)

This cage belongs to one bird. It is the bird's cage.

Use only an apostrophe to write the possessive form of a plural noun that ends in -*s*.

This is a club for boys. It is a boys' club.

Use an apostrophe and -*s* to write the possessive form of a plural noun that does not end in -*s*.

This is a club for men. It is a men's club.

PUNCTUATION 21 ## Colons after greetings in business letters

Use a colon after the greeting in a business letter.

Dear Mrs. Huan:	Dear Sir or Madam:
Dear Senator Rayburn:	To Whom It May Concern:

PUNCTUATION 22 ## Colons in expressions of time

When you write time in numerals, use a colon between the hour and the minutes.

5:45 P.M.   9:00 A.M.   12:17 P.M.

PUNCTUATION 23 ## Hyphens in numbers and fractions

Use a hyphen in a compound number from twenty-one to ninety-nine.

thirty-seven   fifty-eight   seventy-three

Use a hyphen in a fraction.

one-quarter   two-thirds   seven-eighths

Index

Photo Credits